THE PLOT AGAINST
NATIVE AMERICA

THE
PLOT AGAINST
NATIVE AMERICA

The Fateful Story of Native American Boarding
Schools and the Theft of Tribal Lands

BILL VAUGHN

PEGASUS BOOKS
NEW YORK LONDON

THE PLOT AGAINST NATIVE AMERICA

Pegasus Books, Ltd.
148 West 37th Street, 13th Floor
New York, NY 10018

First Pegasus Books cloth edition October 2024

Interior design by Maria Fernandez

Library of Congress Cataloging-in-Publication Data is available.

ISBN: 978-1-63936-746-7

10 9 8 7 6 5 4 3 2 1

Printed in the United States of America
Distributed by Simon & Schuster
www.pegasusbooks.com

For Kitty

The young of the wild bird, though born in captivity, naturally retains the instincts of freedom so strong in the parent and beats the bars to secure it, while after several generations of captivity the young bird will return to the cage after a brief period of freedom. So with the Indian child. The first wild redskin placed in the school chafes at the loss of freedom and longs to return to his wildwood home. His offspring retains some of the habits acquired by the parent. These habits receive fresh development in each successive generation, fixing new rules of conduct, different aspirations, and greater desires to be in touch with the dominant race.

—William A. Jones, Indian Affairs Commissioner, 1902.

CONTENTS

Continental Divide Reserves and Reservations

Reserves by tribal affiliation

① Siksika (Blackfoot)
② Northern Piikani (Piegan)
③ Kanai (Blood)
④ Southern Piikani (Piegan)

Reservations by tribal affiliation

⑤ Chippewa Cree
⑥ A'aninin (Gros Ventre), Nakota (Assiniboine)
⑦ Dakota, Lakota, A'aninin
⑧ Kootenai, Kalispel (Pend d'Oreilles), Salish
⑨ Cree, Métis Ojibwe Tribal Capital
⑩ Apsáalooke (Crow)
⑪ Northern Cheyenne
⑫ Northern Arapaho, Eastern Shoshone

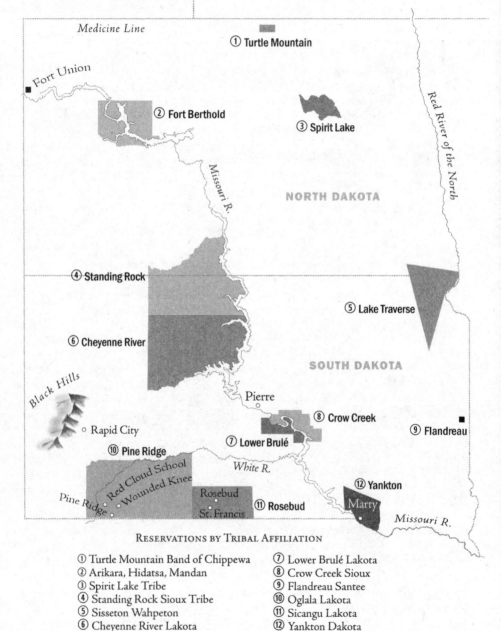

Marievel
Cowesses Reserve
(Salteaux)

PRAIRIE RESERVE AND RESERVATIONS

MANITOBA

SASKATCHEWAN

Winnipeg O

Medicine Line

① Turtle Mountain

Fort Union

② Fort Berthold

③ Spirit Lake

Red River of the North

Missouri R.

NORTH DAKOTA

④ Standing Rock

⑤ Lake Traverse

⑥ Cheyenne River

SOUTH DAKOTA

Black Hills

Pierre

⑧ Crow Creek

○ Rapid City

⑦ Lower Brulé

⑨ Flandreau

⑩ Pine Ridge

Red Cloud School

White R.

⑫ Yankton

Pine Ridge   Wounded Knee

Rosebud

Marty

St. Francis   ⑪ Rosebud

Missouri R.

RESERVATIONS BY TRIBAL AFFILIATION

① Turtle Mountain Band of Chippewa
② Arikara, Hidatsa, Mandan
③ Spirit Lake Tribe
④ Standing Rock Sioux Tribe
⑤ Sisseton Wahpeton
⑥ Cheyenne River Lakota

⑦ Lower Brulé Lakota
⑧ Crow Creek Sioux
⑨ Flandreau Santee
⑩ Oglala Lakota
⑪ Sicangu Lakota
⑫ Yankton Dakota

Desert Tribal Lands

COLORADO

UTAH

① Ute Mountain

② Southern Ute

⑥ Kaibab Paiute

④ Navajo   Red Rock

CA

⑦ Havasupai

⑤ Hopi   Chinle ④ Navajo

Colorado R.

Ft. Defiance

Ganado

③ Jicarilla Apache

Oraivi   St. Michaels

⑭ Canoncito

⑧ Hualapai   ARIZONA

⑫ Acoma

⑨ Fort Mojave

⑩ Yavapai-Prescott

⑰ Chemehuevi

⑯ Yavapai-Apache

⑪ Zuni

⑬ Laguna

⑱ Tonto-Apache

⑮ White Mountain

⑳ Fort McDowell

NEW MEXICO

⑯ San Carlos

㉑ Salt River

㉒ Colorado River

㉓ Gila River

㉖ Fort Yuma

㉔ Pascua Yaqui

㉗ Cocopah

㉕ Tohono O'odham

MEXICO

MEXICO

Reservations and Pueblos by Tribal Affiliation

① Ute Nation	⑮ White Mountain Apache
② Southern Ute	⑯ Yavapai-Apache
③ Jicarillo Apache	⑰ Chemehuevi
④ Diné (Navajo)	⑱ Tonto Apache
⑤ Hopi	⑲ San Carlos Apache
⑥ Kaibab Band of Paiute	⑳ Fort McDowell Yavapai Nation
⑦ Havasupai	㉑ Salt River Pima-Maricopa
⑧ Hualapai	㉒ Colorado River
⑨ Fort Mojave	㉓ Gila River Indian Community
⑩ Yavapai-Prescott	㉔ Pascua Yaqui
⑪ Pueblo of Zuni	㉕ Tohono O'odham Nation
⑫ Acoma Pueblo	㉖ Fort Yuma Quechan
⑬ Laguna Pueblo	㉗ Cocopah
⑭ Canoncito Pueblo	

PREFACE

To get to the Dinwoody Lakes on the Wind River Reservation I drove fifty miles south from Yellowstone Park along a weathered two-lane and turned right onto a trace that barely qualified as a road. Sagebrush sighed against the undercarriage of my Bronco as it heaved and shuddered across eight tortured miles. Although this valley looked to me like the middle of nowhere it had been the sheltered home for a vibrant community of hunter-gatherers whose existence is proven by the document they left behind.

I fell into a trance staring at it. Etched above me on a sheer stone cliff was a menagerie of eerie, otherworldly creatures. Some of them human-sized, it is thought that these petroglyphs were created beginning 5,000 years ago by shamans recording the visions they experienced after fasting, praying, and fending off sleep. They rendered their out-of-body experiences using a pointed stone to peck away the reddish veneer, revealing the pale sandstone underneath. Here were bird-like things with wings, humanoid figures with hands sprouting from their shoulders, little goblin-like beings with feet sprouting from their torsos. The dominant figure had raised its arms to frame its face, a gesture similar to that of the person in Edvard Munch's painting, *The Scream*. Like the confected creatures on the island of Dr. Moreau, none of the figures were exactly human, nor were they exactly animal. The dots and squiggly lines that embellished them created the illusion that they were shimmering.

After taking photographs I headed up a trail to look for more petroglyphs. I was finally turned around by a sign that said only tribal people were allowed to go farther. Back at the cliff I joined two men who had parked their truck next to mine while I was hiking. Paul Revere was a member of the Northern Arapaho, who share this reservation with the Eastern Shoshoni, whose ancestors likely created the Dinwoody petroglyphs. He was here with his priest, the Reverend Harold EagleBull, a Lakota who served as pastor for Our Father's House, the Episcopal church down the road in the town of Ethete.

"What these figures represent is significant," EagleBull said. "To Western culture, to the missionaries, history is in the Bible. But for Native Americans our history is here, in nature. Nature is our Bible."

"I can imagine the people here," Revere said. "I can hear the drums."

"Do you think these pictures are self-portraits?" I asked.

"No. My grandfather told me they used to see these silver things flying in this area. Ones with wings on them. They used to see them out here a long, long time ago."

"You mean UFOs?"

Revere nodded. "They shined. They were spacemen. My grandpa's grandfather told him, and he got it from his grandpa. They were here before the people. I think the people worshiped them, praised them, because they could fly."

In fact, one of the petroglyphs in nearby Torrey Canyon shows what some have interpreted as a representation of the basin from the air. Over the decades White visitors have seen in it a map of buried treasure or hidden cities or lost continents. But like the images in the Dinwoody panel the "map" sprouts arms and legs and a bird-like figure.

I had driven to Wyoming on the first leg of a trip around the Northern Plains to visit tribal sacred sites for an article I would write for my employer at the time, *Outside* magazine.[1]

The significance of my chance meeting at Dinwoody would not strike me until years later, after I and millions of other non-Native Americans learned about what tribal people in the U.S. and Canada have known for generations: Indian boarding and residential schools were used by the government to steal Native land by degrading Indigenous cultures and reducing their communal will to resist the plunder. Revere and EagleBull not only personify the fact that the tribes weathered the storm. They also represent the complex history of conflict and compromise that still exists between Christian and Indigenous spirituality.

What follows is the story of how these assimilation centers were developed and operated by both the U.S. government and several denominations, most notably the Catholic Church, led by Katharine Drexel, the world's wealthiest nun. Although these forces attempted and sometimes succeeded in suppressing Indigenous languages, customs, economies and spirituality, Native people resisted. The occupation of Alcatraz and Wounded Knee are examples, as are the pipeline protests in the Dakotas and the massive class action lawsuit successfully brought by a Blackfeet warrior to regain some of this lost land.

THE PLOT AGAINST
NATIVE AMERICA

Chapter One

CHILDHOOD'S END

T he image is intriguing, disturbing, and ludicrous. Pope Francis is dressed in a virginal white gown, his hands piously clasped as if in prayer. A metal crucifix hangs from a chain around his neck, forged with a shepherd leading his flock, a lamb draped around the shepherd's shoulders. But instead of the pope's traditional peaked skullcap, Francis is wearing an elaborate Cree war bonnet made of white feathers and a beaded head band. As the photograph made its way around the world Indigenous people greeted it with dismay and anger. "The pope," a Canadian tribal leader said, "is a literal figurehead of the colonial systems of oppression that continue to impact Indigenous communities, families and people."[1] On the July day in 2022 when this photo was taken, 15,000 people had gathered in drizzling rain to hear Francis speak at the site of the now-demolished Ermineskin Indian Residential School at Maskwacis, Alberta. Operated by the Catholic Church, it was one of the largest of Canada's Native assimilation centers and notorious for its abuse and mistreatment of children. Riding in a wheelchair, the eighty-five-year-old pontiff had been ushered onto a stage at the center of a pow wow circle, a covered ring over a field used for traditional dancing and drumming.

Surrounding this enclosure were tipis, smoldering campfires, and booths bearing signs that read "Mental Health and Cultural Support."

The audience was mostly First Nations people, some of them dressed in traditional clothing and headdresses. Many of them were residential school survivors. People were excited to be here in the presence of a global luminary. Some of them, of course, were Catholics. But more than those incentives, they had come to hear an apology at last for the Church's role in what the Canadian Truth and Reconciliation Commission called a legacy of "cultural genocide." From 1879 to 1997 some 150,000 Indigenous children were plucked from their homes and families and forced to attend Christian boarding schools, most of them operated by Roman Catholic missionary congregations. In May 2017 Canadian Prime Minister Justin Trudeau met with Francis at the Vatican and asked him to deliver a papal apology for the Catholic Church's role in operating residential schools. The Anglican Church apologized in 1993, followed by the Presbyterian Church a year later, and the United Church in 1998. Trudeau received a letter from a senior representative of the Catholic Church in Canada. The pope, the letter said, could not issue a personal apology. But that was before almost 1,000 suspected unmarked graves of Native children had been discovered on the grounds of two Indian boarding schools operated by the Catholic Church.

In May 2021 a Shuswap tribal leader announced that 215 suspected graves of First Nations children had been discovered in a two-acre apple orchard on the grounds of the Kamloops Indian Residential School in British Columbia. Under the direction of Indian authorities and an anthropologist, Dr. Sarah Beaulieu, workers used a ground-penetrating radar device resembling a large lawn mower to investigate disturbances in the soil that might indicate a burial. Ever since a human tooth and a rib had been found there two decades earlier it had been rumored that the site concealed unmarked graves. From 1892 to 1969 the boarding school, which had been operated by Catholic priests and nuns on Reserve land, was home to hundreds of Indian children. They were forced to attend the school under laws enacted by the Canadian government in the 1920s. They were forbidden to speak their own languages or practice their own spirituality. Native dances were forbidden, replaced by instruction in Irish and Ukrainian folk dancing.

The announcement prompted another search for unmarked graves three weeks later and 700 miles east on the former grounds of the Marieval Indian Industrial School in Saskatchewan. Employing the same technology used at Kamloops, tribal authorities from the Cowessess First Nation announced that it had detected 751 unmarked graves in a grassy field near the former school, which was operated by Catholic nuns from 1898 to 1969. It was determined that the area probably contained the remains of Indian children but also the remains of adults, both White and Indian. It was further speculated that gravestones that once marked the burials had been removed in the 1960s, possibly by a priest.

Although anthropologist Sarah Beulieu advised that her findings at Kamloops could only be verified through excavations, and that the abnormalities she detected could have been caused by the movement of roots, her study sent shock waves across the globe and ignited a media frenzy. The United Nations High Commissioner for Human Rights portrayed the situation as "a large-scale human rights violation" and urged Canadian authorities and the Catholic Church to conduct "thorough investigations." At the United Nations, China and its allies including Russia, Syria, and North Korea issued a statement: "We are deeply concerned about the serious human rights violations against the Indigenous people in Canada." Amnesty International demanded that the individuals and institutions responsible for "the mass grave" at Kamloops be "prosecuted." Prime Minister Justin Trudeau said the discovery revealed "a dark and shameful chapter" in Canadian history. He ordered flags to be flown at half-mast and demanded that Pope Francis travel to Canada to apologize in person. The Premier of British Columbia, John Horgan, said he was "horrified and heartbroken" by the discovery.

Sixty-eight churches in Canada were vandalized or set on fire. Piles of shoes and orange shirts were heaped in protest on the steps of churches of provincial legislatures.[2] Statues of Queen Victoria and Queen Elizabeth II were defaced and pulled down during demonstrations. In 2020 the detached bronze head of John A. Macdonald, Canada's first prime minister, rolled across the cobblestones after his statue was toppled in downtown Montreal by activists protesting the treatment of Black and Indigenous people by the police. Chief Keith Crow of the Lower Similkameen Indian Band, on whose Reserve two Catholic churches were burned to the ground, said that "When all the rest of the residential schools start doing testing, there's just going to be more and more pain that comes out; the 215 was just a start." Kamloops was one of about 130 residential schools attended by about 150,000 Inuit, First Nations, and Métis children between the opening of these institutions, around 1883, and their closing in 1996. Established in 2008, the Truth and Reconciliation Commission of Canada estimated that at least 4,100 children died during their time at these schools. But in 2021 Murray Sinclair, who served as the head of the Commission, said that he believes the number is "well beyond 10,000."[3] According to the Commission, school authorities often gave their families vague explanations or fed them the lie that the child had run away and vanished. And up until the 1960s when the schools did acknowledge a death, they generally refused to return their bodies to their families. Remains were sent back only if it was cheaper than burying them at the schools.

Critics of the hysteria ignited by the media and the government pointed out that because not a single body had been exhumed calling these sites "mass graves" was inflammatory misinformation that suggested a war crime or a massacre. Jacques Rouillard, professor emeritus in the Department of History at the Université de Montréal, pointed out that the Kamloops school was located in the heart of the Kamloops Reserve itself. "With the cemetery so close by," he wrote, "is it really credible that the remains of 200 children were buried clandestinely in a mass grave, on the reserve itself, without any reaction from the band council until last summer?" Historian J. R. Miller of the University of Saskatchewan said that "the remains of children discovered in Marieval and Kamloops had been buried in cemeteries according to Catholic rites, under wooden crosses that quickly crumbled."[4] A conservative columnist named Tristin Hopper wrote that it has never been a secret that the residential schools "abounded" with the graves of dead children. "Communities and survivors knew the bodies were there, as did any investigation or government commission that bothered to ask."[5]

One of these was the Truth and Reconciliation Commission of Canada, which issued a report written by Scott Hamilton, an anthropologist at Lakehead University. In "Where the Bodies are Buried" he reported that dead students were often buried in graveyards near the schools because federal authorities provided no funding to send the bodies home or to conduct proper burials. So they were interred in paupers' graves marked with simple wooden crosses that deteriorated over time and vanished. His report found no evidence that school officials intended to hide the graves. Regardless, after researching the issue between 2008 and 2015 the Commission concluded that the residential school system was guilty of "cultural genocide."

The ongoing absence of a *corpus delicti* contributed to the gradual quelling of destructive acts. While no conclusive body of evidence has been presented yet—in this case actual bodies—resistance to exhuming probable gravesites is understandable. For Indians—as well as all other human beings—the thought of digging up the remains of one's relatives and ancestors is fraught with anxiety, anguish, and grief. Tribal people were offended by the reactionary response to the uproar ignited by the Kamloops revelation. An Indigenous artist named K. J. McCusker said that "This call for bodies is nothing more than a racist rant bordering on genocide denial."[6]

The discovery shocked everyone except Native people in the U.S. and Canada. For decades Inuit, Métis, and First Nations leaders had asked the Vatican for an admission of guilt. On this day they would finally get it. "In the face of this deplorable evil," Francis said in Spanish, the language he grew up speaking in Argentina, "the Church kneels before God and implores His forgiveness for the sins of her children. I myself wish to reaffirm this, with shame and unambiguously. I humbly beg forgiveness for the evil committed by so many Christians against the Indigenous Peoples." Francis said the word "sorry" ten times during his remarks, which were translated by an interpreter into English. And each time the crowd applauded. "I ask forgiveness, in particular, for the ways in which many members of the Church and of religious communities cooperated, not least through their indifference, in projects of cultural destruction and forced assimilation promoted by the governments of that time, which culminated in the system of residential schools."

After Francis finished speaking, Wilton Littlechild, a Cree chief, lawyer, member of Parliament, and residential school survivor, placed the feathered war bonnet on the pope's head as the crowd cheered. Littlechild and other tribal leaders agreed beforehand that the gesture of respect was appropriate, although they were roundly criticized for their decision. Francis had not asked for this high honor and said nothing for the few moments he wore the headdress. However, the Vatican's newspaper, *L'Osservatore Romano*, seized on the symbolism and published the image on its front page under the headline "I humbly beg forgiveness." Unlike other newspapers around the world the Vatican press did not publish the haunting and award-winning photograph of a line of wooden crosses over which girls' dresses had been draped and the image of children's shoes lining the steps of a Catholic church. The furor over what was perceived to be at the very least a tone-deaf moment briefly obscured the implications of the Pope's address. For some, his condemnation of the Church's historic crimes finally made evident for everyone what Indigenous people had known for decades, and mostly kept to themselves. It "was validation that this really happened," said Tony Alexis of the Alexis Nakota Sioux Nation in Alberta. [7]

But would the pope's apology end up just another Catholic mea culpa, one of those easy confessions a priest forgives with nothing more than the confessor's promise to say ten Hail Mary's? Although Francis did not offer reparations on behalf of the Vatican or even define what those might be he made it clear that what he called his six-day "penitential pilgrimage" across Canada was only the first step. "Begging pardon is not the end of the matter," he said, but "the starting point." What might be the starting point for the Vatican was the finish line for most of Canada's twelve million Catholics. In 2007 the Canadian government settled a class action suit filed by 86,000 Indigenous people who had been held captive in boarding schools. The Indian Residential Schools Settlement Agreement provided reparations for the victims that would grow to almost four billion Canadian dollars. Government payments to individuals ranged from $10,000 to $275,000, although in some cases much more, depending on the degree of abuse a victim could document. The Catholic Church in Canada, which is a decentralized collection of organizations, was represented by forty-eight entities complicit in the operation of the boarding school system. These included religious orders and some of the Church's eighteen dioceses. They agreed to pay $29 million to the nonprofit Aboriginal Healing Foundation, plus $25 million worth of "in-kind services." It further agreed to raise an additional $25 million in cash by hiring a professional fundraising team to solicit donations from individuals and businesses, a campaign branded with the brazenly self-promotional tagline "Moving Forward Together." It was a fiasco that raised less than $4 million, half of which the Church claimed was exempt from the agreement because it was spent on lawyers and administration. Critics attacked the Church for not only victimizing aboriginal Canadians but for using legal trickery to renege on its promise to compensate them for the damage it caused. A Church spokesman denied the charge. "There was a cash contribution. There was in-kind payment. There was a best-efforts campaign. We did all those. There wasn't any weaseling out."

After the Church entities hired one of Canada's top attorneys to argue that they had raised all the money they could, in 2015 a judge allowed them to walk away from their commitment. The key phrase in the agreement, the lawyer argued, was "best efforts." One of the challenges the fundraisers faced was the fact that more than half of Canada's Catholics arrived in the country over the last fifty years and don't feel personally responsible for what their newly adopted church did to Indigenous people. But the money was there. In 2021 the *Globe and Mail* newspaper reported that the wealth held by Catholic entities in Canada amounted to $4.1 billion. Since 2005 aggressive fundraising efforts for Catholic cathedrals and other buildings across Canada have yielded almost $300 million for these construction projects. While the Saskatoon diocese and its 80,000 members spent $28.5 million on the Cathedral of the Holy Family that opened in 2012, they raised a

paltry $34,650 for boarding school survivors. The $128-million renovation of St. Michael's Cathedral Basilica in Toronto, whose gala opening
in 2016 featured a brass band, was held one year after the court released
the Catholic entities from its promise. These figures call into question the
church's story about its "best efforts."

In Quebec, three female religious orders that staffed residential schools
raised at least $25 million between 2011 and 2021 by liquidating their
real estate. In 2005 the Grey Nuns sold their motherhouse in downtown
Montreal for $18 million to Concordia University. In 2011 the nuns
sold an island property to the city of Châteauguay on Montreal's South
Shore for $5 million. The same year, they sold two properties in the city
of Nicolet, Quebec near Trois-Rivières, for $1.8 million. The Grey Nuns,
who worked at several residential schools in Western Canada, including
the Holy Angels Indian Residential School in Fort Chipewyan, Alberta,
where at least eighty-nine children died, contributed $2.5 million toward
the $29 million settlement agreement. The Sisters of Providence sold their
motherhouse in Montreal for $7.5 million in 2011 to a nonprofit group
that converted it into housing for seniors. The Sisters of St. Joseph of
St. Hyacinthe, who also signed the agreement, sold their vast mother house
in Saint-Hyacinthe east of Montreal for $4.2 million in 2014. The religious
order sold another property in the same city to a real estate company for
$1.5 million in 2021. Nuns from the St. Hyacinthe order worked at the
Marieval Indian Residential School in Saskatchewan, where a preliminary
investigation suggest that there are 751 unmarked graves at a cemetery
near the institution.

Further evidence of the Church's heel-dragging and dishonesty is a log
kept by the Catholic entities, which documents that the $28 million "in-
kind services" they promised included numerous attempts to evangelize
and convert aboriginal people. Listed are bible-study programs, priests and
nuns inserted into remote northern villages, and translations of religious
material. For example, one order donated $360,000 toward the transcrip-
tion of Jewish and Christian scripture into Innu, a Cree language spoken
by aboriginal people in eastern Quebec. The Sisters of Instruction of the

Child Jesus claimed to have spent $540,000 for "community work" in First Nations reserves and urban environments in Manitoba, Saskatchewan, and B.C. They also claimed that "a variety of services was offered in addition to work that can be classified as 'religiosity.'" Mary Ellen Turpel-Lafond, a former judge and director of the University of British Columbia's Indian Residential School History and Dialogue Centre, called these expenses illegitimate. "This is ordinary church religious work repackaged as in-kind services and reconciliation."[8] The courts allowed the $29 million cash payment to be reduced by $5 million in legal fees and administrative costs, plus an additional $1.6 million the Church claimed it paid out but never specified to whom. And it was also allowed to subtract $8 million that was paid to survivors before the agreement was signed.

Following demands from Indigenous leaders that Catholics stop going to church as a protest, in July 2021 the Saskatoon diocese promised that that it would launch a five-year fundraising effort to raise $1.25 million. It urged other dioceses to follow suit. A year later Saskatoon had raised a fifth of its $1.25 million pledge. Although church leaders are members of a national assembly called the Canadian Conference of Catholic Bishops, which was not party to the original settlement, they acknowledged the Church's public relations disaster and vowed to raise $30 million.

At the conclusion of the pope's Canadian trip he celebrated a sparsely attended mass at the national Shrine in Quebec City. It was interrupted by two Indigenous women who stood in front of the pews and, facing away from Francis, and unfurled a ten-foot banner bearing the words "Rescind the Doctrine." Most Americans and many Canadians who saw the photograph wondered "What Doctrine?" The women were referring to the "Doctrine of Discovery," a distillation of several papal edicts issued in the fifteenth century that represented the Vatican's efforts to adjudicate squabbling among the colonial powers over which nation owned what territory in the New World. The Doctrine gave license to explorers such as Christopher Columbus for Spain and Pedro Álvares Cabral for Portugal to claim vacant land (terra nullius) in the name of their sovereigns, that is, land which was not populated by Christians. If a territory was not occupied by Christians, it was deemed vacant and therefore could be defined as "discovered."

The Indigenous people who had lived for a thousand generations on the lands in question, stretching between Terra del Fuego and the Arctic Circle, were not consulted. The 1455 papal bull titled *Romanus Pontifex* "authorized" King Alfonso of Portugal to conquer Africa and beyond, and to

> invade, search out, capture, vanquish, and subdue all Saracens (Muslims) and pagans whatsoever, and other enemies of Christ wheresoever placed, and the kingdoms, dukedoms, principalities, dominions, possessions, and all movable and immovable goods whatsoever held and possessed by them and to reduce their persons to perpetual slavery, and to apply and appropriate to himself and his successors the kingdoms, dukedoms, counties, principalities, dominions, possessions, and goods, and to convert them to his and their use and profit.

The papal bull titled *Inter Caetera* divided the New World between Spain and Portugal. England also demanded a slice of the pie as did France. In 1496 Henry VII granted a patent to the explorer John Cabot and his sons to claim all land in North America that had not been claimed by Spain.

> [They] may conquer, occupy and possess whatsoever such towns, castles, cities and islands by them thus discovered that they may be able to conquer, occupy and possess, as our vassals and governors, lieutenants and deputies therein, acquiring for us the dominion, title and jurisdiction of the same towns, castles, cities, islands and mainlands so discovered.

In 1534, Jacques Cartier planted a cross in the Gaspé Peninsula in what is now eastern Quebec and claimed what would be Canada in the name of King Francis I. It became the first province of New France. However, North America was hardly vacant when European explorers set sail. By one estimate, on the day in 1492 when Christopher Columbus arrived in Hispaniola North America was home to 54 million Indigenous people, one tenth of the world's population. But the Catholic Church determined that because they were not Christians they could not own the land they occupied. In 1823 the U.S. Supreme Court cited the Doctrine when it ruled that American Indians could not own land because they did not discover it. However, the papal position evolved, sort of. In 1537, Pope Paul III issued the bull *Sublimis Deus,* which forbade the enslavement of the Indigenous peoples of the Americas (called "Indians of the West and the South") and all other people. It states that the Indians were fully rational human beings who have rights to freedom and private property, even if they are not Christian. According to the Doctrine, however, this did not mean that they were granted title to their own land. They were allowed to occupy their land and use it but not own it. This would form the basis of the legal relationship between Indigenous North Americans and the governments of the U.S. and Canada for the next five centuries. On March 30, 2023, the Vatican finally responded to Indigenous demands by announcing its renunciation of the Doctrine, which it said "did not adequately reflect the equal dignity and rights of Indigenous peoples."[9]

In Canada, however, the Doctrine continues to inform the systems of education, health, and housing and it underlies the penal code. The supposition that European Christians could claim land they didn't own laid the foundation for policies such as Canada's "Indian Act" passed by Parliament in 1876, amended numerous times and still in force. The act attempted to assimilate a large and culturally diverse Indigenous population into a White, Christian society, which believed these cultures were inferior. The act replaced traditional native governments with band council elections. In 1885 it banned Indigenous religious ceremonies. In 1894 it made residential school attendance mandatory for First Nations children between the ages of seven and sixteen. In 1927 it forbade members of the First Nations from hiring a lawyer to sue the government. And the act replaced traditional hereditary chiefs with the heads of band councils who were elected. The Pass System was used between 1886 and the 1930s to control the movement of Native people. Never a law, it was enforced through an amendment to the "Indian Act" giving Indian agents the powers of a Justice of the Peace to regulate the provisions of the criminal code dealing with vagrancy and loitering. It required residents of reserves to present a passport issued by reserve agents before they could leave or return to their homes and it restricted the amount of time an individual could stay off-reserve. This was a consequence of the 1885 North-West Rebellion, which pitted Métis against the Canadian government in an effort to establish their own reserve, resulting in a battlefield defeat for the Métis and the execution of its leader, Louis Riel. Authorities were worried that if Indigenous people were free to move around the country they might congregate and foment another revolution.

The Permit System adopted by the government in the 1880s—and not stricken from the "Indian Act" until 1995—regulated the sale of goods by Indigenous people outside the reserves. It was part of an agricultural policy that gave White farmers an advantage over their Indigenous counterparts. For example, the Peasant Farm Policy of 1889 to 1897 prohibited Indigenous farmers on the western prairies from using mechanized equipment, thereby limiting what they could produce. Both the pass and the permit system intentionally damaged Indigenous economies.

Between the late 1950s and the early 1980s child welfare agents on the reserves deemed that because Indigenous children were being deprived of the advantages enjoyed by White children they should be placed in foster homes or adopted out to White families. Some 20,000 children were kidnapped and placed with strangers. They were told nothing about their cultural heritage, and they were not allowed to have any contact with their biological parents. "The Sixties Scoop" was coined to describe the practice. Sharon Boutilier is from the Whitefish River First Nation in Ontario. According to *Calgary City News* she didn't find that out until she was 18 years old. Born in 1966, Boutilier was taken from her family as an infant and placed for adoption with a White Catholic couple in Toronto.

"My adoptive parents always told me that I was 'Indian,'" she told the newspaper. "But I didn't know what that meant, or if it was true. It was like growing up without an identity because you know people would ask me 'where are you from' and 'what nationality are you?' and I didn't even really know who I was." When Boutilier turned eighteen she went to the Catholic Children's Aid Society with her adoptive mother, where she was given some sketchy information about her birth family. Although they were not named because of a nondisclosure clause in the adoption papers, she learned where they lived. Finally certain about her ancestry, Boutilier began to search for her people, hoping to learn more about her culture and background. But she learned that her family had been forcibly converted to Catholicism. "They went to residential schools; they were taught from an early age to disconnect from your identity. Being traditional was sacrilegious." Despite this, she said that when she met her relatives, she experienced an immediate bond with them. "It was freaky but I felt like I was at home on the reserve. It's called Blood Memory—that familiar feeling even though I hadn't been there since I was a baby." [10] Boutilier said the Canadian government's reaction to discoveries of unmarked graves on the grounds of residential schools is insulting to Indigenous communities. "I believe the Prime Minister needs to stand up and stop saying that the Canadian Government is shocked. This was planned by the government, executed by the churches." [11]

At a press conference in June 2021 Trudeau said

> This was an incredibly harmful government policy that was Canada's reality for many, many decades and Canadians today are horrified and ashamed of how our country behaved. The hurt and the trauma that you feel is Canada's responsibility to bear, and the government will continue to provide Indigenous communities across the country with the funding and resources they need to bring these terrible wrongs to light.

But so far he has not indicated that his government was considering a national investigation, suggesting instead that the issue of suspicious unmarked graves is a police matter. However, the federal budget enacted in spring 2022 earmarked almost $210 million over the next five years to fund the investigation by First Nations communities for unmarked graves at residential schools across Canada. Inspections of the cemeteries and grounds of many former schools began as soon as the funding was available. One of the first of these was conducted by the George Gordon First Nation in Saskatchewan, named for a hereditary chief also called Kaneonuskatew. In April 2022 it announced that its crew used ground penetrating radar to identify fourteen potential unmarked gravesites on the grounds of the former Gordon's Indian Residential School. Managed by the Anglican Church, it was the last of the federally funded assimilation centers in Canada. It was closed in 1996 and its main building was demolished.

Each discovery in Canada will bring new demands that the government conduct its own forensic investigation of what some people are calling crime scenes. And pressure will build on the Vatican to put its money where its mouth is and begin paying reparations to the remaining survivors of the boarding school system. A third consequence will be potentially momentous repercussions in the United States, where the Catholic Church is already reeling financially from lawsuits brought by the victims of priests and nuns who sexually exploited them as children.

In 2015, years before the explosive reports about unmarked Native graves in Canada compelled Pope Francis to apologize, a quiet report appeared about the cemetery at an Indian boarding school in Oregon. The investigation was contained in an obscure master's thesis submitted by a graduate student at Montana State University. In her study Marsha F. Small, fifty-three years old at the time and a member of the Northern Cheyenne tribe in Montana, used ground-penetrating radar to survey the half-acre burial ground at the Chemawa Indian School in the northern suburbs of Salem. She detected the remains of as many as 222 human beings, most of whom were children who died at the school between its construction in 1885 and the Depression. The ghostly images that populate the PowerPoint section of her thesis look like murky underwater photographs of sunken ships, vague outlines of prows pointed upward, as if they were trying to surface.

The second oldest boarding school in the U.S., Chemawa was founded by the U.S. government in 1880, a year after the Carlisle Indian Industrial School, and is still in operation as a high school. The cemetery is not a mass burial ground like those found in war zones where bodies were dumped in a pit and covered with lime and dirt to hide them or to prevent disease. The graves at Chemawa were once marked with headstones and catalogued. Some markers were made of wood and others of stone. But all of them were swept away, moved, or leveled in 1960 when groundskeepers used a bulldozer to clear out blackberry and poison oak in an attempt to make the cemetery easier to maintain.

Heavy-gauge copper plates bearing the names of the dead and their death dates were affixed to concrete bars and planted flat at the graves, their positions based on an old plat map of the site. But Marsha Small discovered that over the course of a half century many of the markers had been vandalized or covered by creeping vegetation and soil. Among those she found were some that did not match up with her radar images of the graves, which led her to the question: So who is buried where? Still, a map of the Chemawa cemetery hand-drawn by the school's staff in 1960 shows the approximate location of the graves along with names and death dates. Listed on the map are 174 children who died at the school between 1886 and 1934, mostly from influenza, tuberculosis, meningitis, and pneumonia. Because of the expense of transporting them to their families as they were dying, or shipping their bodies after they were dead, they were buried at Chemawa, never to see home again. Their Indian names had been replaced with "American" names by the school's staff, or Russian names in the case of those students from Alaska, which was "owned" by Russia until 1867. For example, a Tlingit girl renamed "Helen Johnson" died in 1920 of tuberculosis. An Aleut boy renamed "John Ketchikoff" died in 1912 of tuberculosis. A Nez Perce boy renamed "Daniel Boone," who died in 1889 of a pulmonary embolism, had written in a school friend's private autograph book: "Please remember me when I'm in the grave." An additional eighteen gravesites are recorded as containing members of the staff, their children, or others associated with the school who died between 1887 and 1944. Especially troubling for the Native families and clans from California, the Pacific Northwest, and Alaska are some forty plots that likely contain the unrecorded burials of children who just disappeared. "Why is there a cemetery?" Small asked. "It's a school! What the heck? You got money to steal and kidnap a kid but don't have money to send them home if they're ready to die?"

She said she was unmoved by the pope's talk in Canada of penance. "His apology doesn't even qualify as a Band-Aid. It didn't do anything. We need action. They can put in place programs to help our people heal, maybe even economic reparations. It's OK to have equality. It won't break their bank. It's not like they haven't made billions off of us already." If the church released their documents, it would "make my job a whole lot easier," she said in reference to her continuing detective work at Chemawa and other boarding schools in the U.S. "If they open up the archives so we can find our people, our children, that would go a long way in terms of helping us heal."[12]

Small's study was motivated in part by her academic ambitions. While working on her doctoral thesis she also taught anthropology at Willamette University in Oregon. She spent $7,000 of her own money on the Chemawa study, which required leasing equipment and hiring helpers. But her work was deeply personal, as well. Her aunt and three uncles had worn Chemawa's scratchy wool uniforms. Her grandfather and great uncle were shipped to Carlisle. The only international media outlet that reported her findings at the time was Al Jazeera, the Arabic-language radio station financed by the royal family of Qatar. In 2013 a local tribal newspaper published a single article about her work. Nevertheless, the results of Small's study spread through Indian Country by word-of-mouth. Indians were not shocked nor surprised by what they were hearing since almost all Native Americans have a relative who was enrolled in a boarding school. And it's not like the tribes have never sought justice for the kidnapping and abuse of their children.

Between 2001 and 2009 the Oregon Province of the Society of Jesus was barraged by lawsuits filed by the victims of sexual and physical abuse perpetrated by Jesuit priests and brothers at Indian boarding schools in Washington, Oregon, Alaska, Idaho, and Montana over a sixty-year period. The province and its insurer paid $55 million in reparations to these victims. Faced with an additional 200 claims the Jesuits declared bankruptcy in 2009, the only one of the ten U.S. provinces to do so. A statement from the Jesuits said that Chapter 11 bankruptcy "will allow the Oregon Province to resolve pending claims, manage its financial situation and continue its various ministries in the Northwest in which it has been engaged since 1831." The judge overseeing the bankruptcy proceedings gave attorneys a deadline to file new claims on behalf of abuse victims. That led to a massive search and numerous meetings across the West, as scores and then hundreds of Native Americans and several White victims of abuse came forward. In 2011, after a year of negotiations with victims and their lawyers the province and its insurer, Safeco, agreed to pay a whopping $166.1 million to 525 boarding school victims and a few White victims at other Jesuit institutions. Just over $48 million of that settlement was paid by the Jesuits themselves. Payments averaged about $300,000—a lot of money, but hardly life-changing.

Although they claimed to be broke the Jesuits managed to find the cash, mostly through donations from die-hard Catholics and the sale of property. After the province emerged from bankruptcy it sold even more of its real estate to shore up its "ministry" and to care for aging priests. One piece of their portfolio was a $2.2 million building on the campus of Seattle University, where the school once provided a safe harbor for a priest named Michael Toulouse. A serial predator, Toulouse molested boys in Spokane during the 1950s and 1960s before he was transferred to a teaching job at Seattle University. One of the victims was a twelve-year altar boy who was molested at the church where Toulouse celebrated daily Mass. The transfer and coverup were initiated after the father of the boy, waving around a pistol, burst into the office of the president of Gonzaga University and threatened to shoot Toulouse. In Seattle, Toulouse continued molesting young boys. Eight of his victims were among the plaintiffs in the Oregon Province settlement.

Lawyers for some of the victims suggested that they might try to extract money in the future from wealthy Jesuit institutions in the Northwest such as Seattle University and Gonzaga University, although they were not named in the lawsuit. Despite the fact that the colleges and the Jesuits claim no mutual legal or financial bonds their liability cannot be ruled out, especially in light of a shocking revelation issued in 2018. The Diocese of Spokane said that it was "unacceptable" that seven Jesuits credibly accused of sexual abuse lived until 2016 unsupervised at a house on Gonzaga's campus owned by the Oregon Province, a fact neither the diocese, the province or the university shared with the community. They were free to come and go, had unsupervised visits with students and led prayer services at Indian reservations.

A victim's advocacy group reported that the isolation of the boarding schools and the Jesuit policy of shipping "problem" priests to these far-flung assimilation centers accounted for the staggering number of victims. "The victims represent some of the poorest and most vulnerable children in the Pacific Northwest," one of the attorneys representing the plaintiffs said. "We have long suspected the Jesuits used remote villages in Alaska and small towns near reservations in the Pacific Northwest as a place to send its abusive and problem priests, including known pedophiles." Many of the cases involved only a couple of Jesuits, but there were at least two dozen different priests, brothers, or other adults in authority who were implicated. Sixty-six individual claims of sexual abuse were filed against one man, Father John Joseph Morse, who served at St. Mary's Mission near Omak, Washington, on the Colville Reservation. He was accused of molesting a few boys and many girls, some as young as five years old. One accuser said Morse would tell her to come to his office for "a whipping." She said he would whip her and "a whole lot more," and that if she wouldn't participate in "sexual favors" he would lock her in a dark root cellar full of spiders. Another accuser said Morse first raped her when she was an eleven-year-old sixth grader, and that the abuse went on every day through eighth grade. Morse died in 2015 at the age of eighty-five while living at the Jesuit safe house at Gonzaga.

After the federal government and the churches ignored decades of demands that boarding school records be released to the tribes a grassroots movement of Native scholars, researchers, tribal leaders, and boarding school survivors and their descendants joined forces in 2012 and formed the National Native American Boarding School Healing Coalition (NABS). Part of its mission was to lobby Congress for the establishment of a commission on U.S. Indian boarding schools, similar to the Truth and Reconciliation Commission in Canada. The key provisions of the bill they are pushing include a tabulation of the number of children forced to attend residential schools, a compilation of publicly shared information about children who were abused, died, or went missing while enrolled, a study of the long-term impacts on the children and the families of children forced into assimilation, and recommendations for justice.

After NABS spent eight years lobbying Congress, "The Truth and Healing Commission on Indian Boarding School Policies Act" was introduced in the House. Its sponsor was Deb Haaland, a Laguna Pueblo recently elected Democratic Congresswoman from New Mexico. Elizabeth Warren (D-Mass) introduced the same bill in the Senate. Because the legislation didn't reach a committee vote in 2020, it was reintroduced the next year, a common practice. It was cosponsored by sixty-nine Democratic Representatives and six Republicans. Twenty-three Democrats and one Republican, Lisa Murkowski of Alaska, cosponsored the bill in the Senate. Haaland, newly appointed Secretary of the Interior, testified in favor of the bill. Despite the bipartisan support it might takes months or years for the bill to become law, if ever. The reality is that Congress passes only a tiny fraction of the 10,000 bills its members introduce every year. And now that the two parties are increasingly at one another's throats it would take a crisis like a war or a devastating epidemic to compel them to cooperate on any measure.

Haaland, who is the first Native American cabinet member, announced in 2021, following the revelations in Canada about unmarked graves, that she had commissioned the Department of the Interior to compile an extensive report about American Indian boarding schools. In May 2022 the first installment was released. It listed 408 federally financed Indian schools in 37 states, including Alaska and Hawaii. Some 150 of these assimilation centers were operated by Christian denominations, half of them by the Roman Catholic Church. It shocked most Americans by touching on the abuse suffered by children at these establishments. "Federal Indian boarding school rules were often enforced through punishment," the investigation reported, "including corporal punishment such as solitary confinement; flogging; withholding food; whipping; slapping; and cuffing. The Federal Indian boarding school system at times made older Indian children punish younger Indian children."

One conservative's reaction to the report is typical of right-wing efforts to suppress the history of America's human right abuses. "This attempt to create a national scandal over Indian boarding schools," Helen Andrews wrote in the *American Conservative* magazine, "is a thoroughly political scheme contrived by activists to stoke outrage regardless of the facts." She blamed "wokeness" for the uproar over the report and dismissed the use of corporal punishment as something that was meted out at *all* American schools during the boarding school era.[13] Her arguments demonstrate her ignorance of Indigenous child-rearing practices. And she ignores the 1969 hearings during which Congress acknowledged that from "the beginning, Federal policy toward the Indian was based on the desire to dispossess him of his land. Education policy was a function of our land policy."[14]

The Interior report also identified burial sites at more than fifty of the former boarding schools, nineteen of which were the sites where more than five hundred American Indian, Alaska Native, and Native Hawaiian children died, a figure that is expected to grow substantially as subsequent installments of the investigation are completed. While Indigenous leaders praised Haaland's initiative, they believe that a Congressional commission on boarding schools is the only way to give teeth to the struggle for reparations because of the subpoena power of Congress, which compels witnesses to testify or face charges of criminal contempt.

If the course of events in the U.S. follows the Canadian pattern of discovery, investigation, apology, civil action, and reparation, the U.S. government will be making payments to tribal Americans for years. And the churches will be forced to sell off even more of their vast real estate and asset holdings, a process that began after the barrage of sexual abuse lawsuits brought by the victims of predatory priests, nuns, and other clergy. The pope—whether Francis or his successor—will be compelled to release documents illuminating the fate of the Native children who suddenly found themselves trapped inside the big boxes built by White people.

Boarding schools battered Indigenous cultures in their attempt to extinguish Native language and spirituality, while denying several generations of children lessons in how to be parents, all part of the campaign to separate the tribes from their communally controlled land. The U.S. government decided it would be cheaper to absorb Indians into the workforce than sending out the cavalry to annihilate them, but because it lacked the resources to accomplish this goal it turned to the churches for help. The prospect of harvesting thousands of heathen souls lured missionaries from most every Christian denomination to Indian Country. Catholic participation in this spiritual feeding frenzy was enabled by the world's wealthiest nun, who used her fortune to build and finance dozens of boarding schools in the U.S.

But as we shall see, the scheme failed to extinguish Native cultures. Many White Americans, believing that Indians had gone extinct, were surprised when the island of Alcatraz and the village of Wounded Knee were occupied for months by Indigenous protesters fifty years ago. They were reminded again during the eleven-month protest against the Dakota Access Pipeline that the Vanishing Indian is a myth. And at the 2024 Golden Globe Awards Blackfeet actress Lily Gladstone underlined the point after she won for best actress in a dramatic film. "We have come to know the truth," she told the audience in Siksiká, the Blackfeet language, "that our mother tongue is sacred."[15]

Chapter Two

THE INTERPRETERS

At dawn the nuns herded the girls into a pair of white-topped prairie schooners, pulled the bonnet straps tight at each end, and ordered the drivers to get started. Like most travelers on the rough dirt roads of Montana in 1892 the Ursulines and their hired men preferred to walk or ride a saddle horse instead of suffering the bone-jarring lurch of the wagons. But these fifteen Piegan children were put on board because they were precious cargo. The federal government paid the nuns $100 a year for every Indian they enrolled at St. Peter's Mission, compelling Sister Zita and Sister Santa Clara to prevent these little heathens from making a run for it while they were still within running distance of their families.

Among them was Nancy Bird. She had spent two years in the larger world and would have to be watched. Because she spoke Siksiká, Michif, and English she was recruited as interpreter. After she gave directions to the other girls they opened the chests in the wagons and passed around the red wool blankets stored inside. When the wagons began to roll Sister Zita heard Nancy continue to jabber in Indian. The other girls laughed. What was she saying to them? Were they trying to figure out why the nuns dressed like *mamiatsíkimi*—magpies—the one word of Indian Zita could understand?

As the mule-powered caravan plodded its way south from the Black-feet Reservation along the ancient trace the Blackfeet called *miisum apatosiosoko*—the Old North Trail—the temperature rose to 42 degrees. But by late afternoon the November sky darkened. Snow began to fall. And then it was dropping in heavy sheets driven by the wind. The drivers knew that when they could no longer see the 8,000-foot peaks and reefs of the Rocky Mountain Front ten miles west it was time to get indoors. They were not far from the cow town of Dupuyer. The next morning there was a foot of snow on the ground and more coming down. It was Thanksgiving. For thousands of winters Bird's people had raised their lodges in the shelter of the forests growing along streams such as Badger Creek or the Teton River. She must have thought the nuns were insane to even set foot up on the grasslands during a blizzard.

Days later, after slogging across eighty miles of wind-scoured prairie, taking refuge wherever they could find it or beg for it, they spent the night in the village of Sun River. The most daunting part of the journey was still ahead. This was a section of the Mullan Road that climbed a thousand feet from the river's floodplain into the foothills of the Big Belt Mountains. That evening they stopped at a homestead, but they were turned away. The owners were unwilling to share their shelter with Indians. "The dear imitators of the travelers of Bethlehem," a diarist wrote, "spent the night out on the prairie in the black cold." The next evening the nuns looked back down on the flats below. The house was on fire. As they watched, it burned to the ground.[1]

The next day they veered away from the Mullan Road into a narrow valley that looked like a gallery of strange giant sculptures. Rising around them towered a ring of buttes whose American names described them—Fishtail, Haystack, Skull, Lionhead, and the most imposing of all, the Bird Tail, a thousand-foot monolith whose summit was capped by a phalanx of sheer igneous palisades that resembled tail feathers. The Blackfeet called it *piita otoyi*, the Eagle Tail. The nuns hoped that because the butte held a special place in the superstitions of these pagans, living under it might have a calming effect on them.

Four miles farther on they reached the Mission. The Piegan girls—hungry, exhausted, and dehydrated, still wrapped in the blankets they had been huddling under all week—climbed down from the wagons and gazed up at the massive gray stone building studded with towers that would be their new home. The nuns called it Mount Angela Institute. Another huge stone building loomed nearby—the boarding school for boys operated by the Jesuits. Besides Nancy, the girls included Ursula Cutbank, Lizzie Big Eyes, Isabel Bear Chief, and nine-year-old Josephine Hazlett, an orphan who had been traded to a Chinese railroad worker for two ponies. A dissatisfied customer, the man later gave Josephine to George Steell, the agent for the Blackfeet Agency, who gave her to the nuns, who erased her Indian name and substituted it for something they could pronounce. [2]

—⁓⁓—

St. Peter's was one of some ninety Catholic boarding schools spread across more than twenty states, operating between 1819 and 1968. It was a network the Church was fond of calling the "Lord's Vineyard," assimilation centers where Indigenous children such as Nancy Bird were sent so missionaries could harvest their souls. St. Peter's began in spring 1859 after the Society of Jesus ordered two Jesuits to risk their scalps converting the Blackfeet to Christianity. A Dutch Jesuit named Adrianus Hoecken set out that year from St. Ignatius, a mission among the Salish people in western Montana he had cofounded in 1854 with a Flemish Jesuit named Pierre-Jean De Smet. Hoecken's assignment was to select a site for the new outpost. Not the keenest of observers, he chose a spot on the Teton River a mile below the present town of Choteau, Montana, near a rise which is still called Priest Butte. The wind streaming from the Rocky Mountain Front blew constantly, with gusts of 100 miles per hour. Winter low temperatures often dropped below zero. Hoecken and his companion, Brother Vincent Magri, built three small log shacks in the willows and cottonwoods crowding the floodplain and settled down to suffer through the long winter, living on whatever food they could scavenge from the frozen land or cajole from their Blackfeet neighbors—fish, dried bison, roots, moss, and berries. In October they were joined by Johannes Imoda, an Italian Jesuit newly arrived from San Francisco with high hopes. The three of them began pestering the Natives who visited their squalid digs to teach them Siksiká, the Blackfeet language. For the Black Robes this was "a task almost as distasteful to them as being scalped," a fellow Jesuit later wrote.[3] Because of the threat of Blackfeet uprisings and poor choices in choosing sites the Jesuits would move St. Peter's two more times before the mission took root in 1866 under the Bird Tail.

In the records of the American institutions that abducted her, Nancy Bird is listed as a Piegan. But she was in fact Métis, a French word meaning "mixed race." These are people descended from the numerous common-law unions of European fur traders with Indigenous North American women beginning in the 1600s, a practice known as *marriage à la façon du pays*, or "according to the custom of the country." They were also called Bois Brûlé, French for "burned wood," because of how Whites perceived the color of their skin. Numbering 625,000 in North America, according to 2020 census reports, they developed a unique culture composed of aboriginal and European parts. They sang and played cross-tuned fiddles, mixing and mashing First Nations songs with Scottish and French-Canadian tunes, driven by unique beats. This music spawned a dance form called jigging, such as the Rabbit Dance and the Broom Dance. Their chief mode of transport was the Red River cart. This was a two-wheeled conveyance pulled by mules or oxen. It was made entirely of wood and strips of bison hide without any metal parts. Because the oak axles could not be lubricated the carts emitted hideous grinding shrieks as they rolled across the prairies. The Métis practiced a folk Catholicism centered on veneration of the Virgin and St. Paul, and developed several dialects, most commonly the French-Cree hybrid called Michif. Like Nancy Bird, some Métis were simultaneously members of the Métis nation in Canada as well as the Blackfeet Confederacy in

Montana and Alberta. But unlike most Natives and most Whites she was directly descended from professional interpreters.

Nancy's great-grandfather, James Curtis Bird, was born in 1773 in Acton, England. When he was fifteen years old he took a job as a clerk with the Hudson's Bay Company. He traveled to what is now Manitoba in Rupert's Land, a vast swath of North America whose commerce in natural resources was awarded in 1670 to the company by King Charles II of England. Its shareholders would grow fabulously wealthy from the trapping, killing, and skinning of fur-bearing animals such as beaver and mink. In 1809 he was appointed justice of the peace for what the invaders called the "Indian Territories," and from 1816 to 1818 he served as acting governor for the whole of Rupert's Land. He finished his career with the company as one of its chief factors—the agents in charge of buying furs from trappers.

In 1839 Bird was appointed by the Hudson's Bay Company to serve as one of the fifteen governing councilors of Assiniboia, also known as the Red River Colony. Stretching across 116,000 square miles of Rupert's Land from Manitoba south along the Red River into Minnesota and the Dakotas, it was founded in 1812 by a philanthropic Scottish earl named Lord Selkirk. He had purchased enough shares of the company to demand from it a section of land where he intended to create an agricultural haven for his country's tenant farmers driven from their homes during the Highland Clearances. These were evictions carried out over the course of a century by wealthy landlords who wanted to cash in on the increasingly lucrative European wool market by replacing dirt farmers with sheep. In exchange Selkirk agreed to provide workers to the company and allow it to operate posts where it could trade goods to European and Native trappers in exchange for furs. One of Selkirk's problems was the fact that the District of Assiniboia was already occupied by thousands of Assiniboine, Cree, and Saulteaux people and at least 5,000 Métis. Another was increasing pressure from the North West Company, which disputed the commercial monopoly granted by Hudson Bay's charter. The resulting competition between both of these European corporations and the Indigenous population would lead to murder, atrocities, and, later, a war.

Bird partnered with a number of what were called "country wives," probably polygamously, including a high-status Swampy Cree named Oomenahomisk (Well Dressed Woman). He called her Mary—his sister's name. Interracial partnerships were encouraged by the fur trading companies because these unions tended to reinforce networks that delivered furs and later buffalo robes to the trading posts of the Hudson's Bay Company and its rival, the North West Company. They were also sanctioned by tribal leaders seeking to broaden the kinship bonds that buttressed their political power. Bird consulted regularly with his country wives in both domestic and business matters, relying on them because they spoke several languages and served as his interpreters. He was accused by one of his critics in the company of being a "petty coat politician" who was dependent on his "copper colored mate."

Nancy's grandfather, James "Jemmy Jock" Bird, was born in 1798. He became a fur trader, hunter, and guide who worked both sides of the Medicine Line, the imaginary and artificial border established in 1818 between the U.S. and Canada along the forty-ninth parallel. He was also famous across the prairies of both nations as an expert interpreter who spoke French, English, Michif, and five Native tongues. He was fluent in Cree and Siksiká, the sinewy and verb-driven language of the three confederated Blackfeet nations—the Siksikas and Kanais, living north of the Medicine Line, and the Piegans, living primarily in what is now Montana. (Before the European invasion created territories with borders all three bands moved at will throughout the prairies and mountains hunting, foraging, making war, and later stealing horses.)

Bird partnered with a number of "country wives" over the course of his ninety-six years, including Bulls Heart, the daughter of a Piegan chief named Bulls Heart Man. Jemmy Jock called her Sally. The youngest of their children was Philip Bird, Nancy's father. He was born in 1852 among the Piegan, in whose company he would die in 1925 in Montana after dividing his life between the U.S. and Canada. The parish priest of St. James, Manitoba officiated at his wedding in 1870 to Mary Kipling, a Métis and Winnebago. Eight years later Nancy was born to them on the Blackfeet

Reservation. As was common among the Métis, Piegan, and First Nations people the Birds moved back and forth across the Medicine Line in pursuit of opportunity. Philip hunted, trapped, and picked up work as a laborer and a freighter for the Hudson Bay's Company. They were living in what would become Alberta during the brutal Starvation Winter of 1883–1884 on the Blackfeet Reservation, when the U.S. government failed to deliver food to the Piegans following the extermination of the bison herds. This latest broken promise resulted in the deaths of at least 500 people, a quarter of the band, and would significantly reduce the tribe's ability to resist the tyranny of the U.S. government.

In 1884 he landed a job as an interpreter for missionaries from the Church of England at Blackfoot Crossing, a meeting place for the Métis and Siksika in southern Alberta. In May of 1885 the Birds made a two-day trip west to Calgary in their mule-driven Red River cart. After queuing up outside a tent he put his mark on a document stating that he had been residing before July 15, 1870, in the North-West Territories, that he owned no real property and that his net worth was $1,230. He was awarded "scrip" by what was called the North-West Half Breed Commission redeemable for $240.

Scrip was the infamous swindle employed by the federal government in Ottawa to extinguish the Métis Nation's claims to land. It was concocted in response to the long-standing complaints that Indigenous rights were being ignored in the Dominion's rush to settle the Western prairies with White farmers and stockmen. The coupons issued to the Métis resembled fancy engraved currency and were redeemable for 160 or 240 acres or up to $240, which could be used to buy land priced at $1 per acre. The Métis were not allowed to choose specific parcels because the land first had to be surveyed, a process that often took years to complete. Instead of awarding a reserve to the Métis Nation as a whole the Dominion chose to deal with individuals, thus weakening their ability to press their territorial claims as a collective. Meanwhile, many Métis sold their money scrip for less than their value to speculators and con men. The scheme so impressed U.S. lawmakers that Congress passed its own Native land swindle in 1877 called the General Allotment Act. At the very moment Philip was putting his mark on his scrip application some 300 Métis and First Nations fighters were shooting at Canadian soldiers on a battlefield 700 miles away. The outcome of that armed resistance would set Nancy Bird's young life on a bizarre new course.

—⁓—

In 1879 an army officer named Captain Richard Henry Pratt successfully lobbied Congress to fund an Indian boarding school at the Carlisle Barracks in Pennsylvania, an abandoned fort built by the British in 1745. It was chosen for its proximity to Washington, D.C., policy makers and because it was on a rail line. Plus, it was on the other side of the continent from the nomadic cultures whose children he would soon begin attempting to reprogram. After the Barracks was transferred from the War Department to the Interior Department, Pratt set about recruiting students. The Indian Bureau required that at least half of them should come from the most troublesome tribes, and ideally would be the children of their most important chiefs. The government was especially interested in extracting Sioux children because they could be used as leverage to carve more land from their reservations. Commissioner of Indian Affairs Ezra Hayt ordered Pratt to get his first students from the agencies at Pine Ridge and Rosebud in South Dakota "because the children would be hostages for the good behavior of their people." Pratt traveled west and arranged a meeting with Spotted Tail, White Thunder, and Two Strikes. "The white people" Spotted Tail told Pratt, "are all thieves and liars. We do not want our children to learn such things."[4] But Pratt pressed on, arguing that because the Sioux were illiterate they had no way of knowing what was written in the treaties they were signing. At Carlisle, Pratt promised, your children will be taught to read and write.

His first shipment of Indians arrived on the Cumberland Valley Rail Road just before 1:00 A.M. on October 6, 1879. Although the late hour was designed to discourage gawkers an excited crowd of hundreds had gathered around the Carlisle station, expecting to see exotic savages in cages. Instead, what stepped down from the train were eighty-nine sleepy and confused Sioux teenagers exhausted from their week-long journey across America, packed inside what one of them described as "a moving house." The sixty-three boys were dressed in blankets, moccasins, and leggings. The twenty-six girls wore bright shawls and carried baskets containing their meager belongings. Captain Pratt reported to the local newspaper that a crowd of 3,000 had gathered at the Rosebud Agency to see the children off and "made the night terrible with their incessant howling."[5] Surrounded by this friendly and curious crowd of White people Pratt's conscripts were marched in the moonlight a mile from the station to the Barracks. Among them were four of Spotted Tail's sons. Two weeks later another group of fifty-eight children arrived at the station. They were members of nine different tribes including Cheyenne, Apache, and Arapahoe. People in the crowd were disappointed that they were dressed in what a newspaper called "citizen" clothes rather than their native garb. And so it went, year after year, what the Carlisle newspaper called "Pratt's young braves and squaws" stepping down from the train into a new life removed a continent away from their families and their culture.

In March 1890, five years after the Birds joined thousands of Métis fleeing Canada following the collapse of the rebellion, Nancy was driven by wagon across the Blackfeet Reservation and loaded on an eastbound Great Northern train along with thirty-seven other Piegan and Métis children, ranging in age from six to eighteen. The group included her brother, Henry, two years older. A week later the Birds arrived at Carlisle. Fatigued and disoriented, they were marched a mile in the dark from the depot to the gates of Pratt's school. They crossed the parade grounds to an administrative building where they were examined briefly by a doctor, who recorded Nancy's height at four feet, eleven inches and her weight at ninety-six pounds. Thirteen-year-old Henry weighed in at 106 pounds and stood five feet, two inches tall. She was led to a bathroom where another girl showed her how to use the hot and cold spigots. After her bath she was ordered to put on the clothes she had been issued—leather boots studded with buttons and hooks and a heavy ankle-length Victorian dress made of wool. Next, she was ushered to her quarters. This was a fourteen-by-sixteen-foot sleeping room she would share with two other girls. They were not from home, however, they were from two far-flung tribes whose languages were based in linguistic families that had nothing in common. This was a tactic the institution believed would force students to learn English if they wanted to get along with their roommates.

Like that of all the boys, Henry's long, black braids were lopped off. Many Native children perceived this as a shocking invasion of their personal space. Native people would only cut their hair in mourning. The school sheared its students, it maintained, to control head lice. But the practice was also intended to strip them of their individuality, make them look more like White children, and distance them from their cultures, in which long hair was a traditional source of spiritual strength. After his bath Henry was outfitted in boots, scratchy red flannel underwear, a military-style McClellan cap, a stiff-collared white shirt, and a blue wool uniform studded with red stripes, brass buttons, and faux-epaulets. He was assigned the rank of private. If he performed the right tricks at Carlisle he could advance up the ranks and become a lieutenant or even a captain, entitled to carry a saber on ceremonial occasions. The military-school aspects of Carlisle that included the organization of boys into squads, forced marches, and special privileges and status for cadet officers turned out to be one of the few things about Carlisle that appealed to the sons of warrior cultures such as the Piegan and the Lakota. Henry was then taken to a room in the Large Boys' Quarters, while younger Blackfeet were taken to the Small Boys' Quarters. Like his sister, he would share this room with two conscripts from linguistically remote cultures.

The Birds were placed in the first grade and enrolled for a five-year stint. They had no say in the matter. Tribal police had been rounding up the children of reservation families who refused to enroll them in government or Christian schools. In response, some parents hid their children. It's possible that Philip and Mary Bird volunteered to send Nancy and Henry to the other side of America because they believed that Carlisle would be a better place for them than the reservation, which was still reeling from the Starvation Winter and the Great Die-Up, when 90 percent of the cattle across Montana were killed by a relentless blizzard that raged across the territory in January 1887, dropping temperatures to minus 46 degrees. Because she could speak some English she was assigned to interpret for her Piegan classmates, who were not allowed to speak Siksiká. Her assimilation began immediately. This included traditional American schoolroom classes in English, history, drawing, composition, arithmetic, geography, and music. She was compelled to learn what today would be called home economics—cooking, baking, laundering, and cleaning. She was given instruction in Christianity and was expected to attend daily services at a local church and two services on Sundays. Exercise sessions in the gymnasium were mandatory. She could choose to join one of two literary societies.

The next day was dizzying. The regimen the Birds would have to endure resembled boot camp more than it did a school for children. Every moment for the 750 young Native Americans enrolled at Carlisle was regulated and controlled. They rose at 6 A.M. after the bugle played reveille and turned off the lights in their rooms at 9 P.M. when it played taps. They were marched in formation to breakfast. At mealtime they were fed things they had never before tasted. One of the staples was cow's milk, a food unknown to Plains Indians. Although most Native Americans were and still are lactose intolerant, in 1880 Pratt wrote the Commissioner of Indian Affairs pleading for funds to feed his students milk, a relatively cheap and plentiful commodity he said the school's physicians recommended be given to its children "in abundance." For a few years Carlisle bought milk from local dairymen, but later relied on its own herd. It can be speculated that the inevitable digestive problems the Carlisle diet likely caused was one reason so many students suffered from health problems.

Each block of their time was marked by bells and whistles, an alien and jarring way to live for children raised in a culture that marked the passage of time by the silent flow of the sun and the heavens. The disorientation produced by the dictatorship of the clock was compounded by the hierarchical structure of Carlisle. At its apex was Richard Pratt. Below him were teachers and staff. Below them were cadet officers. On the bottom rung were the other students, who had been shipped here from societies built not around bosses but kinship networks and the rule of consensus.

Nancy spent her first morning at Carlisle in what was called the Industrial Departments, which offered home economics. Henry's three-hour morning was spent in the Academic Departments, where beginning students were immersed through rote repetition in the difficult and often illogical English language. In the afternoon Nancy went to school in the Academic Departments and Henry went to work in the Industrial Departments learning such trades as carpentry, harness-making, tin-smithing, shoemaking, and printing. Again, all instruction was given in English. Not until a student could master at least some of the language was she given instruction in arithmetic, art, history, and science. Music was part of the required regimen—singing for most students, musical instruments for those who showed an interest. The Birds were required to attend daily church services and workouts in the school's gymnasium. What was called "physical culture" included hefting "Indian" clubs and stretching on the parallel bars.

Carlisle's theory was that by prohibiting students from speaking their own tongues and forcing them to learn English they would also absorb lessons embedded in the language about Western notions of hygiene, God, individuality, and capitalism—consider, for example, the hundreds of words related to money. This was not a radical idea—modern speakers of Siksiká believe that the only way to understand traditional Blackfeet culture and spirituality is to become fluent in the language. Some children circumvented the prohibition by simply ignoring it. Others communicated with Hand Talk, the sign language of the Plains spoken in 1890 by 100,000 people from three-dozen tribes. And they further reached out to one another by sharing pictographs they drew on their slates with slate pencils, portraying most often the horses, riders, battles, and hunts that were central to the cultures they refused to leave behind. Plains Indian pictographs called "winter counts" were drawn on buffalo hides and, similar to the Bayeux Tapestry, usually featured a significant event that happened during the previous four seasons. The school tried to enforce its will with jail time, corporal punishment, or by shaming Native-speaking students in the pages of *The Red Man*, the school's student newspaper.

When that didn't work, Carlisle decided to employ reason rather than restraint. At a regular Saturday night assembly in the school chapel called "English Speaking Meeting," Pratt stood at the podium ramrod straight and told his 700 charges that it was in their best interests to obey. A person who knew only his Indian language was a prisoner of his reservation, he argued, and a prisoner to the thoughts of his people. A person fluent in English was a free person who could always get a job and travel anywhere he wanted. Tall, barrel-chested, possessed of a large head and wearing a long, black Prince Albert coat, Pratt sometimes used call-and-response to enliven his lectures. After reciting a Bible passage and a prayer, then reading the names of students caught using tobacco that week or speaking their native languages, he might call out "How shall we solve the Indian problem?" Several children would shout back various responses such as "abolish the Reservation system" and "abolish the ration system" and "get the Indian into civilization and citizenship and keep him there." These were not their own thoughts, of course, but those of Captain Pratt.

The Birds sensed an excitement building around them as their first noontime meal approached. That's because Thursday was Pot Pie Day. The entire student body was marched in platoons to the Dining Hall. The Large Boys were seated at one long row of tables, the Girls at another and the Small Boys in the middle row between them. Laughter and chatter ceased as one of the older girls stood and began singing "Praise God from Whom All Blessings Flow." Many of the students joined in. When the song was over the cadet officers and some older girls began passing the pies around. [6] Much of the food at Carlisle was grown on the school's farm and prepared in its kitchens. The farmers were the students themselves as were the cooks and dishwashers. Students washed and dried the laundry. All custodial work was performed by students, including scrubbing the floors and cleaning the latrines. Student carpenters, masons, and painters repaired the buildings. Much of the clothing distributed by the institution was cut and sewn by students. Student mechanics repaired the farm equipment. *The Red Man* was printed by students as were the many brochures, pamphlets, envelopes, and letterheads used by the school's administration. In the winter student crews fed coal to the school's boiler twenty-four hours a day. Today most of the nonfarm work at Carlisle would constitute violations of the child labor laws. But during the same era many American children were pulled from school and forced to work. For example, kids as young as seven clocked sixty-hour weeks spinning cotton in North Carolina mills.

After working in the mornings for a year and attending school in the afternoons Nancy was sent in May 1891 to a farm in West Grove, Pennsylvania, ninety miles east of Carlisle. Like many rural families in the borough the Joneses were Quakers by denomination and rose growers by occupation. But Nancy did not work in the gardens; she was employed as a domestic servant working as a housekeeper and a babysitter. Quaker racial attitudes regarding Indians were often more tolerant than those of most other White Americans. And they welcomed the cheap labor Nancy supplied. She was paid $5 per week and provided room and board. Carlisle called this practice the "outing" system. In 1891 boys who were outed earned a total of $17,000 and the girls $5,000. Girls chosen to be outed to "the country" were required to speak some English and relinquish their wages to Carlisle, which held them in trust. It's not known if Nancy saw any of this money. It can be assumed that during the five months she lived with the Jones family their Pennsylvania Dutch accents crept into her speech.

Most of the Blackfeet who arrived with the Birds were outed, including Henry. In June 1890 he was sent to a farm in Dolington, Pennsylvania, owned by a prominent family called the Beans. After a summer of working in the fields he was sent back to Carlisle. In April 1892 he was outed again, this time to a farm on the left bank of the Delaware river near Trenton, New Jersey. In 1893 he was outed yet again. This time he ran away. But he was soon caught and returned to Carlisle. In September he was expelled and sent back to the reservation. But Carlisle was persuaded to give Henry another chance. Two months later he was shipped back to school, where in 1895 he "timed out," that is, finished his five-year stint. He was one of only a

dozen in his group to do so, a relatively large percentage when compared to
the mere 7 percent of the 10,600 Native Americans who finished Carlisle's
course of instruction. That is not to say they earned high school diplomas.
Because very few students could master English in the time allotted them
and finish the academic courses that would earn them a diploma, only
158 Native Americans graduated from the school during its thirty-nine-
year history. This is a matriculation rate of 1.5 percent, compared to the
3.5 percent of Americans as a whole who finished high school in 1890, a
figure that rose to 16 percent in 1918.

Only one member of the group that stepped off the train with the Birds
actually earned a high school diploma. This was William Hazlett, a veteran of five summer outings. He left Carlisle when he was nineteen and
enrolled at the Haskell Institute in Lawrence, Kansas, originally called
the United States Indian Industrial Training School, and renamed again
in 1993 as the Haskell Indian Nations University. Founded in 1884, it
was one of the many boarding schools that copied Carlisle's military-style
assimilation-by-immersion model. There Hazlett, who was tall, broad-
shouldered, and strikingly good-looking, met his future wife, Nora Guy,
a Caddo who was snatched as a young girl from the Indian camps around
Fort Cobb, Oklahoma, and sent to Haskell. She entered school speaking
no English. After six years at Haskell she could no longer converse with
her mother in the Caddo language. William Hazlett became a newspaper
editor, a teacher, and a farmer—a photograph shows him standing with
his tenants in his five-acre cabbage patch in Oklahoma. He sat on the
founding Board of Directors of the Society of American Indians, which
was the first national rights organization run by and for Native Americans. He waged an unsuccessful campaign for Oklahoma State Senator
on the Democratic ticket in 1910, losing by five votes in the primary,
before moving his wife and three kids to Aberdeen, Washington, where
he worked as a real estate salesman.

Two other classmates of the Birds made a life together after they timed
out at Carlisle. Charles Walter Buck and Spyna Devereaux returned to the
Blackfeet Reservation in 1895 and got married. Buck, whose Piegan name

"Brockey," short for Tail Feathers Coming Over The Hill, was replaced with westernized names. Through the General Allotment Act and land purchases the Bucks took title to 960 acres of grazing land near the tribal seat at Browning, Montana, where they raised cattle and horses. In 1909 they adopted a Canadian Cree girl named Emma Cooper and built a frame house with a porch and a mudroom. They sent photographs back to Carlisle showing their dining room and the piano in the parlor, which the Bucks learned to play at Carlisle. In 1910 they had become prosperous ranchers living near Browning, Montana. By their account they had $6,000 in the bank and owned a solid frame house, 450 cattle and seventy horses. By 1918 Charles had become the president of the Stockman's State Bank in Browning, the tribal seat, was one of the owners of the Mercantile store, served on the executive committee of the Montana Stockgrowers Association, and ran some 6,000 head of cattle on his multi-ranch operation. A Montana newspaper described him as "probably the most influential man on the reservation."[7]

Buck played on Carlisle's 1894 football team, the Indians. It was inexperienced and poorly coached, posting a 1-6-2 record, the only win a shutout against nearby Harrisburg High School. Two of their losses—against Bucknell and Navy—were also shutouts. From the team's beginning in 1893 the Indians focused their strategy for competing with their heaver and taller White opponents on using speed, agility, cunning, and deception in what at the time was considered a blood sport like boxing. They played without pads or any sort of protective head gear, and injuries were common. By 1911 Carlisle had developed into the best amateur football team in the nation. Under Coach Glenn "Pop" Warner, a profane, cigarette-smoking former lawyer and cowboy, the Indians posted an 11-1 record that year, beating Georgetown, Pittsburgh, Brown, and Penn and shocking the Harvard Crimson 18-15, losing only to Syracuse, by one point. The best football player in the country played for the Indians. This was Wa-Tho-Huk, translated from the Sauk and Fox language as "Bright Path." Baptized in Oklahoma in 1887 as Jacobus Franciscus Thorpe, Jim Thorpe was also a track-and-field star at Carlisle. At the 1912 Summer Olympics in Stockholm he won two gold medals for the U.S. and was named "The World's Greatest Athlete" by King Gustav of Sweden.

Also arriving at Carlisle with Buck and the Birds on that 1890 train was Pressly Houk. His mother was Piegan and his father was a White man who served for a time as a city marshal in Great Falls, Montana. While at school he worked as one of Carlisle's printers. After he timed out in 1895 Pressly returned to Montana and married a fellow Carlisle student named Maggie Abbott, four years his junior. Only eight years old when she arrived in Pennsylvania on the 1890 train, she was returned to the Blackfeet Reservation after a few months due to illness. Together they acquired 960 acres near Browning. After he worked for a while as a partner in a wholesale business they moved to Lethbridge, Alberta, where they bought a house with his income as a passenger train conductor. He wrote a note to the school in which he mentioned "dear old Capt. R. H. Pratt—he is loved by all of us." Eleanor, the Houks' daughter, was admitted to Carlisle in 1912 when she was eleven years old. After the school closed in 1918 she transferred to the Chemawa Indian School in Oregon. In 1921 she became the first Indigenous woman admitted to the University of Oregon, where she was elected president of the Cosmopolitan Club, an organization of foreign students.[8] In 1915 during a midnight street fight in Great Falls with a gang of Austrians, Pressly died after one of them slit his throat.[9]

Richard Sanderville entered Carlisle with Nancy and Henry Bird in 1890, and like her, returned to Montana two years later because of "ill health." He was also descended from interpreters. His grandfather, Isidoro Sandoval, was a Spanish adventurer who went to work in the early 1800s for the American Fur Company at Fort Union in what is now North Dakota. He partnered with a Blackfeet country wife named Catch For Nothing and served as an interpreter facilitating trade between Native trappers and the Company. In 1833 he was shot in the head and killed during a drunken brawl with a fellow employee named Alexander Harvey. Isidoro Sandoval Jr., known as Hair Coat among the Blackfeet, followed his father's lead, taking a job with the Company and marrying three Native women, Buffalo Painted Lodge, Blood Woman, and Bird Tail, who was Richard's mother (somewhere along the way the name Sandoval morphed into Sanderville). Fluent in English and Siksiká, he was hired by the Blackfeet Indian Agent at Fort Benton, where Richard Sanderville was born. As a boy Sanderville was forced to work in the fields and shops for three years at the Catholic Mission school in St. Ignatius, Montana. Then, at the age of twenty-four he was shipped off to Carlisle after his sponsor, Major J. B. Catlin, lied by telling the school that Richard was eighteen.

Back in Montana Sanderville went to work for the Office of Indian Affairs as disciplinarian of the boys who boarded at the Fort Shaw Industrial Indian School. Then he was transferred to the Blackfeet Agency, where he worked as a clerk and a tribal interpreter. He was appointed one of three interpreters during the signing of the 1895 agreement transferring what is now most of Glacier Park from the Blackfeet to the U.S. government, which mistakenly believed the land was laden with gold and copper. Indian Agent George Steell—a morphine addict—was instrumental in convincing Piegan chiefs such as White Calf to accept a ludicrous payment of $1.5 million payable over the course of a decade. The Blackfeet believed this contract was a lease, not a sale, and that they would be allowed to continue hunting, foraging, and gathering firewood in the mountains as they had been doing for millennia. The government tried to end to that practice in 1903 when it strung a barbed wire fence around the entire 2,200-square-mile reservation.

In the 1920s Sanderville helped organize the Piegan Farming and Livestock Association to promote Blackfeet beef and wheat. He helped develop the *Dictionary of the Indian Sign Language* with the Smithsonian Institute in Washington, D.C., in the 1930s. And in an effort to preserve tribal history he was instrumental in establishing the Museum of the Plains Indian in Browning. The stunning dioramas and exhibits feature beaded clothing, horse gear, weapons, musical instruments, household implements, baby carriers, and toys. He later served on the Blackfoot tribal council.

Most of the thirty-seven Piegans on the train with the Birds—and the 146 Blackfeet children to follow them over the years—experienced far different outcomes at Carlisle. Besides Bird and Sanderville ten others suffered from what were listed as health problems and returned to Montana. Four children went back home after their families demanded that the school release them. Six students were expelled for running away, or what the school called "desertion," which became a common act of resistance in both Federal and Christian boarding schools. Another of Buck and Houk's teammates on the 1894 Indians squad was a full-blooded Piegan named Anthony Austin. He was expelled after five years at Carlisle for what his student card said was "drunkenness." He returned to the Blackfeet Reservation, married a woman thirteen years his senior, and died of unknown causes at the age of thirty-four.

Two of the Birds' Piegan classmates—Lawney Shorty and George Ell—died at Carlisle and were buried in the school's cemetery. An article in *The Red Man* reported that Ell, "while jumping some three weeks ago burst a blood vessel in the lungs and died on Tuesday from the effects. All was done for the dear boy as he lay on his bed of sickness that human agency could contrive, but in spite of every effort of skill and patience, although at times there was a shadow of hope, the flow of life blood continued until he peacibly [*sic*] passed away." It's unlikely that Ell, who was six feet tall and weighed 165 pounds, could suffer a ruptured blood vessel simply by "jumping." It's more likely that he died of tuberculosis; although the remains of most of the hundreds of students who died at the school were returned to the reservations, the bodies of TB victims were interred at Carlisle because of the fear of contamination. At that time the disease had no cure, and doctors didn't know enough to quarantine sick patients.

Louie and Mary Ell were not informed of their son's death until more than a year after he was buried. His friends at Carlisle pitched in and bought him a headstone. But it was destroyed in 1927 when the Department of War, which took control of the Carlisle campus after the school folded in 1918, dug up 186 graves and moved them to a new location to make way for a parking lot. In the 1990s a relative of the Ell family attending graduate school at Penn State came across a white limestone marker engraved with Ell's name at what is now called the Post Cemetery on the grounds of what became the U.S. Army War College in 1951. Although tribal police had abducted Ell from his family's home on Livermore Creek in 1890, the Army refused to return his body. According to George's nephew, Dale Ell, "We were told by the U.S. government that once a person is buried in U.S. government property, he can't be taken out of the ground and moved someplace else." But another relative, Leon Chief Elk, was determined to bring his uncle home. He made no headway until 2017, when the Army reversed course under increasing pressure from tribal nations and announced that it would comply with their demands for the return of their relatives. By the end of 2023 the remains of thirty-two Carlisle students had been exhumed and sent home for reburial. Finally, on a summer day in 2018, George Ell was laid to rest at the family's cemetery on the Blackfeet Reservation in a flowered meadow under a 12,000-foot monolith called Flattop Mountain.[10]

Shorty was sixteen years old when he was shipped to the school and assigned "Lawney" as his first name. He was outed twice to White families in Pennsylvania and would likely have been outed several more times during his scheduled enrollment of five years, but he contracted tuberculosis and never recovered. Its victims slowly wasted away as their skin turned gray, they lost weight, and coughed up blood. (Some New Englanders believed that some people killed by "consumption" were vampires that preyed on their families after they died.) When the Army informed the Blackfeet Tribal Historic Preservation Office that the tribe's request would be granted and Shorty's remains would be disinterred, William Gladstone was assigned to bring him back to the reservation for reburial. He was offered two options: the Army could fly Shorty's casket from Pennsylvania to Great Falls, Montana, accompanied by a military escort, or the Blackfeet could arrange for his transportation home themselves. "In my eyes, (this boy) was trusted to the U.S. government, to the military, and they let him demise in their care," Gladstone said. "The military, at this point in time, had simply done enough." Gladstone and his cousin Joe Wagner soon began driving the 2,100 miles to Carlisle in Wagner's Toyota Tundra. The cousins both work for the Preservation Office and are member of the Crazy Dog Society, a Blackfeet guild which, as part of its responsibility to maintain good relationships with grizzly bears, is promoting the use of bear-proof dumpsters in grizzly country.

The cousins watched as archeologists and a forensic anthropologist from the U.S. Army Corps of Engineers unearthed Shorty's grave and took his bones to a laboratory for cleaning and analysis. After determining that these bones were those of a male Shorty's age they transferred them to a simple wooden casket measuring eight inches deep and thirty-three inches long. The calcium deposit on his ribs was likely produced by a lung infection. The cousins were also told that deer, cattle, and pig bones were found in his grave, the result of that fact that the cemetery grounds had previously been used as a dump for animal scraps from the school's kitchen.

Shorty was buried in Holy Family Mission Cemetery on the reservation as a gathering of Blackfeet people looked on. "We are the same as him," Gladstone said. "That could be me. That could be Joe. That could be my cousin. His life was just as important as any member of our tribe." Because the cousins had learned at Carlisle that one of the few things Shorty liked about Carlisle was its sports programs, they put a football and a baseball mitt in his casket before it was lowered into the ground. [11]

Chapter Three

UNDER THE BIRD TAIL

In November 1892 Nancy Bird entered Mount Angela Institute at St. Peter's Mission the same way she entered Carlisle—with a lice check, a bath, and a change of clothes that included boots and a heavy, ankle-length wool dress. This time her parents had no choice about enrolling her in school. Congress had passed a compulsory attendance law the year before that authorized the Commissioner of Indian Affairs to withhold rations, clothing, and other annuities from families who did not offer to send their children to an assimilation center. Fathers who refused could be jailed. Nineteen Hopi leaders from the village of Orayvi in what is now Arizona were arrested in 1894 after refusing to send their pueblo's children to a government boarding school thirty miles away. They spent almost a year at hard labor on Alcatraz Island. Perched on a mesa, the 1,200-year-old adobe town is the oldest continuously inhabited built community in North America.

The Blackfeet Indian Agent, George Steell, ordered tribal police armed with rifles and revolvers to round up kids at gunpoint if necessary and ship them to one Montana school or another. Besides St. Peter's those included Holy Family Mission on the reservation, which was operated by the Jesuits, and the federal government's Industrial Indian School at Fort Shaw. Steell continued shipping Piegan children to Carlisle until he quit his job in 1896 after realizing he could make more money selling his ranch's beef to the reservation than administering Indians for the government. Because the spirituality of the Birds included both Blackfeet and Catholic elements, and because unlike some other Métis girls Nancy could speak English, she was shipped to St. Peter's, where she joined 110 Métis and full-blooded Native American girls. The school also boarded or day-schooled children from White settler families in facilities strictly segregated by sex and race. Records indicate that Nancy left Carlisle because of ill health. If her malady was diagnosed the results were never recorded. But it's likely she wasn't suffering from a physical ailment. She was probably homesick.

The daily routine was similar to that of Carlisle. In the morning and afternoon sessions Ursuline nuns showed the girls how to sew, make dresses, cook American food, sweep, and do the laundry. Once they got the hang of these tasks they were shown how to bake bread, skim the cream from raw milk, and churn butter, alien food Nancy would eat only if she had nothing else. There would be some minimal instruction in arithmetic, reading, and penmanship. More "advanced" girls might also get some experience playing instruments, singing, painting, drawing, and carving wood. Three periods of manual labor occupied hour-long slots throughout the day beginning at 8:00 A.M and ending at 6:00 P.M. Nancy and the others were put to work cutting and hemming sheets, pillow cases, bedspreads, and towels. The goal was to teach these daughters of animistic, seminomadic hunter-gatherers the skills required of housewives and domestic servants. Very few of the hundreds of thousands of Native American girls forced into government and denominational institutions during the boarding school era actually found domestic work because it didn't exist on the reservations most of them returned to after their stints in the boarding schools.

St. Peter's, however, differed somewhat from Carlisle in both philosophy and practice, mirroring the divide between government schools and those of the denominations. Although the girls wore matching dresses, these were not military uniforms and there were no forced marches. Also, neither girls nor boys were "outed" to White families to work as indentured servants, and many of them stayed at St. Peter's during the summer. Although they were obliged to sit through a half-hour of religious indoctrination every day they were not prohibited from speaking their own languages while also learning English. At a recital on a spring day in 1897, for example, the nuns were greeted by Native girls in their own languages. Louise Pepion spoke in Siksiká, Aliza Azure in Nakota, and Jennie Heureux in Cree. In allowing children their native tongues the Jesuits and nuns ignored the Indian Bureau's orders to allow only English. This flaunting of the rules made St. Peter's more palatable to the tribes, and it reflected the fact that some of the Jesuits attempted to learn Indigenous languages.

The girls despised their household chores. For one thing, they were carried out behind locked doors instead of under the sheltering sky where they had spent their first years blowing here and there like little whirlwinds. Learning English was essential to this campaign mostly because literacy would allow girls to read the Bible, which the nuns believed would facilitate their complete acceptance of Catholicism and a total rejection of Native spirituality. However, like the staff at Carlisle, the nuns harbored no pretense that they were preparing their charges for higher education. They did their best, however, to immerse the girls in the canon of White American history. For example, On October 21, 1892, the girls were obliged to celebrate the four-hundredth anniversary of the "discovery" of America by putting on a play titled *Christopher Columbus*. It's unlikely the nuns had read accounts of the 500 Taíno Indian slaves Columbus shipped back to Spain from the island of Hispaniola, many of whom died on the voyage, or the enslaved natives whose hands he ordered chopped off because they failed to bring him any gold. It is estimated that in two years under the Columbus regime the island lost a quarter of a million of its aboriginal inhabitants, killed by European violence and disease.

Advocates for Indian boarding schools believed that their campaign of assimilation should focus on the daughters. "The girls will need the training more than the boys & they will wield a greater influence in the future," a Wisconsin Presbyterian missionary named Isaac Baird wrote in 1883. "If we get the girls, we get the race." Richard Pratt believed incorrectly that because Plains Indian women were "drudges" who did most of the work, their men withheld them from his recruiters. He told a reporter that the reason his first conscripts for Carlisle in 1879 included three times as many Lakota boys as girls was due to the fact that girls "bring, in open market, after arriving at marriageable age, a certain price in horses or other valuable property." In that regard boys, he said, were "valueless." But he maintained that in order to "lift up the Indian Race" converting girls was crucial because it was Native women more than men who were responsible for passing on the culture from one generation to another. [1]

Although Nancy Bird was enrolled in St. Peter's under the Christianized name her parents gave her, other girls arrived at the Institute with their Piegan names, onto which the Ursulines appended the monikers of saints—Isabelle, Ursula, Francesca, Elizabeth and so on. Sister Zita saw this renaming as proper and beneficial. After all, she had been baptized Sarah A. Chance by her White Catholic parents, and like all Ursulines had taken the name of a martyr or a confessor whose good qualities were believed to match their own. Saint Zita endeavored to perform ordinary tasks extremely well and was the patron saint of maids and domestic workers. Considering the nature of her work at St. Peter's this was a prophetic choice for Miss Chance. Saint Zita was also appealed to in prayer when keys were lost. However, something about the life she had chosen must have troubled Sister Zita. A year after freighting Nancy Bird across Montana in that horrific blizzard Sister Zita, according to a diarist, was "dismissed" from St. Peter's. She renounced her vows, left St. Peter's a month later and booked a room at the McDermott Hotel in Butte, Montana. Then she disappeared from the records.

A photographer recorded Nancy Bird soon after her arrival using a camera that exposed glass plate negatives lit with a magnesium flash. That is to say, she is probably pictured in an arranged group of some eighty unnamed girls ranging in age from five or six to seventeen or eighteen. It's possible she also appears in a photo of girls working at sewing machines, or in another group pictured with musical instruments and art supplies staged to make the scene appear as if they are being guided by three nuns, one of whom, according to a diarist, is "teaching catechism to Big Eyes" (Lizzie Big Eyes, one of the girls who arrived with Bird). None of the girls looks happy. But then, almost no one in early American photographs smiled. That affectation didn't appear until the 1920s, when showing one's teeth in photographs was no longer believed to be a symptom of insanity or drunkenness.

The nuns may have rationalized keeping their charges indoors so much of the time by citing the weather or the danger of wolves, mountain lions, and rattlesnakes. Montana's climate in the 1890s was much colder than it is now. On January 31, 1894, the Academy's thermometer registered minus 39 degrees; the temperature in Helena, Montana's capital 60 miles south, dropped to minus 52 degrees. Nuns venturing outside in the winter were sometimes blown over by the wind. However, the Native American girls were taken on sleigh rides in the winter and were allowed to go out "sliding" on a pond that was created by damming Mission Creek. In the summer they played tennis on the lawns in their heavy wool dresses and were driven by wagon to various streams for picnics. But they were closely watched to prevent them from running away.

Because St. Peter's was dependent on the Mission farm for much of its food most of the ninety boys enrolled in 1892 were required to work in the barns, the kitchen garden, and the fields during growing season—planting, weeding, harvesting, and operating the irrigation ditches. Both summer and winter they tended to the Mission's horses, herded, and fed its 133 head of beef cattle, including twenty-one calves, and milked its thirty-one dairy cows. This was forced labor, but the Jesuits rationalized the practice as essential in preparing a boy for what they believed would be a farmer's life. This goal was a delusion propagated by people who didn't understand that most of the Blackfeet Reservation is short grass prairie unsuited for planting. Some Piegan and Métis, however, became successful ranchers on land that once fed vast herds of bison, and by 1890 was supporting 25,000 head of cattle. Because St. Peter's was chronically underfunded—like most Indian boarding schools—the unpaid labor of students was essential to keep the place afloat, which allowed the nuns and Jesuits to believe that they were doing good work. A diarist reported that the nuns observed New Year's Day 1893 "without a cent of money in the treasury."[2]

The St. Peter's method of forced learning for both girls and boys was the opposite of how Blackfeet children were taught to be Blackfeet adults. Children wandered around the village, dressed in soft moccasins and loose clothing, watching as their elders made pemmican, tanned hides, beaded with dyed porcupine quills, crafted tools and weapons, practiced with them, trained horses, and prayed. For the girls, grandmothers were their primary teachers. Their goal, besides passing on practical skills, was to teach cooperation, tradition, and spirituality. The widespread corporal punishment of children administered in Indian boarding schools—and in White society, as well—was a rarity among most tribal societies. The Blackfeet considered spanking or slapping as abusive, preferring instead to admonish, tease, ridicule, or frighten with outcomes involving wild animals or scary spirits.

Like Carlisle, St. Peter's had a problem with runaways, although the school didn't call them deserters. Soon after Nancy Bird arrived, Francesca Sleeping Bear and Susie Lard slipped out of the Institute during evening prayers and made their way to a nearby horse ranch, where they spent a frigid December night in a haystack. A ranch hand discovered the girls in the morning and returned them. They were lucky; many runaways during the boarding school era died of exposure because they chose winter to make their escape. A Métis named Carrie Belgarde recalled her lonesome first weeks at St. Peter's. "I had never been away from my parents. My sister, Jenny was with me at the time. I told her 'Let's run away.' She said 'If you want to go, go ahead.' After I stayed there awhile, and after I got acquainted with all the girls, I liked it."

The first Native American children conscripted by the Mission were rounded up on the Blackfeet Reservation in 1885. A newspaper recorded the event: "Father Imoda last week visited the Piegan agency and selected 22 little reds, whom he took with him to St. Peter's where they will at once commence going to school."[3] Thereafter, while some children tried to flee St. Peter's others were regularly freighted in. Some of these new conscripts included not just Piegan and Métis but A'aninin (Gros Ventre) and those of nine other tribes. A diarist recorded on that on September 18, 1893, "A wagonload of children reached us from Depuyer. Four were girls." On October 11 five girls from the Blackfeet Reservation arrived by wagon. A priest named Markham brought a load of nine Piegan boys and two girls in January 1893.

A Jesuit named Schuler arrived with a cargo of eleven boys and three girls in December 1892, and nine months later returned with twenty-two boys and eleven girls. These were the children of the Spring Creek band of Métis, who in 1879 founded Lewistown, 135 miles east of St. Peter's. Trailing after the dwindling herds of bison that were at the center of their culture and economy, in the 1860s the Métis began moving west from the Red River to the Milk River country of northern Montana, where they built a permanent community of cottonwood cabins on Frenchman's Creek. Both men and women processed the bison they hunted into hides and pemmican. Some of this bounty they kept for their own use, but most of it was traded for hardware, weapons, cloth, and horses. The tribes were not amused by the depletion of the herds these commercial hunters caused. It was reported that when smallpox was spreading across the Northern Plains, Indians visited the Métis camps hoping to infect them with the disease, but the plan didn't work. After the Métis began hunting bison on the newly formed reservations the U.S. government ordered them to leave the Milk River. Under the leadership of Pierre Berger some twenty-five families loaded their Red River carts with their meager possessions and headed south to the Judith Basin, where they had been told that there was an abundance of bison.

Unlike the Plains tribes these Métis were not nomadic. Their moves were attempts to find a place where they could create a permanent settlement and continue to hunt buffalo. Forested and watered by a ring of mountain ranges, they saw Judith Basin as their Shangri-la. The first to arrive at Spring Creek filed homestead claims. The government awarded land to the Métis who looked more White than Indian and denied claims to those deemed to look more like Indians. Those who failed to earn a land patent moved onto the reservations or became part of a growing population of landless Indians, many of whom took up residence in the shacks and later abandoned cars in a hilltop squatter's camp called Hill 57 on the edge of Great Falls, Montana (so named after a salesman for the Heinz food company arranged rocks on the hill in a huge "57" shape and painted them white).[4] Hill 57 also became home to landless Ojibwe and Cree people. Along with the Métis, they were finally recognized in 2019 by the Federal government as the Little Shell Tribe and awarded 718 acres of land in and around Great Falls. Named Montana's poet laureate in 2023, Chris La Tray is one of some 6,500 Little Shell members.

By 1880 there were 150 families living in settlements along Spring Creek. They built their log cabins in a circle around a dance hall, a testament to the centrality of jigging and fiddle playing in Métis culture. They buried their dead in a cemetery on land that was later bought by a White rancher and County Commissioner named Jacob Corbly, who wanted the remains moved off his property. Working for three days and at night by the light of bonfires, the Métis built wooden caskets and exhumed the remains. They were reburied in what would become Lewistown's Calvary Cemetery on land donated to the Catholic Church by a Métis family. Records of who was reburied exist for only half of the seventy-five deceased, of whom a dozen were infants. In September 2023 Métis descendants gathered at the cemetery for the unveiling of a monument to the dead.

In the winter of 1880–1881 the Spring Creek Métis traded 3,200 buffalo robes and as many pelts, a result of their successful hunts. But by 1893 the bison were gone. Without their reaffirming connection to the bison trade the Métis floundered and turned for comfort to their faith in Catholicism. Some of the most ardent wore crucifixes. Their children were prepared for their first communion with instructions in both French and Cree, which had been developed as a written script a half century earlier. In 1889 a Jesuit named Leopold Van Gorp persuaded the Spring Creek Métis to send their sons and daughters to St. Peter's. That autumn some thirty children were taken in Red River carts across Montana to the boarding schools in the Mission Valley.[5] By 1895 St. Peter's enrolled more than 200 boys and girls, including Métis day students from the area and Native American and Métis boarding students, each one earning the Catholics a monthly $9 voucher. In addition to this income, the schools took in a few White boarders. Also, settlers in the area paid St. Peter's to have their children educated in the White schools. The Catholics believed this arrangement would benefit both races and would help prepare Indian children for their inevitable life in the predominant society.

The two small communities that had gathered around St. Peter's by 1892 included a village of twenty-five Métis families in the Sullivan Valley three miles south, and a few settlers on nearby homesteads. Two of these White pioneers had been left in charge of the Mission as caretakers when the Jesuits fled for their lives during the 1866 guerilla war that flared between colonists and the Blackfeet, who were riled up by a flood of fortune-hunters invading their territory. The reason that Edward Lewis and Thomas Moran kept their scalps was because Lewis had wisely married Sycowwastakapi, the daughter of Meekiappy or Heavy Shield, a Piegan war chief.

Lewis had worked on Mississippi and Missouri River steamboats before signing with the American Fur Company to ferry goods between Fort Union and Fort Benton in a mackinaw boat. At the end of the Civil War he and his partner, Malcolm Clarke, were granted a charter to build a toll road through the canyon of the Little Prickly Pear Creek, which would connect Fort Benton with Helena, the Territorial capitol. The next year Clarke was killed at his ranch on the creek by a band of Piegans. After settlers demanded that the U.S. Army bring the savages to justice a force commanded by Capt. Eugene Baker attacked a sleeping village of Piegans camped along the Marias River and slaughtered 200 of them with bullets and axes. None of Clarke's assailants were among the dead because Baker had attacked the wrong band. These were mostly women, children, and old men, many of them suffering from smallpox. The Piegan Massacre ended Blackfeet resistance to the invasion. The Jesuits returned to St. Peter's.

Lewis and Sycowwastakapi begat three daughters, who were among the first students of the Ursulines. Their primary teacher, however, was an old Piegan woman named Sikeykio (Black Bear), who lived with the family for years. The 1880 census listed her age at 115. While her band was camped at the mouth of the Sun River on July 11, 1806, she was shocked by her first sight of White men—members of the Lewis and Clark Expedition. She was living on Malcolm Clarke's ranch the day he was killed. But she saved the life of his wife, a Piegan named Cothcocona, by hiding her out of sight.

Thomas Moran, with his mother in tow, fled County Waterford, Ireland, in the wake of the 1840s Potato Famine. It was just as well that he was illiterate because the signs posted all over Boston said "No Irish Need Apply." After he was rejected for service on the Union side in the Civil War he said goodbye to his mother, sailed to Panama, crossed the isthmus, and sailed up the Pacific coast to San Francisco, where he milked cows for a living. Dreaming of gold he headed to Montana with another man and one horse, which they shared using the ride-and-tie method, Moran riding for a way, tying the horse to a tree, and walking on, while his partner walked up from behind, then rode ahead. And so on. In January 1866 while prospecting in Last Chance Gulch he heard a rumor that gold had been discovered on the Sun River. Alongside hundreds of other fools he galloped seventy miles north from what is now Helena during a chinook that was followed by an arctic blast that sent temperatures to minus forty. He was dressed in a shirt, canvas breeches and leather boots without socks or underwear. As the Sun River Stampede ground to a halt dozens of men lost extremities to frostbite, and some of them lost their lives. The Jesuits at St. Peter's Mission, which at the time was a collection of rough log shacks located inside a loop of the Missouri River near present-day Ulm, gave Moran shelter from the storm. In return, he would never leave the Mission, although the Jesuits would abandon *him* for eight years.

After becoming prosperous farmers on sizable spreads in the Mission Valley, Lewis and Moran would bail out St. Peter's time and again with gifts of coal, hay, potatoes, grain, chickens, apples, and money. Although illiterate, Moran served as the Mission's first postmaster. When a St. Peter's Jesuit named Philip Rappagliosi died in 1878 at the age of thirty-seven while proselytizing among a Métis encampment on the Milk River, Moran ferried his body by wagon to Helena, where he was buried. A widespread but unconfirmed rumor accused a Swiss priest named Jean Baptiste Genin of poisoning Rappagliosi in retaliation for going after the Métis souls Genin had marked as his own.

Another denizen of St. Peter's who helped keep the facility afloat was its de facto foreman, Mary Fields. She was born into slavery somewhere in the South around 1832. During the years before the Civil War she was owned by a Virginia family named Warner. When the family moved to Cleveland, Ohio, they took Fields with them as a domestic servant. Sometime after the 1863 Emancipation Proclamation she told a reporter that she worked as a chambermaid aboard the *Robert E. Lee*, a Mississippi River paddleboat, and was on board during its famous triumphant race in 1870 against the *Natchez*. That year she returned to the Warner household as a free agent, working again as a house maid, this time for wages. When daughter Mary Warner decided to enter the Ursuline Convent of the Sacred Heart in Toledo, the family sent Mary Fields along to help. She hired on as the convent's groundskeeper, earning a reputation as a diligent but cranky worker. "God help anyone who walked on the lawn after Mary had cut it," recalled one of the Toledo nuns.[6] Fields stood almost six feet tall and weighed 200 pounds.

The Ursuline mother superior, Sarah Theresa Dunne, who had christened herself Mother Amadeus, was related to the Warners by the marriage of her brother, Judge Edmund Francis Dunne, to Mary Warner's older sister, Josephine. In 1875 President Ulysses S. Grant removed Dunne as Chief Justice of the Arizona Territorial Supreme Court because of his campaign urging Catholics to withhold taxes used to finance public schools, arguing that the Church should be in charge of Arizona's education. In 1881 Dunne founded a faith-based colony in Florida during an era of fierce anti-Catholic sentiments across the U.S. incited by the Irish diaspora into the U.S. (An 1875 Thomas Nast cartoon portrayed Catholic bishops in their white mitres as crocodiles slithering from a river to attack a public school.) In 1883, after thirty-eight-year-old Josephine died of pneumonia at the Dunnes' Florida settlement, Amadeus sent Fields south to take care of her brother's house and his five children. Fields eventually returned to Toledo with the girls, who were later enrolled in a convent boarding school in Canada.

The sheltered convent life Amadeus had been leading for more than two decades was about to end. In 1883 the Bishop of Montana begged Church authorities in Ohio to send him a priest and some nuns to establish a mission among destitute Cheyenne people who were barely surviving along the Tongue River south of Miles City, Montana. Roaming the floodplain without land or homes, harassed by homesteaders and cowboys who wanted the valley for themselves, the Cheyenne, it was rumored, were killing cattle in order to stave off starvation. Amadeus, a Jesuit priest and five Ursulines arrived in Miles City on a Northern Pacific train in January 1884. In March they traveled eighty miles south by wagon, escorted by soldiers, to a log hut roofed in mud and papered with copies of the *Police Gazette*. It was here at the mouth of Otter Creek that St. Labre Mission was established and the task of converting the savages began. "We studied their language part of the time and taught them ours," one of the nuns wrote. "We taught them sewing and games."[7] In November 1884 a federal executive order created the Tongue River Reservation next door to the 160-acre Mission, later renamed the Northern Cheyenne Reservation.

St. Labre was still operating in 2023, offering a free K–12 education. Cheyenne children enroll as day students or boarding students, who are bused home on the weekends if they live more than forty miles away. The Church also runs two satellite schools for children on the Crow Reservation next door. The curriculum includes instruction in Indigenous culture, languages, and tribal government. A 2012 lawsuit filed against the Great Falls-Billings diocese alleged that children at St. Labre and several other Church schools located on eastern Montana reservations were sexually, physically, and emotionally abused by nuns and priests. According to court documents the oldest alleged crimes occurred in 1943 and the most recent case was that of a twelve-year-old boy abused by an older resident of the St. Labre Mission orphanage in 1993. (There is no statute of limitations in Montana affecting the sexual abuse of children under the age of eighteen.) In 2018 the diocese settled the lawsuit by paying eighty-six plaintiffs $20 million as part of its bankruptcy reorganization.[8] Most of the money came from Catholic Mutual, the Church's insurer, but St. Labre paid

$1 million out of its own coffers. The payment underlined the fact that the school is wealthy—its assets in 2021 were valued at $145 million. Every year it wages an aggressive fundraising campaign that includes sending out 17 million direct-mail solicitations, a blitz that netted the school $46 million in 2021.[9] (Because of the volume of mail, the postal service awarded the school its own zip code.) The tribal council was paying attention to the school's harvest of cash extracted from well-meaning doners. Between 2014 and 2019 St. Labre paid the tribe $11 million as the result of a lawsuit accusing the school of marketing the poverty of the Cheyenne in order to raise money.[10]

In 1884 the Jesuits at St. Peter's begged the Bishop of Montana to send them some nuns willing to teach Indian girls. The priests promised them a house, a farm, two wagon horses, two milk cows, and some food. They would also pitch in $200 if the sisters could also bring a nun willing to assimilate Indian boys. Amadeus arrived by stagecoach several months later with three novices and a postulant. The "house" they had been promised was a motel-like row of log cabins stitched together under a bell tower. This first crude Indian school for girls opened in 1885 with eleven Blackfeet and Métis children, including a Piegan named Kaminiki and three Métis—the Coquette sisters. A few months later Amadeus was near death, bedridden with pneumonia. The Jesuits contacted the Toledo convent pleading for help with her care. Mary Fields was dispatched west with three nuns, who nursed Amadeus until she recovered.

Fields went to work immediately for St. Peter's. Over the next decade she planted vegetable gardens and potatoes, kept huge broods of chickens, and hunted wild birds to help feed the school. She washed clothes and bed linens and hauled freight and passengers. One winter night while she was delivering goods to the Mission during a blizzard her horses got spooked by a pack of wolves and overturned her wagon. Rather than surrender her load to the wolves she stood guard over it all night until help arrived. She smoked cigars, drank whiskey in saloons, swore like a drunken sailor, and was often armed. The Indians named her White Crow because she acted like a White person but her skin was black. Although she had been paid $50 a month while under contract to the convent in Toledo, she refused to sign any such agreement with St. Peter's, taking from the Ursulines only room and board and some occasional walk-around cash for tobacco and ammunition. She preferred to come and go as she pleased, accepting short-term gigs from time to time, leaving the nuns to do her work or go without. They complained that her absence compelled them to weed and debug her potato patches and wash the laundry. During one of her outings they determined to clean the laundry room where she worked. As they burned a pile a rubbish one of her bullets exploded, barely missing Sister St. Gertrude's eye.

During a quarrel with a ranch foreman over a harness she nailed him with a fist-sized rock. A dust-up with another man ended without violence when the belligerents "touched rifles," according to one source. Although other published accounts of her brawling, gunslinging outbursts are lively frontier stories they most likely are not true. However, in 1894 the Bishop of Montana decided that Fields cast a shadow over the pious pretensions of the convent and ordered her to leave St. Peter's. The Ursulines were devastated. She had been unflinchingly loyal to them and one of the Mission's hardest workers. She moved into Cascade and landed a contract to deliver mail between the village and St. Peter's, the first African-American woman and only the second woman to work for the U.S. Postal Service. Rain or shine, she picked up the mail bags on the train platform in Cascade and heaved them onto her conveyance, a buckboard pulled by horses and her pet mule, Moses. To ward off bandits and wolves she carried a rifle and a .38 Smith & Wesson revolver. It was during her eight years servicing this star route that people began calling her Stagecoach Mary.

After she retired in 1903 she spent much of her time growing flowers, baby-sitting, and volunteering as the equipment manager and head cheerleader for the Cascade baseball team. In June 1912 she joined 200 other Cascadians on a charter train to Fort Benton to root for her beloved team, whose members regularly received flower boutonnieres from her garden and bouquets she awarded to players who hit home runs. She had high hopes that the day would result in a victory, since her team stepped on the diamond with a winning 5-0 record. But the Fort Benton Nine defeated

Cascade 4-0. In the typically florid and inaccurate newspaper language of the day a reporter noted that "Among the Cascade visitors was their mascot, Aunt Mary, a 300-pound mass of colored femininity whose features are familiar to nearly everybody who has passed through Cascade."[11]

The most famous teacher at St. Peter's was not an Ursuline or a Jesuit but a brooding Métis mystic and political leader named Louis Riel. Well, famous is how some remember him; notorious is another. One-eighth Indigenous, he was born in 1844 in Assiniboia. At the age of thirteen he was sent to the College of Montreal to study for the priesthood, where he wrote poetry, read copiously, and kept to himself. Homesick for the prairies, he became disenchanted with his pious, cloistered life, fell in love with a French-Canadian girl named Marie-Julie Guernon, let his grades slip and was expelled in 1865. To support the woman he hoped would be his future wife he apprenticed at a law firm. When her parents discovered he was Métis they broke off the engagement. Heartbroken, he returned to the Red River Colony. But it's likely he left a legacy of his life in Montreal—a love child named Ernest.

Back in the Métis world Riel would be called to action by secular rather than religious forces. By 1869 the declining demand in Europe for North American furs compelled the Hudson's Bay Company to sell Rupert's Land. The stockholders looked first to the United States, which had such deep pockets its leaders had thought nothing about forking over $7 million to Russia in 1867 to buy Seward's Folly. But Britain pressured the company to sell instead to the Dominion of Canada, which the Crown ruled. Hudson's Bay buckled under the pressure and agreed to part with one-quarter of North America for the ludicrous sum of $1.5 million. The Dominion made immediate plans to populate its vast new territory with White settlers, especially what the governor of Rupert's Land called the "most desirable emigrant," the Protestant Anglo-Saxon from Ontario, rather than the French-speaking Papist from Quebec. That scheme was undermined by one major flaw: The territory was already home to millions of First Nations, Métis, and Inuit people who were not consulted about the transaction.

The cradle of Assiniboia had developed around the confluence of the Red and the Assiniboine Rivers, what is now Winnipeg. More than 10,000 Métis lived along the banks on ribbon farms granted to them by the Hudson's Bay Company, so named because their holdings were long lots with narrow frontages abutting the rivers. Each plot, which extended back for two miles, was endowed with "hay privileges," grazing rights on unfenced prairie that served as an open range shared by many families. This was a configuration imported from France that allowed every landowner access to water for irrigation and navigation. And it brought neighbors close to one another, a function of their geography that reinforced kinship ties. The Métis farmed just enough to put produce and bread on the table and kept small herds of cattle that largely fended for themselves. This casual affair with agriculture allowed hunters to chase after buffalo whenever they wanted while the old people tended to the gardens. Even before the documents were signed transferring this land to Canada, and before Queen Victoria announced the transaction, surveyors were ordered to measure up the colony according to the American system of square sections. The Métis were not amused. Sensing rightly that the government wanted to subjugate the "half-breeds" and extinguish their land titles they threatened violence if surveys were carried out on their properties.

Although the surveyors were ordered to stay away from the ribbon farms one crew made the mistake of trespassing on land owned by a White French settler. He ordered the government men off his property. But because he spoke no English they didn't understand him. After he called for help, sixteen unarmed Métis showed up behind a man whose family the farmer had married into. This was Louis Riel. He stepped on the survey chain with his moccasined foot and said: "You go no farther."

When word spread that Canadians were attempting to transport rifles into the Red River Colony a force of 500 armed and mounted Métis reported for duty. The man they voted to lead them was Riel, selected not because he had any military experience, but because he was a writer and a good speaker who could effectively present the Métis cause to their White neighbors and the Dominion. (The Métis form of political organization centered around the democratic election of leaders, a meritocracy that was different than the hereditary transfer of control employed by other tribal people on the Northern Plains.)

Riel and his supporters seized Fort Garry, a trading post that was built on what is now Winnipeg's main drag. They also erected a barricaded checkpoint ten miles south across the only wagon road into the colony in order to prevent Canadians and their weapons to penetrate from the Dakota Territory. Then they convened the first meeting of their provisional government, the Convention of the People of Rupert's Land, and drafted a bill of rights that demanded Canada recognize their claims to land and their authority to reject any Canadian law they didn't like. They raised a flag the world had never seen before—a gold fleur-de-lis on a white background. Riel would be elected President.

A faction of Canadians living in the Colony mustered a brief and ludicrous resistance to the coup d'état. Forty-five armed men holed up in a house twenty miles north of Fort Garry and dared the insurgents to do something about it. Riel surrounded the house with 300 Métis riflemen and aimed a pair of cannons at the front door. The Canadians immediately surrendered. The whole gang was marched to Fort Gary and jailed. Some would escape and the rest were eventually released after signing pledges not to bear arms against Riel's government. Two months later a mob of 500, most of them Canadian farmers armed with clubs and a few rifles, stormed southeast on foot from Portage au Prairie towards Fort Garry vowing to bring Riel down and release his prisoners. When they learned that the captives had in fact been released most of them turned around and headed home. A group of four dozen, however, mushed on across the snow-covered prairie. When a company from a force of 600 mounted and heavily armed Métis galloped from the fort the mob surrendered. Its members were arrested, filling the cells that had recently been occupied by their equally foolish countrymen. One of them, Thomas Scott, a Protestant, was court-marshaled and executed by firing squad. This was a serious tactical mistake on the part of the insurgents because it would cast them as murderers instead of freedom fighters.

On July 15, 1870, the Canadian Parliament voted to accept the Red River Colony and the portion of Assiniboia north of the Medicine Line as the Dominion's fifth province. Riel's provisional government suggested a Native name for what was dubbed the "postage stamp province" because of its size. It would be called Manitoba. As part of the deal Riel and his lieutenants were promised amnesty for their part in what is called the Red River Rebellion. A governor and a military force of 1,200 was dispatched from Ontario to accept the negotiated transfer of power from the provisional government of the Métis. As the army made its way slowly west Riel received reports that the troops were vowing revenge for the execution of Thomas Scott and that Canada's amnesty promise was a lie. Riel was urged to attack the soldiers before they could capture Fort Garry. Instead, he fled south across the Medicine Line into Dakota. Searching for him, Canadian soldiers ransacked the house where he and his mother and sister were living. A warrant for his arrest was issued and a reward of $5000 was offered for his capture.

Even so, in 1873 Riel was elected to the Canadian House of Commons. But because of his impending arrest he fled to the United States. He won reelection to his vacated seat the next year but was expelled from Parliament two months later. The same year his Métis supporters elected him for a third time. Fed up, Parliament voted to offer unconditional amnesty to every one of the Red River rebels except Riel—he would have to accept a five-year banishment from Canada before charges would be dropped.

During his exile he went crazy. He had a vision in which he saw himself as the "prophet of the New World" and the voice of God's favorite people, the Métis. He announced that he was King David of the Old Testament. He gave $1,000 to a blind beggar. From time to time he threw off his clothes because, after all, Adam and Eve had lived naked in the Garden. He wept and shouted in public. He argued with a priest during Mass. He was committed under a false name to a Montreal mental asylum. For the next two years was periodically confined by a straitjacket.

After his mental health improved, Riel moved to Fort Benton where he worked as a trader selling goods to Indians and the growing number of

Métis abandoning Canada. He then tried his hand as a woodchopper and a shepherd, but wasn't much good at either. In 1880 he visited the Spring Creek Colony to muster support for his campaign to convince Congress that it should establish a reservation for the Métis in Montana and supply them with farm implements, seeds, and livestock. In exchange, he promised, the mixed bloods would ban alcohol from their land and serve the government in any way it saw fit. "If the Government would wish to use our influence, such as it is, among the Indians we freely offer it," he wrote.[12] And he urged the Spring Creek Métis to get behind candidates who supported his cause. Although it was illegal for a Métis man to vote, one observer claimed that Riel convinced 200 Spring Creek residents to cast their ballot for the Republican candidate for territorial delegate to Congress.[13] But Riel's dream of a Métis reservation was never realized.

In 1881 he married a Métis woman named Marguerite Monet, and they began traveling with a wandering band of Métis buffalo hunters. After becoming a naturalized U.S. citizen in 1883 he was approached by the head of St. Peter's, Father Joseph Damiani, who offered him a job teaching the children of the sixty Métis families living in cabins and tipis around the Mission. Riel jumped at the opportunity. Marguerite was pregnant with their second child and wanted a more permanent environment for the baby than a hunting camp. But during the Starvation Winter they were held captive by temperatures that plunged to 60 degrees below zero, nearly freezing to death inside the Mission's rough log cabins, which were built in 1865. He taught English, French, and arithmetic to Métis boys.

Meanwhile, conditions for the Métis in the former Red River Colony had steadily deteriorated since the day it became Manitoba. Chronic poverty grew as the bison herds disappeared. This was a catastrophe to which the Métis as well as Indians and Whites had contributed by overhunting. Canada had continued its hated resurvey of land using the American square system. The scrip swindle had stripped hundreds of families of any claim to land whatsoever. And the Canadian Pacific railroad had flooded the prairies by selling off its land grant to White settlers, many of them claim jumpers.

Besides Montana and Dakota, Métis from the Colony moved to a string of villages collectively known as the Southbranch Settlement. Because of the intransigence of the Canadian government regarding Métis land claims conditions there deteriorated just as they had in Manitoba.

During Sunday Mass in June 1884 Riel was summoned from the little whitewashed church at St. Peter's to meet with four visitors from the Southbranch Settlement. He believed that their request for him to help them organize a Métis protest against the Dominion was divine intervention. After he finished teaching his last class he packed up his family and headed north. In March of 1885 after his petitions to the Dominion were ignored he and his followers organized the Provisional government of Saskatchewan, whose de facto capital was the town of Batoche. Riel was elected president. Push came to shove soon after when a firefight erupted between some of Riel's rebels and a company of Royal Canadian Mounted Police that left twelve Canadians and five Métis dead. The Dominion sent 2,000 soldiers to put down what would be called the North-West Rebellion. The conflict's climactic battle near Batoche May 9–12, 1885, pitted as many as 400 Métis and Cree rebels against 900 soldiers. Riel's forces ran out of ammunition and were overwhelmed.

When the smoke cleared eight Canadians and fifty-one rebels lay dead, although historians have argued about these figures. There may have been as many as 200 casualties. After Riel surrendered, the Dominion of Canada tried him for treason and he was convicted. On the morning of November 16, 1884, he was led from his cell to a scaffold, a rope was put around his neck, and with a priest by his side, he began reciting the Lord's Prayer. Just as he reached "deliver us from evil" the trap door fell.

Chapter Four

THE WORLD'S
WEALTHIEST NUN

Although Luis Riel, Mary Fields, Edward Lewis, Thomas Moran, and others gave their time and labor to St. Peter's Mission the individual most responsible for financing its construction and operation was Katharine Mary Drexel. Born in 1858, she was the second daughter of Francis Anthony Drexel, a fabulously successful Philadelphia banker and financier whose father had been J. P. Morgan's partner. Her mother died of complications from childbirth five weeks later. In 1860 Francis Drexel married Emma Bouvier—the great-great-aunt of Jackie Bouvier Kennedy—and a daughter was born to them in 1864. The three Drexel girls were homeschooled by tutors and studied history and geography by touring extensively in the U.S. and Europe.

Brought up in luxury yet surrounded by poverty, they were raised in a family that not only preached altruism but practiced it. When they weren't traveling the world, twice a week the girls handed out food, clothing, and cash to poor people at the family's three-story brownstone on Philly's posh Rittenhouse Square. Emma insisted her daughters help her keep strict accounts of who got what in order to prevent the Drexel's charity from being squandered on alcohol or gambling. Like her parents, Katharine developed a savvy sense of money management. While the Drexels were so devout they went to Mass every day, by the age of fourteen Katharine was developing the obsessive-compulsive behavior of a religious fanatic, much like Louis Riel. While other teenaged girls confided to their diaries their giddy secret crushes and longing for what they imagined was romance, Katharine confided to her "spiritual journal" an unusual resolution. "Men I abhor," she wrote. "I have recorded a vow before the shrine of an unmarried saint never to be aught but the purest celibate." At the age of eighteen she wrote: "Jesus has given his life for me. It is but just that I should give Him mine."[1]

In 1884 Francis Drexel took his daughters across the country on a business trip to Portland, Oregon. Traveling on a private railway car they stopped every day to find a church where they could celebrate Mass. While praying, their car was sidetracked, to be recoupled later to the next train coming down the line in their direction. In a Bismarck church they missed their ride and weren't picked up until twelve hours later. The delay saved them from being robbed, assaulted, kidnapped, or all three in Cinnabar, Montana. A gang of thieves had tied up the stationmaster there and had been waiting to pounce on the wealthy Easterners. When the family didn't show, the thieves abandoned their scheme and left town. In Yellowstone Park the young ladies got soaked by Old Faithful. They were arrested for removing small stones they wanted to keep as mementos, but an amused justice of the peace presiding over their trial in a local general store allowed the family to go on its way.

On the Puyallup Indian Reservation near Tacoma, Washington, the Drexel girls approached a small Catholic chapel to inquire about the schedule of services and were surprised to find that the priest who greeted them was a man they had befriended while on one of their visits to Rome. He took them to look at an even smaller chapel deep inside the reservation. Katharine noticed that although the chapel was called Our Lady of Grace Church it had no statue of Mary. Back home in Philly she ordered an enormous Virgin for what in today's currency is $3,000 and had it shipped to Tacoma.[2] This was the last thing the Puyallup people needed. Their

salmon-based economy had been decimated when they were herded onto
the reservation and given individual allotments of land that were then stolen
from them through the transformation of illegal leases into titles owned
by Whites. The sight of their wretched poverty would be an unforgettable
impression that would shape the rest of Katharine's long life.

In 1883 Emma Bouvier died a lingering death from cancer. Two years
later Kate was at her father's side when he died of a heart attack after
coming down with a cold that developed into pleurisy. She fell into a deep
depression. "I am not happy in the world," she wrote. "There is a void in
my heart which only God can fill." What would have been the good news
for anyone except Kate was the fact that she and her sisters were named
in their father's will as the majority beneficiaries of his estate. Their share
amounted to $470 million. This vast fortune would be held in a permanent
trust from which each daughter would receive an annual interest payment
equivalent to almost $12 million. The breathless newspaper accounts of
their inheritance did not escape the attention of two Catholic clerics,
who soon visited the sisters with their hands out for money. These were a
German priest named Joseph Stephan and Bishop Martin Marty, a Swiss
Jesuit whose face had been disfigured after drinking acid in his father's
shoemaking shop. Katharine jumped at the chance to serve God and give
her existence meaning. In 1885 Drexel wrote her first check to St. Peter's
for $5,000 to be used as seed money to help kick-start the construction of
Mount Angela Institute. Over the next five years she would donate $11,300
more, contributions that would be worth almost $544,000 today. Word of
her largesse spread throughout Catholic missions across Indian Country,
where the clergy was fighting to retain its federal funding.

President U. S. Grant's so-called Peace Policy of 1868 had replaced corrupt Indian agents administering reservations with Christian missionaries
he deemed morally superior. Like Richard Pratt he was of the nineteenth
century assimilationist school of thought holding that Indians could be
brought into White society if they were taught to farm or get jobs, speak
English, adopt Christianity, embrace democracy, and acquire private
property. Unlike Pratt, who believed that the strong kinship and cultural

ties on reservations made assimilation efforts there doomed to failure, Grant believed reservations were a necessary albeit temporary refuge from the White invaders. Exterminationists such as George Armstrong Custer believed that Indians were savages who could not be transformed into imitation White people.

After Chester Arthur became an accidental President in 1881 following James Garfield's assassination, the government began re-evaluating its funding for Christian missions due to his belief that government assimilation centers such as Carlisle in Pennsylvania and Chemawa Industrial School in Oregon were more effective than religious schools. "They are doubtless much more potent for good than the day schools upon the reservation," he said in his first state of the union address, "as the pupils are altogether separated from the surroundings of savage life and brought into constant contact with civilization." There was also a rising chorus of anti-Catholic voices in the wake of the diaspora that flooded America with European Papists who threatened the economic and political control of Protestants and, critics argued, were loyal not to the United States, but to the pope. The loudest of these voices belonged to a secret society, the American Protective Association, which circulated fake documents declaring that Catholics had started the Civil War and were intending to "exterminate all heretics" on September 5, 1893.

In 1887 the sisters traveled to Rome and met with Pope Leo XIII, begging him to order Jesuits to staff the Indian missions the Drexels were beginning to build and finance. The Pope suggested that Katharine ought to serve as her own missionary. Two years later she entered a convent in Pittsburgh. Her "withdrawal from the world" shocked polite society. She chose the name Mother Katharine and spent the rest of her ninety-six years giving away her fortune as the founder of the Sisters of the Blessed Sacrament for Indians and Colored People. Her money went to establish twelve schools for Indians, forty-five missions, and fifty schools for African Americans, including Xavier University in Louisiana, the only Catholic college in the U.S. that was exclusively intended to educate Blacks.

The network of so-called Drexel mission schools for Indians stretched from Wisconsin to Puget Sound to the Mexican border. The reservations where she constructed facilities included those of the Puyallup, Cheyenne, Arapaho, Sioux, Blackfeet, Crow, Coeur d'Alene, Nez Perce, Chippewa, Cherokee, Comanche, Osage, Pueblo, and the Morongo in California. Her attack plan rarely varied. She bought the land, hired contractors to erect the buildings, and then deeded her real estate to the Bureau of Catholic Indian Missions. [3]

In recognition of Drexel's financial support Catholics lobbied to see her named a saint. This required evidence of at least one miracle. Two cases were submitted to the Vatican. First, in 1974 a fourteen-year-old Pennsylvania boy named Robert Gutherman reportedly regained the hearing in one of his ears following an infection after his family prayed exclusively to Mother Katharine—then dead for nineteen years. Second, in 1994 a girl named Amy Wall was born deaf but gained her hearing at the age of two after her family watched a PBS special on Katharine Drexel and prayed to her for a miracle. People of faith had no problem accepting these unsubstantiated anecdotes as proof of the Miracle Ears. In 1988 Drexel was beatified after the Vatican recognized her first miracle and canonized in 2000 for her second. (Beatification is the step before sainthood. By beatifying someone, the Church says that the person is definitely in Heaven, and definitely able to plead to God on your behalf if you pray to her.)

Saint Katharine, who is regarded as the patron saint of racial justice, donated $45 million to Indian boarding schools. In 1903 the Bureau of Catholic Indian Missions reported that Drexel "gives every year to Indian missions more than all the Catholics of the United States combined." [4] The following year the Director of the Bureau reported that if it had not been for Drexel "The whole system of Catholic Indian schools would have collapsed. And the Indian children been given over to schools decidedly anti-Catholic." [5] Clearly, if one individual could be held more responsible than anyone else for the assault on Native American society waged by these assimilation centers it would be Drexel.

The gloomy fortress she built for the Ursulines at St. Peter's was a building only the Addams family could love. Designed in the Queen Anne and Second Empire styles, it rose three stories and covered a footprint of 10,000 square feet. Dormers housing the nuns were built into a mansard roof, towers were capped with cupolas, and a centrally located four-story tower loomed above the entrance. A kitchen and dining room occupied the lower ground floor under thirteen-foot ceilings. Above that an arched hall ran the length of building through its center, dividing the classrooms on the first floor into two halves, one for Native American girls and the other for Whites. The second floor contained equally segregated dormitories large enough on each side to house 100 girls, who slept in iron beds surrounded by privacy curtains suspended from the ceiling. All the doors were made of heavy oak. Addressing the literal walls separating the races a newspaper reported, "As far as studies and social customs are concerned, they have no interests in common and neither is assisted nor elevated by co-education with the other, so an entire separation is found to be advisable."[6]

A huge stone school for the boys had been completed in 1887 a hundred yards away on the south side of Mission Creek at a cost of $400,000. Its construction was financed by private donations and federal funding through the "contract school" program that paid religious orders to assimilate Native Americans. Equally gloomy, it was four-stories tall and also featured dormers built into a mansard roof and a cupola above the front entrance. Although a bridge spanned the creek between the two schools a row of cottonwoods was planted between them to visually reinforce the fact that boys and girls were strictly segregated. The boys school contained dormitories, classrooms, kitchens, bathrooms, and dining facilities. In the workshops boys fabricated items from metal and leather, some of which were sold to the locals. In the carpentry shop they learned how to build a proper frame house, although when they returned to the reservation most of them would live in the tipis in which their people had always lived. Like the convent, the building segregated Natives from Whites. Attached to it was a three-story frame structure that served as a residence for the

Jesuits. St. Peter's regularly paid for newspaper advertising to entice White families to board their children in its schools. Tuition was free; room and board was $10 per month per child.

Both the Institute and the Jesuit school were built from blocks of stone quarried by stonecutters from Square Butte twelve miles northeast and hauled to the construction sites in wagons. This was shonkinite, a rare igneous mineral forced upward from a subterranean volcano as magma, which cooled just before it reached the surface and was eventually revealed by erosion. The word comes from the Blackfeet name for the nearby Highwood Mountains, which, besides the Mission Valley and the Indonesian island of Timor, is one of the only places on earth where shonkinite is found. This extremely hard and adamant grey stone is studded with small hunks of a black crystal called augite, in the manner of chocolate chip cookies. To a traveler unprepared for these colorless monoliths—rising in a remote valley three-hours by stagecoach from the nearest village—the sight of them would have been as jarring as a cathedral in Antarctica. One scholar called them "visual absurdities." But the Catholics assumed that their strongholds would last forever.

These buildings—and those of Carlisle and other Indian boarding schools—were in themselves a significant weapon in the federal and parochial arsenal of assimilation. Native American children from the Plains who had lived in a world of circles suddenly found themselves confined to square boxes. "Birds make their nests in circles," observed Black Elk, an Oglala spiritual leader who also became a Catholic.

> The sun comes forth and goes down again in a circle. The moon does the same, and both are round. Even the seasons form a great circle from childhood to childhood, and so it is in everything where power moves. Our teepees were round like the nests of birds, and these were always set in a circle. The nation's hoop, a nest of many nests, where the Great Spirit meant for us to hatch our children. But the Wasi'chus [White people] have put us in these square boxes. [7]

The Jesuits and their boys moved into their fortress in August 1887. In January 1892 the nuns moved their White and Native girls and themselves from their crude log cabins into Mount Angela. In terms of ideology and architecture these moves connected St. Peter's directly to the day in 1609 when Spanish Jesuits founded San Ignacio Guazú in what is now Paraguay. The tumultuous decades that followed represented the first Catholic campaign to convert the New World's Indigenous people into Christians and confected Europeans. The Jesuits built walled compounds in the jungle among the Guaraní, whose population at the time numbered about 100,000 people spread across an area the size of Indiana. In what was called the Paraguay Reduction System the compounds—called reductions—were built environments of enclosed workshops, dormitories, barns, and fenced fields where Natives worked year-round under the constant supervision and surveillance of the priests.

The Guaraní were physically separated from their villages, where they had lived in large, thatched houses, each one shared by a dozen or so sedentary families working communally to grow manioc and maze. The Jesuits believed that the artificial configuration of space manifested by the compounds was necessary to isolate the Guaraní from their shamans and the contamination of European settlers so they could be converted to Christianity and taught to read. Confine wild birds to a henhouse, the Jesuits reasoned, and they would eventually produce chicken eggs. The reductions were met initially with violent resistance during which a number of Jesuits were transformed into their favorite things: martyrs. But eventually many Guaraní accepted the rigid and regimented life in the reductions because they were offered material benefits such as metal tools and domesticated animals. More compelling, the compounds were sanctuaries from bandits who conscripted Indigenous people to work as serfs and slaves on settler plantations called *encomiendas*. To defend the reductions from slave raiders the Jesuits armed the Guaraní and organized them into militias. By saving the Natives the priests could rationalize exploiting them. However, the oppressive environment of the reductions was part of the same conquest mentality that facilitated Columbus' enslavement of

500 Taíno Indians on Hispaniola Island. By 1740 some thirty reductions were successfully competing with the *encomiendas*, whose owners were not amused. Because of their meddling in local politics, among other reasons, the Jesuits were expelled from South America in 1759. The Swiss historian Clovis Lugon called the reductions a "communist Christian republic," a description that pleased neither communists nor Christians.[8]

In *The Mission*, a 1986 film starring Robert DeNiro and Jeremy Irons, the Guaraní tie the first Jesuit they meet to a crucifix and send him to his death over a waterfall. But they eventually succumb to the Church and in the end fight a disastrous battle against a superior force of European soldiers, who gun down the Jesuits and everyone else in the reduction—including women and children. In 2015, Pope Francis received thunderous applause in Bolivia after apologizing for the sins and crimes of the Catholic Church against Indigenous people in Latin America. At a similar gathering of Native and nongovernmental groups a few days later in Paraguay he praised the reductions as "one of the most important experiences of evangelization and social organization in history." They were where "the Gospel was the soul and the life of communities which did not know hunger, unemployment, illiteracy, or oppression." His comments elicited from the audience a stony silence.[9]

After the 1854 founding of St. Ignatius Mission in western Montana the Jesuits were successful in converting a number of Salish people to Catholicism, at least temporarily. Much of this accomplishment centered on baptism. Some tribal leaders believed that the ritual opened a portal to a mysterious force granting them new-found success in battle against their traditional enemy, the Blackfeet. Pierre-Jean De Smet, the Flemish Jesuit who founded St. Ignatius, wrote that the Blackfeet were "murderers, thieves, traitors, and all that is wicked."[10] He determined that in order to convert them the Church would need more than beads and the Good Book. It would need to kidnap Blackfeet children and confine them. This scheme, spawned by the Paraguay Reduction System, is an extreme example of architectural determinism, the idea that the built environment is the chief or even the sole determinant of how people act. Reformers of the late nineteenth century such as John Wesley Powell believed that Native Americans acted like "savages" because of their physically challenging lives in the natural world huddled in tents. Move them into proper houses and buildings and they would morph into the imitation White people. Lawrence Palladino, a Jesuit at St. Ignatius, told a Congressional committee in 1892 that the Indian boarding school and the tipi village brought "civilization and uncivilization face to face—the former with its home and dwelling, its food, its industries, its cleanliness, its field and garden, its stock, its ease, its comfort and its plenty, and the latter with the whole train of wretched contrasts." The contrast would compel Indians, he said, "to see, hear, smell, touch, taste, and compare the blessings of the one with the wretchedness of the other."[11] Palladino's testimony was a criticism of establishing Indian industrial schools such as Carlisle in locales far removed from the reservations. It was not the first nor the last salvo fired between Jesuits and Richard Pratt.

The first of the built environments at St. Peter's consisted of a crude log chapel and a few whitewashed cabins thrown together in 1874. Unfortunately for the Jesuits, that was the same year the federal government significantly reduced the size of the Blackfeet Reservation by shifting its southern boundary sixty miles north to Birch Creek. This sudden physical separation of the Mission from the reservation would make St. Peter's considerably less attractive to tribal leaders. Although the federal government hath taketh away by moving the border it would also giveth to St. Peter's by making Indian education mandatory. "Only by complete isolation of the Indian child from his savage antecedents," Indian School Superintendent John B. Riley declared in 1886, "can he be satisfactorily educated." Even when the boys escaped the vertical and horizontal confinement of their fortress to work outside on some of the Mission's 1,100 acres they found themselves still hemmed in, this time by fences and barns and corrals. Wrapping Indians in stone, reformers believed, would encourage their untapped intellectual potential to flourish so they could become useful members of American society.

When stonecutters excavated the cornerstone of Mount Angela Institute from the shonkinite quarry at Square Butte they uncovered a nest of prairie rattlesnakes underneath and killed thirty of them. Although the moral of the story is more fantasy than fact, according to an Ursuline biographer the demise of the serpents was symbolic of the "evil that Mother Amadeus had already driven out of the country." Did the writer believe the "evil" was Native American culture or did she mean the general unchristian nature of this rough frontier world? The cornerstone, which was laid in 1888, contained a time capsule with a document that included a prayer: "May the Peace of Christ dwell in this house of education. May it be erected for the greater honor and glory of God." There were no prayers for Nancy Bird or the hundreds of other Native American girls who would be confined here between 1892 and 1918.

As the tolling of the church bell echoed off Skull Butte the funeral processions at St. Peter's wound their way from the little whitewashed chapel to the cemetery on a rise overlooking Mission Creek. It's not known exactly how many Native American children were buried there, but according to diocese records there were at least ninety, none of them named. The original whitewashed wooden crosses marking their graves rotted away. Some family members arrived to take their dead boys and girls home to the reservations or to the Métis communities, and some stayed to march behind a simple pine casket to the Mission cemetery.

In 1885 a Jesuit named Frederick Eberschweiler, who had established his presence among the A'aninin (Gros Ventre) and Nakota (Assiniboine) people on the Fort Belknap Reservation, sent Amadeus what her Ursuline biographer called "a priceless gift: a wagonload of Indian girls." The passengers included the daughters of the chiefs leading the twelve A'aninin bands. Agessa was the daughter of Bushy Head; Watzinitha was Eyahe's girl, and Atathan was the granddaughter of Akipinaki. "A perfect type of Indian," a diarist wrote of Agessa, "she had a high forehead, long aquiline nose, a profusion of straight black hair, and lovely white teeth."

A nun named Angela Lincoln, who wrote the biography of Amadeus, described the moment of their arrival in 1887: "Mother Amadeus enfolded each child in her maternal arms whilst the wondrous smile of her eye and lips won and subjugated the trembling, wild little hearts beneath the buckskin, and sunned away the first tears of lonesomeness and shyness." The little girls were scoured with soap and tubs of hot water and their long hair was combed free of lice, which were dropped in vats of coal tar. "Together they lived their little lives at St. Pete's Mission," the biographer continued with grotesque hyperbole. "Together they learned from Mother Amadeus to love Jesus, Mary, and Joseph, and together they died in her loving arms, little virgins consecrated to God."[12] In June 1892 Agessa came down with pneumonia and was visited by Bushy Head and his wife. She died at midnight three weeks later. Her pallbearers were Itathan (renamed Ursula by the Ursulines after the patron saint of schoolgirls), Bathnay, Watzinitha and a Nakota girl named Isca, all of whom the nuns dressed up in white gowns with wreaths of orange-colored blossoms.

Native American children confined at St. Peter's got sick from a range of ailments, many of them undiagnosed, untreated, or mistreated. Although the Institute maintained what the Sisters called their "infirmary" the nearest doctors were forty miles away in Great Falls. Although they occasionally made the long trip to the Mission they had very little in their medical bags to combat infectious disease. In July 1892 the diarist wrote that a doctor examined the girls. "We prayed for good news and lived all day in its expectation, but we were answered by no bad news, which is good news nowadays." However, Mary Rose Swan came down with what the nuns described as "cerebral trouble" and died. Martini Berger died soon after the nuns administered the last rites to her. A month after Agessa's burial Atathan died, followed by the death of Katharine Landry. In February 1895 fifteen-year-old Theresa Lewis, the youngest daughter of Ed Lewis and Sycowwastakapi, "breathed her last," according to the diarist. These deaths were followed by those of Mary LaRance, Philomena Berger, Ursula Cutbank, Lilly Allis, and a baby surnamed Azure. In 1898 after undergoing surgery at the hospital in Great Falls three years earlier Watzinitha died. In winter 1896 an outbreak of measles spread through the girls' dormitory.

The federal government's growing doubts about Indian boarding schools came too late to save Nancy Bird. The diarist recorded without elaboration that while some of the nuns were off enjoying a picnic on August 7, 1894, Nancy "died suddenly of a hemorrhage." She was fifteen years old. The lack of clarity about her death was typical of the documentation at St. Peter's and that of most Indian boarding schools of the era, where records of the demise of Native American children were often opaque or guesses made by people with no medical training. If Bird died of a ruptured blood vessel, in what part of her body was it located? Could it have been in her lungs, which would suggest she had tuberculosis? Since no death certificate for her exists in the records of the Cascade County Clerk and Recorder, whose records go back to 1893, the Ursulines apparently did not summon a physician from Great Falls to determine the cause of death or sign any documents. It's not known if her family claimed her body or if she was buried at St. Peter's. But unlike the 186 children laid to rest in the cemetery at the Carlisle Indian School between 1880 and 1918 at least she died on the land where she was born.

Native children also suffered from accidents. In 1897 six young unattended Métis girls ate a commercial poison called "Rough on Rats" that had been spread on the floor of the art room to kill mice. They were fed gruel, milk toast, and barley broth until they recovered. A kindergarten girl named Annie Barnaby drowned in a stream while out walking with some nuns. The diarist did not reveal how they could have let this happen. On a picnic outing two wagonloads of nuns and Native children were returning to St. Peter's when the horses bolted, breaking the tongue and sending the wagon over an embankment into the creek below. Katie Redd suffered a broken jaw that took months to heal.

The state of mortality at the Jesuit school was similar. Thirty boys came down with pneumonia in 1892. Soon after, diphtheria ran rampant through the dormitories, forcing the Jesuits to quarantine sick boys in the Mission's unoccupied log cabins. While sixteen Native girls dressed in pink dresses with white veils and green wreaths were about to receive their First Communion the Mission bell began to toll for the death of a Métis boy named Joe Barrow, who had just died of pneumonia, which would later strike

Edie Ford. James Tabor and Cash Allis died of causes that weren't known or weren't recorded.

By 1895 it was becoming apparent to some government officials that the assimilation program at St. Peter's was failing. A supervisor for the federal Indian Office named William Moss reported that "everything here is so fine and nice that when the children go home the contrast will be too great for them to bear." His cultural bias allowed him to ignore the fact that most of the Native American children hated their work, their class-rooms, and most of all their confinement inside these ludicrous, artificial environments. They had been brought into the world by tribal people who moved continuously under the sun and the stars to extract food and fiber from the natural world, guided by a deep knowledge of plants, animals, and weather. In 1901 William A. Jones, the Commissioner of Indian Affairs, understated the failure of boarding schools when he reported that "the methods of education which have been pursued for the past genera-tion have not produced the results anticipated." Further, boarding schools wasted resources because of their "fallacious idea of bringing the Indian into civilization and keeping him there."

This ideological failure can be traced to the Civilization Fund Act passed by Congress in 1819. It granted the President the power to hire "capable persons of good moral character" to teach Native Americans the "arts of civilization." Because aboriginal people controlled the entirety of North America at the time except for narrow strips of settler territory along the Eastern Seaboard and north of Lakes Erie and Ontario this law was the epitome of hubris. Maps showing the 1819 political boundaries of the twenty-two states were cartographically nothing more than wishful thinking. However, the law provided funds for Catholic and Protestant missionaries to establish schools in Indian Country, where it was believed that Native American societies could be replaced with Christianity and a Euro-American monoculture. Five years later the War Department established the Office of Indian Affairs to oversee this doomed assimila-tion scheme. Luke Lea, its commissioner from 1850 to 1853, said it was "indispensably necessary that [Indians] be placed in positions where they can be controlled, and finally compelled by stern necessity . . . until such time as their general improvement and good conduct may supersede the necessity of such restrictions."

Like ravens and magpies fighting over crusts of bread, as soon as money from the Civilization Fund Act became available Catholics began competing with Protestants for Indian conscripts. During the 1870s the government expanded its partnerships with Christians by awarding their schools contracts that paid a set price for every Native American they enrolled. In 1874 the Church established the Bureau of Catholic Indian Missions, which marked a new surge in Catholic activity in Montana. That year its mission schools received only $264,000 in federal contracts. But by 1890 Catholics controlled 75 percent of the lucrative Indian education industry, enrolling more than 2,000 Native American children in thirty-eight schools and raking in $16.5 million in contracts. Congress had helped grow enrollment by passing the compulsory Indian Education Act in 1887, followed by the 1891 law that enabled federal officers to forcibly take Native American children from their homes and reservations.[13]

But a Protestant movement called Friends of the Indians, encouraged by the growing anti-Catholic bias sweeping the nation, stepped up its campaign to defund religious schools and transfer the chore of assimilating Native Americans to the federal government. Richard Pratt relentlessly attacked the Indian Bureau and the reservation system. The argument of The Friends rested on the First Amendment provision separating church from state, which they conveniently ignored when confronted by Catholics with the fact that the government's schools were essentially Protestant schools operated by evangelicals such as Pratt. Founded in 1861, the Friends believed that they were more qualified to speak on behalf of Indians than Indians themselves. Many of its members had worked in the Office of Indian Affairs and other government agencies. Some of them were founders of the new "science" of ethnography and moved in with Native Americans in order to "study" them. Having witnessed the abuse of tribal people firsthand, they believed that the reservation system was an immoral and oppressive form of segregation; Indians would be better off as members of the dominant culture, they reasoned. While some of these self-styled reformers were compassionate others wanted the tribes stripped of what land they still controlled and given to White settlers. As their lobbying in Congress intensified, the Protestant schools withdrew from the contract system, knowing that government schools such as Carlisle and Chemawa were operated by like-minded evangelicals. For example, Richard Pratt, saw his work with Native Americans as an evangelical mission. "In Indian civilization I am a Baptist," he said, "because I believe in immersing the Indians in our civilization and when we get them under holding them there until they are thoroughly soaked." By 1895 Protestants got what they wanted: Congress voted to phase out all Catholic contracts over a five-year period.

However, the Ursulines began the year 1896 brimming with optimism. They constructed a large two-story frame building containing an auditorium and a stage for performances. The nuns called it the Opera House. The girls were expected to learn European-style dance there, as well as embroidery, painting, wood carving, and musical instruments. They put on plays and entertained visitors with recitals. But in August the federal government abruptly canceled its contract, making St. Peter's one of the first Catholic boarding schools to get axed. After Amadeus deposited the final federal check in the amount of $1,944 she knew that come winter the wolves would be at the door—literally. She wrote Drexel begging for help. Saint Katharine promptly sent a check for $750 with a promise to send the same amount every quarter. This would finance the boarding of thirty Native American girls to replace the government's payments of $100 per child per year. Drexel would send $750 every quarter for the next twenty years.

Life continued at the Institute much as it had before Drexel's largesse. Fire was a constant problem. The log cabin serving as the bake house burst into flames, one of the hot water heaters caught on fire, the chimney in the Jesuits residence began smoldering, a box of candles and "benediction charcoal" were ignited by some unknown source and began to spread up one wall of the chapel, and a fire broke out in the washhouse, spreading from smoldering blankets. A January wind blew the curtains in the "art room" up against hot water pipes, and the resulting flames threatened to consume the girls' infirmary. Except for two catastrophic infernos all of these blazes were quickly extinguished.

With the loss of its federal contract the Jesuits shut down their school at St. Peter's in July 1896 and shipped their Native American boys to other Catholic facilities, notably the boarding school at St. Ignatius and the Holy Family Mission on the Blackfeet Reservation. Two years later they abandoned St. Peter's altogether. The Ursulines, who had always complained about having to take care of the fathers, were not sad to see them go. "Throughout the missions," a Catholic historian wrote, "sisters labored in the school, cooked, cleaned, and did the priests' laundry."[14] In fact, at St. Peter's it was the Native girls who did most of this domestic work for the Jesuits. Without the boys to do the gardening, field work, and stock-raising the Ursulines would come to rely on the generosity of neighboring White farmers such as Thomas Moran and Ed Lewis. But these families couldn't feed everyone.

Like all Indian boarding schools St. Peter's was chronically under-funded. "We have had much suffering of late," the Ursuline diarist wrote during winter 1892. "Yesterday there was nothing in the house but corn meal—no butter, eggs, syrup, not a drop of coal oil or a bit of money." The seven years of operating the Indian girls' school, she continued, had been "seven years of famine." The next seven years, it was recorded, were "seven years of not so plenty." Some of the White families paid for their children's room and board with cows and other barter goods but even with Drexel's charity what the nuns needed was money. Their financial problems were compounded when one of these families paid with a hundred-dollar bill that was confiscated by the police.

Eddie Curry was enrolled at St. Peter's on April 24, 1899, when he was three or four years old, one of the few White boys in the area the nuns agreed to educate after the Jesuits retreated. Six weeks later his father would hold up a Union Pacific mail train near Wilcox, Wyoming, with five other members of the Wild Bunch. After the gang used dynamite to blow open the doors of the express car the stunned clerk refused to unlock the safe.

So they dynamited that, as well, using so much explosive the whole car was destroyed. The scene was reprised in the film *Butch Cassidy and the Sundance Kid*. After the explosion The Kid asks his partner: "Think you used enough dynamite there, Butch?" (Although Butch Cassidy was probably the mastermind, he likely didn't take part in the actual robbery.) The gang fled north to their Wyoming hideout at the Hole-in-the-Wall with $50,000 in gold, jewelry, watches, and currency.

One member of the gang was Lonny Logan, alias Lonny Curry, who took his nom de guerre from another member of the Bunch named Flat Nose George Curry. Lonnie's brother and fellow train robber was Harvey Logan—known as Kid Curry. The brothers turned from working as cowboys to robbing things for a living after a deadly altercation in 1894 at Jew Jake's saloon in the Bears Paw Mountains of Montana. A rancher and gold miner named Powell "Pike" Landusky and Harvey Logan were neighbors who became enemies. The source of their animosity was Logan's alleged romantic entanglement with Pike's daughter, Elfie. Or maybe they had quarreled over a plow. Whatever, Logan reportedly marched into the saloon and slugged Landusky, who reached for his pistol. When it misfired Logan shot him in the head, killing him. Elfie later revealed that in fact the father of her son, Eddie, was not Harvey but his brother Lonny.

On March 10, 1900, Amadeus received a hundred-dollar bill on the Curry account to pay the Mission's monthly $10 fee for board and laundry. After she deposited the bill in Helena the president of the bank wrote to inform her that because of the serial number he determined it was part of the loot from the Wilcox train robbery and would be confiscated. Now a hunted man, Lonny Curry fled to his aunt's farm outside Kansas City. In 1900 a group of Pinkerton agents tried to arrest him there. In the shootout that followed Lonny was killed.

Until he enlisted as a career soldier there was nothing in Richard Pratt's life to suggest that he would become the chief architect of the federal government's bizarre campaign to transform Native Americans into White Americans. But to paraphrase Vladimir Lenin, war breaks some people and enlightens others. Pratt had fought for four years on the Union side during the Civil War. After the South surrendered he ran an unsuccessful hardware store in Indiana for two years, then reupped in the Army, which commissioned him a lieutenant in 1867. He was assigned to the 10th Cavalry, a segregated unit composed of freed slaves commanded by White officers at Fort Sill in the Oklahoma Territory. The Indians had nicknamed the enlisted men "Buffalo Soldiers" because of the bison coats they wore in the winter or maybe because of the color and texture of their hair or their ferocity in battle. He participated in the Red River campaign of 1874, a series of skirmishes across the southern Great Plains in which twenty-five Indians and ten soldiers were killed. Although casualties were relatively light the conflict exhausted the dwindling resources of the tribes and ended the ancient nomadic rhythms of Comanche, Kiowa, Southern Cheyenne, and Arapaho people, who were herded onto reservations. Their fate was hastened by the wholesale slaughter of bison on the southern Plains by the Army and White hunters.

It was Pratt's interpretation of the proposed Fourteenth Amendment to the Constitution that sparked his interest in what were then America's two largest minorities. "All persons born or naturalized in the United States . . . are citizens of the United States," the amendment begins, adding that no state shall deprive any citizen of "life, liberty, or property without due process of law." Pratt believed that when the amendment was ratified it would put an end to the segregation of Blacks in the regular Army and the segregation of Indians on reservations. (It was Pratt who first coined the term "racism" in a 1902 speech railing against the segregation of Indians and Blacks.) Equal opportunity and education would allow both populations to compete as the equals of Whites in the American economy. Although the amendment clearly overturned the Supreme Court's Dredd Scott ruling in 1857 that denied citizenship to Blacks, in 1870 the Senate Judiciary committee determined that the only Indians who were eligible for citizenship were the 8 percent who were taxed for allotted land they had accepted. The balance of an estimated aboriginal population of 330,000 were considered members of sovereign nations. Native Americans were not granted universal citizenship until 1924, two months after Pratt died. Finally, in 1948, Harry Truman ordered the desegregation of the U.S. military.

Pratt would get a chance to try out his theories about Indian assimilation at the end of the Red River Campaign. In 1875 he was commanded to shackle seventy-two warriors charged with murder and rape and transport them by wagon and rail to Fort Marion in St. Augustine, Florida. A massive bulwark constructed of quarried blocks of coquina, an accretion of seashells that grows stronger the longer it's exposed to air, the fort had a secret dungeon and was surrounded by a moat. The only access was over a drawbridge. Soon after arriving Pratt ordered the removal of the prisoners' chains. They were given free range of the fort, and several of them were appointed security guards. Wealthy people from throughout the world wintering in the posh St. Augustine hotels came to gaze at the savages, who were never tried for their alleged crimes. Pratt had their hair cut short and replaced their blankets and moccasins with pants, shirts, and boots. Then he introduced them to classes in the English language and arts and crafts taught by White ladies from the community, because he didn't have the money to hire trained instructors. It was the beginning of his life-long obsession with immersion education designed to finally solve what was called "the Indian problem," which was defined by the military historian Robert Utley as "that perennial source of disturbance that flowed from the Indian's insistence on keeping what he had always owned and leading the life he had always lived."[15]

At Rosebud Pratt met with White Thunder, Two Strike, and Sinte Gleska (Spotted Tail), important Sicangu chiefs. Two years earlier Spotted Tail had asked the government to send the Sicangu some Black Robes to teach his people's children how to read English. Pratt argued that because the Sioux were illiterate they had no way of knowing what was contained in the treaties they were signing. At Carlisle, he promised, your children will be taught to read and write English. His emphasis on literacy was inspired by the Massachusetts Puritans, who believed that the children of Plymouth Colony should be literate for only one reason—so they could read the Bible. They passed laws such as The Old Deluder Satan Act of 1647 that mandated classrooms and schoolmasters in order to prevent the devil—the "Old Deluder"—from deceiving otherwise ignorant people. After Pratt met with the Sicangu he headed west to Pine Ridge and met with five Oglala chiefs, including Red Cloud, American Horse, and Black Bear. They reluctantly agreed to send thirty-six boys and girls to Carlisle.

Surrounded by a curious crowd of White people, Pratt's conscripts were marched in the moonlight a mile from the station to the Barracks. Among them were four of Spotted Tail's sons. These were nine-year-old Little Scout, renamed Pollock by the school; Bugler, age twelve, renamed Oliver; Talks With Bears, fourteen, renamed Max, and Stays At Home, eighteen, renamed William. A year later Spotted Tail visited his sons at Carlisle while on a trip to Washington, D.C., with a large Lakota delegation negotiating the passage of rail lines through the Sioux Nation. Although the studio photograph showing him posed with his sons at Carlisle could be interpreted as his approval of the school, he was disgusted by what he saw there. His boys and all of the others were dressed in military uniforms and forced to march under the flag of the invading nation that had killed so many of his own people. One of his sons had faced court martial for fighting and had been jailed in the guardhouse for a week. The imprisonment and corporal punishment common at Carlisle were abhorrent practices that had no place in Lakota society. When Spotted Tail left Pennsylvania for the trip home he took his boys with him. Another Lakota boy named Knocks Off, renamed Ernest, disliked Carlisle so much that when they climbed aboard the train he stowed away with them. But he was soon caught by the authorities and taken back to school. He was the first Carlisle student to run away. But he was far from the last. After studying school records Australian anthropologist Genevieve Bell estimated that there were at least 1,850 attempts to escape Carlisle during its history. The eighteen-year-old son of a Sicangu chief named White Thunder, Knocks Off was photographed with several other students in the school's tin smithing shop as they fabricated pails. Pratt appears in the photo, as well, inspecting one of their products (as a boy he had apprenticed to a tinsmith). Six months after his foiled escape Knocks Off was diagnosed with diphtheria. For days he refused food, water, and medicine, possibly because his sore throat and swollen glands made swallowing difficult. Finally, he ate a bit of steak and pudding, drank some tea, and took some medicine. Pratt wrote daily letters to White Thunder reassuring him that Carlisle was doing everything in its power to nurse his only son back to health. In a letter to the Secretary of the Interior, however, Pratt said that Knocks Off's condition was "entirely his fault" and that he "wants to die."

Finally, Pratt sent White Thunder the news that his son had passed away. "It was because you loved him so much that you gave him to me," Pratt wrote. In a subsequent letter he described the details of Knocks Off's burial. "I had them make a good coffin and he was dressed in his uniform with a white shirt and nice collar and necktie. The minister read from the good book and told all the teachers and the boys and girls that some time they would have to die too . . . I want you to learn about the good book and what it says. That was the best thing we taught your son." The school newspaper called Ernest a "bright, studious, ambitious boy, standing first in his class, and of so tractable a disposition as to be no trouble to his teachers." His immediate burial must have also caused his parents additional grief because it was not a ritual that the Lakota practiced. They typically painted the body red and wrapped it in a buffalo robe or a blanket. Then they placed it on a scaffold or in a tree so the deceased's spirit would be closer to the sky. Loved ones would visit the site, bringing food, gifts, and conversation. When Spotted Tail's teenaged daughter, Brings Water Home, died in 1866 of pneumonia or tuberculosis her body was placed in a wooden coffin that was transported in an Army wagon to a seven-foot-high scaffold on the prairie near Fort Laramie, as scores of Sicangu people and White soldiers walked behind. The girl's relatives covered the coffin with a buffalo robe and a red wool blanket, raised it to the platform, and tied it down with leather thongs.[16]

A few hours before Knocks Off died a seventeen-year-old Sicangu named Little Girl succumbed to what the doctor's report said was "phthisis," known today as tuberculosis. Her lungs were also compromised by bronchitis and pneumonia. The school newspaper described her as a "bright, impulsive, warm-hearted girl, much beloved by her school mates." She was the daughter of a chief named Swift Bear, leader of the Corn band of Sicangu, and an advocate of peaceful relations with White settlers. Little Girl and Knocks Off were buried at the same time in Carlisle's new cemetery. Their deaths came as a shock to their parents, who had no idea from the tone of Pratt's letters that their children were on the verge of death. A year after the funerals Spotted Tail and White Thunder wrote the Commissioner of Indian Affairs asking that the remains be returned to Rosebud. "We cannot bear to have them sleep so far from their earthly home," they wrote. But Pratt refused their request, believing that it would set an expensive precedent. In 1881 a Rosebud council that included Spotted Tail, Two Strike, White Thunder, and Swift Bear wrote Pratt and government officials a letter protesting the "constant sickness and frequent deaths of our children" and asking for a school that was closer to home.

Shipments of Native Americans would continue until 1918, when the school was closed and the Carlisle Barracks handed back to the Army for use as a military base (it is now home to the U.S. Army War College). Until his death in 1924 Pratt would continue to rail against the reservation system, the Bureau of Indian Affairs, government-operated reservation schools, and Catholic missionaries whose schools, he argued, didn't teach Indians anything but Catholicism. In 1904 he was forced to retire by the Interior Department because of his unrelenting rhetoric about the corruption and incompetence of the BIA. During the thirty-nine-year existence of the institution that he founded, almost 7,800 children stepped down from the train into a new and alien life removed a continent away from their families and their culture.

The first Native American child buried on the grounds of Carlisle, at what would be referred to as the Bureau of Indian Affairs cemetery, was a thirteen-year-old boy from the Sisseton-Wahpeton Oyate named Amos La Framboise. The son of a prominent Métis leader who helped establish the Lake Traverse Reservation government in South Dakota, Amos and his

sister Emily arrived with the first group of Sioux Nation conscripts in 1879.
He died twenty days later of an unrecorded illness. His sister spent three
years at Carlisle and then went home. Pratt was apparently unprepared for
student deaths despite a spike in U.S. child mortality in the 1870s due to
outbreaks of cholera, yellow fever, and smallpox. He arranged to have La
Framboise buried at Ashland Cemetery in the town of Carlisle. A lot had
been set aside for use by the U.S. government, which had interred 500
Union soldiers there in a mass grave. After townspeople objected to the
presence of an Indian in their cemetery the Army's judge advocate ruled
that in fact the deed limited burials in the soldiers' lot to "white persons
only." La Framboise was disinterred and reburied on the grounds of the
school. He would be reburied yet again in 1927 after the entire school
cemetery was moved to make way for a parking lot. Although the new
graveyard was located in a spot out of sight at the back of the base, for
security reasons the Army moved the main gate from the front of the base
to the rear in 2001, making the cemetery the first thing visitors see. Most
of the original grave markers were replaced with simple white headstones
issued by the military, similar to those at Arlington Cemetery Administration, which is in charge of all U.S. military graveyards. During the school's
first two years fifteen other students would die on the grounds, including
another Sisseton-Wahpeton boy named Edward Upright. The son of a
prominent chief named Waanatan, he died from measles and pneumonia
at the age of twelve.

Chapter Five

THE HOSTAGES

Whenever moonlight streamed through the tall French windows in their second-floor dormitory its glow cast weird shadows across the boys while they slept or tried to sleep. Sometimes a silent figure appeared, drifting between the rows of beds. It was dressed in a black habit. But it had no head.

Most everyone on the Pine Ridge Indian Reservation in South Dakota has heard stories about the headless nun and other eerie apparitions occurring in old Drexel Hall. Down in the girls' dorm on the first floor a child brushing her long hair before bed suddenly sensed that she was being watched. When she turned toward the window she was confronted by the horrid face of an ogre. The girl's screams alerted a nun, who rushed outside and trudged through a foot of new snow. But she found no monster or peeping Tom at the window. Nor did she see any footprints beneath it. Then there are the stories of doors that open and close by themselves, playground swings moving with no child in them, and the sound of organ music late at night, although Holy Rosary Mission did not own an organ.

Like many buildings where generations of children lived and sometimes died Drexel Hall is indeed haunted, by bad memories if nothing else. The first Oglala Lakota sons and daughters were snatched from their families and enrolled here beginning in 1888, the year Jesuits and Franciscan nuns from Germany completed the building's construction. Holy Rosary was typical of most Indian boarding schools run by the Catholics. In the beginning the nuns and the Jesuits tolerated Native language and culture, knowing that trying to prohibit free speech and spirituality would backfire. But later, especially after mandatory enrollment became the law, children were punished for speaking Lakota, required to dress in uniforms, had their long hair cut short, and were subjected to corporal punishment. "We were abused and mistreated but no one ever did anything about it," Vivian Locust Nelson recalls of her four years at the school in the 1940s.[1] "One nun had a ring of big skeleton keys. I don't remember what I did but she beat me in the head with those keys. I had big old bumps on my head. I hated that place. I hate it to this day."

In 1981 Tim Giago (Oglala Lakota) founded the *Lakȟóta Times*, the first independently owned Native American newspaper in the U.S., later renamed *Indian Country Today*, then *ICT*. He was enrolled at Holy Rosary during World War II. "Many of those who came out west to educate the Indian children were misfits," he wrote.

> They were sent out here by the Bureau of Indian Affairs or the Catholic Church on a mission of killing the Indian while saving the child. Among the teachers finding their way to the Indian reservations were many that came here as a form of punishment. In the Catholic Church many came out to the reservations as a form of penance. Among those teachers were many pedophiles. They found an easy place to prey on innocent children because we were so isolated that no one really cared what happened to us. The most prevalent form of punishment was the leather strap. After observing and receiving many severe beatings with the strap I cannot help but conclude that many of the teachers sent out west were also sadists.[2]

Giago told the story of a classmate named Gabby Brewer, whose brother and father had drowned while fishing. Previously a lively, chattering boy, he was returned to Holy Rosary following the funerals grieving and depressed. Like many boarding school children he ran away. A prefect tracked him down at his family's home in the village of Pine Ridge, four miles south. After ordering all the boys to watch, a priest used his belt to beat Gabby across the bare buttocks. Cardboard signs were draped across his chest and back that said "I am a runaway." Giago also recounted the story of his sister, Shirley, and another girl named Goldie Walks Under the Ground, who shared a terrible secret. They had both been raped by a groundskeeper who lived in a house at the Mission. The girls, who were two of this predator's many victims, finally took their story to the Franciscan Sisters. But the nuns did nothing. One day the man vanished and was never seen at the school again.

Giago also wrote about the account of a boy named Buzzy Torres who witnessed the savage beating of a ten-year-old classmate named Pinky Merrival. A school prefect began lashing Pinky with a belt and became so enraged that soon he began beating him with the belt buckle. All of the little boys who witnessed this were screaming and begging the man to stop. "You're killing him," they shouted, but the beating went on until Pinky finally collapsed.[3] "One of my friends," Giago told a reporter, "a sixteen-year-old young man got an ear infection and he died. So they assigned me and my friend Red Elk to dig his grave. So we were up at the Holy Rosary Mission cemetery digging his grave. And I dug down, we were about five feet down and I hit something with my pick. And when I lifted it up over my head, it was a little child's skull."[4]

In 1939 when he was six years old Basil Brave Heart was taken from his family and enrolled in Holy Rosary. "I was in a state of shock, traumatized," he told a reporter named Hilary Giovale. "I couldn't understand what was happening. I didn't cognitively understand what abandonment meant, but I knew what it feels like being left at a school. I felt taken away from my parents. It was very traumatizing. You block your emotions." His grandmother, Mary Red Hair, was enrolled in 1888 as one of the first female students. Brave Heart's father, brothers, and sisters, all went to school there. "They cut our hair. That again, was to me, a very spiritual violation because in our culture, only maternal grandmother had the right to cut my hair. So when they started to cut my hair and let it fall to the floor and stepping on it, I felt disrespected."

Brave Heart described his experience in the school's church. "There was a time to kneel down, a time to stand up, and there were special gestures we had to make. Someone said prayers with his back toward us. I looked on the wall and there was a man with long hair hanging from a cross. I thought, 'They told us a little while ago that they were going to cut our hair, but now they are talking reverently about this man with long hair, and saying he gave his life for us.' They tried to explain that we were sinful, and this man died to take our sins away."

He said there was never enough food and "they yelled at us." The physical abuse began soon after he was enrolled. These included lashing with leather straps, paddling with wooden boards, hands held to radiators, punishments for the smallest things, which included uttering words in Lakota. He was forced to bite down on one end of a rubber band, stretch it with his fingers, then let it snap back against his mouth. "Physical abuse was difficult," he said. "But when they took my language away, they took my moral compass."

For Brave Heart, another disturbing place was the dormitory. "After they turned the lights out at 8:30, a door would open and someone would come in. This dormitory was very old and you could hear the floor squeaking with the person's footsteps. One night, I heard whimpering, muffled crying. It was like someone put their hands over the person's mouth. And after a while, I figured out that this guy was coming in and taking a little boy to the back room. As time passed, I heard some of the boys say, 'A man came and took me out of my bed; it was not good.'" Brave Heart said that many of his classmates drank to dull their pain. Some of them committed suicide. Others, like himself, fled the reservation and went to war. "I came from a caring, loving home and community, and [Holy Rosary] was an unfriendly place. I felt betrayed.

I didn't trust these people." After he survived school he became a Korean War combat veteran, a school administrator, an addiction counselor, and the author of *The Spiritual Journey of a Brave Heart.*[5]

Maria Hazel Stands was enrolled at Holy Rosary from 1968 to 1969 just as it was changing its name to Red Cloud Indian School in honor of the famous Oglala war chief. "I remember I tried to speak my language. I said '*lowáčhiŋ.*' That means 'I'm hungry,' and a nun heard me. They said, 'We don't want ever, ever to hear you speak your language.'" She pointed to the tall white steeple that towers over the school. "You see that steeple? They put me up there. They said, 'You're gonna live here. You're a monster. You're a little monster for speaking your language. We don't want that here,' and I was up there almost a week."[6]

———

Maȟpíya Lúta (Red Cloud) was the only Native American military commander to win a war against the United States. A brilliant tactician, he developed his skills fighting for control of hunting grounds against the Oglala's traditional enemies—the Crows, Arikiras, Pawnees, and Shoshones. Because of his courage in battle his stature rose from that of a foot soldier to the undisputed leader of the allied Lakota, Arapaho, and Cheyenne fighters who launched a guerilla war in 1866 against the rising flood of prospectors and settlers passing through tribal hunting grounds on their way to the gold fields in Montana. To protect these travelers the U.S. built three stockaded forts in present-day Wyoming and Montana along what became known as the Bozeman Trail. Red Cloud's forces laid siege to these fortifications, cut off their supplies and attacked soldiers who ventured outside. After they annihilated a cavalry and infantry detachment near Fort Phil Kearny in December 1866, killing all eighty-one soldiers, civilian traffic ceased. By the time the government surrendered, some 200 White soldiers and settlers lay dead, killed mostly by Indian arrows. Fort Kearny's garrison abandoned its post. As the column marched away Cheyenne warriors burned it to the ground.

The Fort Laramie Treaty of 1868 brought a halt to the fighting by establishing the Great Sioux Reservation, a huge swath of territory covering the western half of what is now South Dakota, including hunting rights on land in what is now five other states, and a promise to return surplus federal land to the tribes. Except for the Indian agent and a few federal employees Whites were banned from setting foot on the reservation without tribal permission. In exchange, Red Cloud and the other chiefs agreed not to "kill or scalp white men" or attack railroads on land bordering the reservation, specifically the Union Pacific along the Platte River south of the reservation. They also agreed "to compel their children, male and female, between the ages of six and sixteen years, to attend school, and it is hereby made the duty of the agent for said Indians to see that this stipulation is strictly complied with." The treaty also stipulates that "for every thirty children between said ages, who can be induced or compelled to attend school, a house shall be provided, and a teacher competent to teach the elementary branches of an English education shall be furnished, who will reside among said Indians and faithfully discharge his or her duties as a teacher." According to one of Red Cloud's direct descendants, Dusty Lee Nelson, if you were a leader at that time and you had a chance to secure a future for your people, you would do it. "You would do it out of the love of your people because you want them to survive, and I'm certain he had no idea the violence that would be unfolded on us when he signed that treaty."

White trespassers began violating the terms of the treaty before Red Cloud's mark was dry. In June 1870 he traveled to Washington, D.C., to petition President U. S. Grant in person. "We do not want riches," he said, "but we want to train our children right. Riches will do us no good. We could not take them with us to the other world. We do not want riches. We want peace and love . . . In 1868 men came out and brought papers. We could not read them and they did not tell us truly what was in them. We thought the treaty was to remove the forts and for us to cease from fighting."[7] The treaty was also violated by the U.S. government. In 1874 it ordered Gen. George Armstrong Custer to trespass on Oglala land in the Black Hills to prospect for gold.

Red Cloud understood that the nomadic, halcyon days of the Lakota were over and the restricted life of the reservation would be the new normal. To survive, the Oglala would have to learn to speak and read English to ensure that they would not be deceived again. But because the government officials who had lied to him were Protestants, he decided that Catholics, if not more trustworthy, could be used as an ally in his ongoing transactions with the federal government. An enemy of my enemy is my friend, he reasoned. Red Cloud had developed connections with several Catholics, including Pierre-Jean De Smet, the Flemish Jesuit who had founded two missions in Montana, traveled widely as he visited tribes across the Northern Plains, and was considered someone whose word the Lakota could believe. Red Cloud's daughter Louise had married a White Catholic named Peter Menard Richard, and Red Cloud and his wife, Pretty Owl, had adopted into their family a Métis Catholic translator named Baptiste Pourier.

President U. S. Grant's 1869 "peace policy" included the appointment of a Seneca tribal member named Ely Parker as Commissioner of Indian Affairs. Parker appointed dozens of army officers to administer agencies and reservations west of the Mississippi. The Grant administration also chose specific Christian denominations to establish ministries and missions on seventy-two specific Indian agencies and reservations. Although the policy was ostensibly designed to create a more humane relationship between Euro-Americans and Indigenous people, in practice it was intended to counter the notorious corruption of Indian agents who had been appointed to these lucrative positions at the urging of certain congressmen as a reward for their political support.

To Red Cloud's disappointment Pine Ridge was not one of the eight agencies assigned to Catholics. Ignoring questions about the separation of church and state and the religious freedom of the Oglalas, the Pine Ridge Agency was turned over to the Episcopalians. Their bishop wrote that the politically appointed agents he and other missionaries had replaced were "men without any fitness, . . . a disgrace to a Christian nation; whiskey sellers, barroom loungers, [and] debauchers."[8] Grant also created a ten-man

Board of Indian Commissioners, composed strictly of wealthy members from Protestant denominations, to audit the finances of Indian agencies. In response Catholics created the Bureau of Catholic Indian Missions in 1879 to oversee their meager slice of the pie and to lobby the government for something bigger.

In September 1877 Red Cloud met in Washington, D.C., with Rutherford B. Hayes. He was accompanied by Spotted Tail. "I would like to say something about a teacher," he told Hayes. "My children, all of them, would like to learn how to talk English. They would like to learn how to read and write. We have teachers there, but all they teach us is to talk Sioux, and to write Sioux, and that is not necessary. I would like to get Catholic priests. Those who wear black dresses. These men will teach us how to read and write English." Red Cloud also asked Hayes for reservation schoolteachers. "Catholic priests are good and I want you to give me one of them, also."[9] During his trips to the East Coast he became the most photographed Indian in the United States.

But unlike his alcoholic predecessor Hayes was opposed to schools operated by churches, and nothing came of the request during his presidency. Regardless, in 1879 the Catholic Church sent a Benedictine father to Pine Ridge with a letter from Church authorities directing him to establish a Catholic mission. After the agent ordered him to leave he moved to a ranch across the White River on the agency's northern border and began fishing for Oglala souls at a distance. Meanwhile, the government built its own school at Pine Ridge, partially delivering on one of the promises it made in the 1868 Fort Laramie Treaty. Although Red Cloud was present when its cornerstone was laid this was not the Black Robe facility he had been lobbying for on behalf of the Oglala. But for the time being it would have to do. The one-story wood frame building that went up was a hundred feet long and thirty-four feet wide. It was not intended as a boarding school but rather an assimilation center where families would be persuaded to send their children during the day, returning to their homes in the evening.

In 1881 federal officials suspended Grant's policy of assigning selected missionaries to Indian agencies after a group of brazen Catholic priests escorted Protestant missionaries off the Devil's Lake Agency (now Spirit Lake Reservation), in what is now North Dakota. The restrictions were officially revoked in 1883, giving Catholics a shot at any tribe it wanted to go after. But the Church ran into problems finding Benedictine priests qualified to establish a mission and a school at Pine Ridge and the Rosebud Agency next door. After some failed attempts the bishop was forced to recruit German Jesuits and nuns from the Sisters of St. Francis of Penance and Christian Charity, who maintained an exile colony in Buffalo, New York. German Chancellor Otto von Bismarck had ordered most Catholic religious orders to leave the country beginning in the 1871 during what was called the *Kulturkampf* (culture struggle), a conflict that was more about tariffs and consolidating power than it was about religion.

To build boarding schools and other mission buildings the Church needed a significant amount of cash. Officials had read about the enormous inheritance awarded to Katharine Drexel, the patron saint of patronage, and begged her for funding. Between 1886 and 1890 she donated the money to build what would be called Holy Rosary Mission at the Pine Ridge Agency and St. Francis Mission at the Rosebud Agency. The boarding schools at each mission were called Drexel Hall, of course. When St. Francis opened in 1886 Drexel's wealth had constructed facilities to house 100 Sicangu children.

Later she would send nuns to teach at St. Francis from the order she founded in 1891, Sisters of the Blessed Sacrament. Unlike St. Peter's there was no available stone for construction of Holy Rosary so the Jesuits pressed the Oglala into service fabricating bricks from the clay that was abundant along White Clay Creek, which had carved the valley selected for the site of the school. This was back-breaking work that involved digging the material from the banks of the creek, mixing it with water and lime produced by burning locally quarried limestone, ladling the paste into molds, and firing the bricks after they dried, which gave them a reddish tinge. Completed in 1888 the result was a sprawling, unimaginative fortress underlaid with a warren of basements. A collection of rectangles two stories high surrounding two interior courtyards under a towering white spire above the

entrance, the building covered a footprint of 30,000 square feet. Generations of Lakota children carved their names into the building's old bricks
as a small act of resistance and remembrance. It wasn't until 1980 that the
school stopped boarding students.

A photograph shows the school's first conscripts lined up in front of the
newly completed fortress. The girls, ranging in age from tiny to teen, are
dressed in identical dark pinafores and white aprons. A similar number of
boys are dressed in high boots and uniforms. Holding their round, wide-
brimmed hats in their hands we can see that their hair has been cut short.
The hat they're wearing was called the "Boss of the Plains." It's unknown
if the Oglala were amused or insulted by the trade name. After all, these
were the sons and daughters of one of the tribes that annihilated Custer
and the Seventh Cavalry on the hills above the Little Big Horn. Because
Custer had not listened to a warning to stay away from the Black Hills,
sewing awls had been driven into his ears to improve his hearing in the
next world. And because he had raped a young woman named Monahsetah
during his unit's 1868 attack on the Northern Cheyenne at the Washita
River in present-day Oklahoma, an arrow had been driven into his penis. [10]

———

At her 1887 meeting with Pope Leo XIII Katharine Drexel experienced a
spiritual panic attack. She had spent five weeks in a German spa to which
her worried sisters had admitted her after the death of their father triggered
a deterioration of her physical and mental health. Her vitality restored, the
sisters set out on a lavish Grand Tour of the Continent before traveling
to the Vatican, where Katharine begged the pope to send missionaries to
covert the aboriginals of the western United States. Leo shocked her by
suggesting instead that she herself become a missionary. Suddenly faint and
feeling sick, she interpreted his suggestion as a commandment from God.

After the sisters returned to Philadelphia Joseph Stephan, the German
priest who had begged them for money the year before, invited the Drexels
to inspect the results of their investment in the conversion of Indians on

the Great Sioux Reservation. Consequently, three years after their 1884 trip to the Puyallup Reservation, the sisters returned to Indian Country to indulge themselves with four weeks of adventure travel. According to the website of the order of nuns Katharine Drexel founded, the group "roughed it" as they bounced across the Dakota prairie in a buckboard (rail lines have never penetrated either reservation, and horses are still a common means of transportation). Accompanied by Stephan and Katharine's spiritual adviser, Bishop James O'Connor, they first paid an unannounced visit to St. Francis. A huge frame building had been thrown up quickly there to house the Sicangu boarding school. An addition was later added. Drexel's sister Louise described the crowd that had gathered. "Squaws in bright colored shawls and dresses, some with faces painted red, some yellow, some with paint down the hair part . . . Men wrapped in unbleached sheets, some in fancy costumes, some in European clothes. All with long hair." An ox was butchered for a feast, she continued, which the Indians ate raw. They met with Sicangu chief named Numpkahapa (Two Strike). Two Strike had succeeded Spotted Tail, who was murdered in 1881 by a subchief named Crow Dog, the culmination of a feud. Like his predecessor Two Strike believed that the survival of his people depended on Lakota children learning to read and write English in order to coexist with the White invaders (and like Spotted Tail he did not immediately grasp that Catholics wanted to turn Indians into Christian farmers).

He got his wish when three German Jesuits arrived in 1885 followed by a crew of Franciscan nuns, who were also German. Because they were trained as teachers the nuns handled the academic instruction at St. Francis and Holy Rosary. The German Jesuits, who, unlike many Blackrobes, were more tradesmen than they were scholars, offered boys training in the manual arts. They were also responsible for selling the Lakota on Catholicism. Their strategy included translating the seven sacraments into the Lakota language, appropriating the concept of *wakan*—the mysterious force—into rites such as the eucharist, which they rendered as *Yutapi wakan or* "sacred meal." *Wakankiciyuzapi* or "sacred union" described the rite of marriage. Between 1883 and 1885 the Jesuits baptized some 800 Lakota, including

Red Cloud. Spotted Tail wanted to be baptized, as well, but because he refused to give up his eight wives he was denied on the grounds that the Lord abhorred polygamy. This zeal to convert Indians had unintended consequences. Because many of the newly baptized were old and sick they soon died. The Lakota blamed the Jesuits for their deaths, trembling with fear whenever a Blackrobe showed up at the door bearing holy water. Finally, after a generation, the Jesuits overcame these concerns by pointing out that rate of death following baptism was about the same as that death rate among people treated by Native healers. After visiting Rosebud the Drexel party headed west and were shown Drexel Hall at Pine Ridge. They met with Red Cloud and gave him a bridle and saddle and his wife a shawl.

Like Richard Pratt, Joseph Stephan had no use for Indigenous cultures and was a hardliner in the matter of the "Indian Problem." He believed that Indians must be "civilized" by teaching them English, converting them to Catholicism, and replacing their hunting and gathering economies with farming and trades for the boys and domestic servitude for the girls. Trained as an engineer in Germany, after he sailed to America he was ordained a priest in 1850. In 1863 he was commissioned a chaplain in the Union Army and designed a pontoon bridge that so impressed his superior officers he was offered a permanent military career, which he declined. But the "Fighting Priest" got his nickname not from his war experiences but because he was hot-headed, stubborn, and eccentric. During his brief posting as the Indian agent at the Standing Rock Reservation in Dakota he accused the Benedictine monks of incompetence in their administration of three assimilation centers for Lakota and Dakota children. These included boys and girls boarding schools and an industrial farm where boys were compelled to endure instruction in agriculture, carpentry, shoemaking, and Euro-American tailoring. He cited an instance when they "should have pulled and hoed weeds out of the field, the brother sent them to cut wood." To remedy the situation Stephan ordered "20 squaws" into the field to do the work the boys should have done. He also criticized the monks for speaking with the boys in

Lakota and Dakota instead of English, which he believed slowed their transformation into facsimiles of White Americans. The monks, he wrote, sneered and laughed at him.

As Standing Rock's agent he was responsible for doling out government rations. He used this power to reward "farming Indians" and withheld annuities from the chiefs and others who clung to the old ways. This was part of the strategy facilitated by the recently passed Dawes Act, which shifted communal ownership of land by the tribes to individuals, a process that eroded the power of the chiefs while opening up unallocated "surplus" Native land to White settlers. Stephan wrote that the sooner the hereditary leaders lost their power and the "farming Indian treated as his own chief, the nearer the end will be of all Indian troubles."[11] Stephan also quarreled with the U.S. Army garrison stationed on the reservation at Fort Yates. Accusing soldiers of debasing the morals of Indian children he moved the girls' school fifteen miles to the boys' industrial farm. He also claimed that the army harvested timber for its own uses that was a source of income for the tribe. After he declared that the army was no longer needed because of the organization of a tribal police force, the garrison commander wrote a diatribe to the Army's Adjutant General of the Territory claiming that Stephan was "too old and too infirm of body and too irascible in mind, to be a safe or an efficient Agent for this Agency."

In 1884 Stephan was appointed Commissioner of the Bureau of Catholic Indian Missions, the conduit through which money flowed from patrons such as Drexel to the Church's outposts in Indian Country. In 1893, Stephan asserted that in order to "civilize the Indian, to awaken and vivify his moral nature, he must be brought to an understanding of the existence, the power, the omnipresence, and the perfect justice and goodness of the Supreme Being." The drive to secularize Indian schools, he claimed, was a "dishonest, hypocritical one, whose sole aim and purpose it is to drive the Catholic Church out of the Indian educational and missionary field."[12]

In 2003 six members of the Sioux Nation filed a $25 billion lawsuit against the Bureau of Indian Affairs alleging sexual, physical, and mental abuse at two South Dakota boarding schools formerly overseen the BIA and operated by the Jesuits and other entities of the Catholic Church. They sought class action status on behalf of all former students who suffered abuse at the St. Paul's School in the town of Marty on the Yankton Sioux Reservation and the St. Francis Mission School. In their argument they accused the federal government of violating the 1868 Treaty of Fort Laramie by allowing "Bad Men" to come onto the reservation and abuse them. According to the treaty "If bad men among the whites, or among people subject to the authority of the United States, shall commit any wrong upon the person or property of the Indians, the United States will, upon proof made . . . reimburse the injured person for the loss sustained." The language was common in treaties signed by other tribes in the late 1800s, but the BIA violated the treaties by failing to establish regulations to deal with "Bad Men" cases.

One of these was a Jesuit brother names Francis Chapman. In 1968 officials at St. Francis wrote in a breezy and bizarre letter to their superiors at the Rapid City Diocese that although most of the mission school's faculty were of high quality "there are troublesome staffers . . . including 'Chappy,' who is fooling around with little girls—he had them down in the basement of our building in the dark, where we found a pair of panties torn." Over at St. Paul's a report to Sioux Falls Diocese official recount that two nuns have an excessive "interest in" dealing with older male students. Another nun, the report said, has "too close a circle of friends, especially two boys."[13]

Izzy Zephier described a prison-like daily routine at St. Paul's when he attended boarding school there. "We were marched along barbed-wire-lined sidewalks from locked dorms to locked classrooms and back again; in grade school, we went outdoors within a barbed-wire-topped pen." Native parents faced penalties, including jail time, if they did not enroll their children in the boarding schools. As a young teenager Zephier stumbled into an unexpected way out. "School had just let out for the day, and I realized I'd forgotten a couple of books. I ran back into the building, where I found that a priest had a girl on the floor. She was fighting and screaming, 'let me go!' When the priest saw me, he got up and backhanded me hard. I hit him back and yelled to the girl, 'run, get out of here!' I hit the priest five times and knocked him down. The girl took off. The next day I was expelled."[14]

Despite the presentation of this and other damning testimony a Federal Claims Court judge appointed by George H. W. Bush dismissed the lawsuit, arguing that the plaintiffs didn't follow an arcane procedure set out in the treaties. The former students, she wrote, should have asked the BIA to adjudicate the case before coming to the courts. Less than a year later the judge stepped down from the bench. Rather than waste any more time with the federal government the plaintiffs filed their lawsuits in South Dakota district courts, which dismissed them. Appeals to the state supreme court were also dismissed.

After the Claims Court threw out the lawsuit, Sam Brownback, a conservative Republican from Kansas, introduced a resolution in the U.S. Senate that would apologize for "official depredations and ill-conceived policies" towards Native peoples. The admission of guilt cited "the forcible removal of Native children from their families to faraway boarding schools where their Native practices and languages were degraded and forbidden." Although backed by Senators Ben Nighthorse Campbell (R-Colorado), Daniel Inouye (D-Hawaii) and other lawmakers, the resolution failed to pass. But the floodgates in South Dakota had been opened. By the summer of 2010 more than 100 lawsuits had been filed against the dioceses in Rapid City and Sioux Falls.

In 2008 Izzy Zephier's brother, D. Z. Iron Wing, filed suit in a South Dakota district court against the Sioux Falls Diocese and several Catholic entities associated with St. Paul's where, he claimed, he had been sexually assaulted forty years earlier by a nun and a Jesuit priest, both of whom molested him repeatedly over a decade, from 1953 to 1964. After he transferred to a secular high school, he finally told his father and stepmother about the abuse. According to Iron Wing his stepmother "walked up beside me and slapped me alongside the head. She said how dare you talk about those people, those priests, those nuns, how dare you talk about them like that. She said those are people of God. They don't do those kinds of things." The court dismissed Iron Wing's case. He appealed to the South Dakota Supreme Court, which in 2011 affirmed the lower court's ruling.

At issue in these cases was a law passed by the state legislature in 2010 that was written to protect the Catholic Church, whose priests and nuns operated St. Paul's and four similar schools in South Dakota. Replacing a much less stringent statute of limitations passed in 1996, the 2010 law requires that anyone seeking damages for childhood sexual abuse must file a lawsuit within three years of the alleged abuse or within three years of the time the victim discovered or should have discovered that an injury was caused by the abuse, injury in this case being damage to the victim's mental health. In addition, "no person who has reached the age of forty," the law states, "may recover damages from any person or entity other than the person who perpetrated the actual act of sexual abuse."

The South Dakota legislature, which was at the time and still is dominated by a supermajority of Republicans, shrank its statute of limitations to prevent Indians from bringing claims related to sexual abuse that occurred during the boarding school era against the Catholic Church, other Christian denominations, and the federal government. The law, which was applied retroactively in numerous cases, is a clear violation of the Fourteenth Amendment to the U.S. Constitution, which was adopted during Reconstruction following the Civil War to guarantee equal protection of the laws to every American citizen. It is a product written in legalese of systemic racism that has infected South Dakota since the 1800s. For example, an 1875 report issued to the U.S. Commissioner of Indian Affairs declared that hundreds of Northern Cheyenne and Lakota Sioux in Wyoming, Montana, and South Dakota were openly hostile to the United States. The report stated that Indians who associated with Crazy Horse and Chief Sitting Bull "set at defiance all law and authority . . . laugh at the futile efforts that have thus far been made to subjugate them and scorn the idea of white civilization" and suggested that the Army should "whip them into subjection."[15] D. Z. Iron Wing is the grandson of Chief Iron Wing, one of those defiant associates of the Lakota leaders who killed Custer.

In its dismissal of Iron Wing's lawsuit the South Dakota Supreme Court argued that "He knew he had been abused by two members of a religious order beginning when he was age ten and resuming at age thirteen. Because of this abuse he was angry and harbored hatred against the church and its priests and nuns from the time he was in the eleventh grade, he left the school because of the abuse, and he never forgot the abuse. These circumstances were sufficient to prompt a reasonably prudent person to seek out information regarding his injury or condition and its cause." A lawyer for one of the defendants, the Oblate Sisters of the Blessed Sacrament, said there is no proof that Iron Wing was molested. A lawyer named Steve Smith, the bill's author, described the previous statute of limitations his bill replaced as impossible to defend because it would permit sexual abuse claims to be brought even when the perpetrators were dead. During the bill's passage one of Smith's clients was the Congregation of the Priests of the Sacred Heart, which was the defendant in a dozen boarding school sexual abuse cases. Smith accused the plaintiffs of "trying to grab the brass ring, seeing someone else grab the brass ring, thinking that's [their] ticket out of squalor." He also attacked one of the attorneys for the plaintiffs, who practiced law in both Los Angeles and Rapid City, South Dakota, claiming that the old statute was a welfare bill for carpetbagging California lawyers flying out to The Mount Rushmore State to recruit Indian plaintiffs willing to say they were abused as children. By March 2011 a Circuit Court judge named Bradley Zell had used Smith's racist law to retroactively dismiss the sexual abuse claims of eighteen former St. Paul's students. Although South Dakota's legal code says that no law "shall be construed as retroactive unless such intention plainly appears," Zell claims that his decision was based on a 1996 Supreme Court ruling that made retroactive an expansion of opportunities to bring sexual abuse claims. The state's Supreme Court sided with Zell.

But the victims have never given up. Geraldine Charbonneau Dubourt and her eight sisters were enrolled by their parents at St. Paul's during the

1950s and 1960s in the hopes that they would get a decent education, not knowing that Indian boarding schools didn't teach much more than basic skills such as carpentry and sewing. Members of the Turtle Mountain band of Chippewa in North Dakota claimed in a 2008 civil suit against the Sioux Falls Diocese and the other Catholic entities running the school that the girls suffered sexual and physical abuse at the hands of four priests, six nuns and two school workers, who are all now dead. Dubourt said the abuse began as inappropriate touching shortly after she arrived as a six-year-old, then escalated. In her deposition she said when she was sixteen years old a priest raped her multiple times in a basement. After she got pregnant she was forced to undergo an abortion; one of her sisters was ordered to destroy the fetus in an incinerator. In their depositions the sisters said they were sexually abused by both priests and nuns, deloused with DDT, shown Nazi propaganda to frighten them into submission, and warned that if they told their mother and father about the abuse their parents would burn in Hell. The dozen weathered and deteriorating buildings on the grounds of this remote campus contained warrens of dormitories, classrooms, offices, closets, storage rooms, and dark basements fitted with doors opening into underground tunnels through which priests, nuns, and school workers scurried from building to building. Looming over this remote campus is St. Paul's church, whose gleaming white steeple rises 200 feet from the prairie.

The sisters' lawsuit was dismissed by both the circuit court in 2008 and the Supreme Court three years later on the basis of the 2010 statute of limitations. But the struggle of what people in Indian Country call "The Nine Little Girls" moved immediately from the courts to the arena of public opinion. Rallies were organized in Pierre, the South Dakota capital, and billboard ads went up in an attempt to shame lawmakers. But South Dakota Republicans are shameless and have repeatedly voted down attempts to rescind the 2010 statute. This is despite warnings that the Civil Rights Division of the U.S. Department of Justice was investigating whether the state, through its legislature, had committed a civil rights violation. In February 2020 the Charbonneau sisters testified before a committee considering a bill to open a two-year window for abuse victims such as those who attended St. Paul's to sue organizations such as the Sioux Falls Diocese. It was voted down in committee. The legislature's strategy to shield the Catholic Church is to keep the statute alive at least until the victims of the diocese are dead. Three of the Charbonneau sisters have in fact died and the other six are in their seventies and eighties.

The diocese has apologized publicly for the child sexual abuse committed by its priests decades ago but it hasn't said anything about the allegations leveled at it by the Charbonneau sisters and other Native Americans enrolled at St. Paul's. Since 2003 more than a hundred former students have sued the diocese. It has weaseled out of its responsibility by falsely claiming that it did not have direct control of the clergy who staffed the school. This is common tactic used by dioceses across the U.S., successfully employed by Sioux Falls so far but a failing ploy for at least twenty-six dioceses that have declared bankruptcy in the wake of sexual abuse lawsuits. The chancellor of the Sioux Falls Diocese, Matt Althoff, said that regardless of statutes and civil law the diocese promises to help victims in the form of "spiritual accompaniment" and counseling. "The Church recognizes God's law as superior to all other laws," he added. His gesture is comparable to a wife beater offering to fetch a Band-Aid from the medicine cabinet.

The most visited gravesite on the campus surrounding Drexel Hall is that of Red Cloud, who died in 1910 at the age of eighty-seven or eighty-eight. Baptized a Catholic in 1884, he was buried in a crypt under a tall stone botonée cross. Chiseled in the base of the cross is his name in English and Lakota and his likeness portrayed in a full feathered war bonnet. As an homage visitors leave stones and pouches on his crypt and festoon the cross with bright strips of cloth called prayer ties.

But it was the suspected unmarked graves of children who may have died at Holy Rosary that brought together a tense gathering in May 2022 of Pine Ridge tribal members, academics, school officials, and protesters on horseback. At the center of the storm was Marsha Small. The school had invited her to use the ground-penetrating radar technology she had employed at Oregon's Chemawa Indian School in 2015 to investigate one of the basements under Drexel Hall. In winter 1995 a twenty-eight-year-old Oglala maintenance worker named Justin Pourier descended a narrow flight of wooden stairs to look for a leak in the steam pipes used to warm the building. Following the course of Drexel's ancient plumbing through a maze of dimly lit tunnels he made his way to a door that opened into a cramped dirt-floored room with a low ceiling, next to the boiler room. He said he doesn't remember whether he found the leak in the room. What he does remember is the chilling sight of three small child-sized mounds of dirt lined up in a row, topped with white crosses. He quickly turned around and climbed back up the stairs. When he told his Jesuit boss about what he had seen he was ordered not to enter that room ever again. "I just let it go," he says. "It bothered me, but at the time I just took care of myself with prayer and sweat lodge ceremonies. I knew it was there, and I knew somehow, eventually, it was going to come to light."[16]

By 1980 the dormitories in old Drexel Hall had been closed and the building converted to offices, a heritage center and a residence for the Jesuits and Sisters. The gardens on campus where children were forced to work have been replaced by sports fields and parking lots. And there have been structural changes made to Drexel Hall, which some people in the community would like to see demolished because of the abuses that occurred there when it boarded children. After the news broke in 2021 about unmarked graves at First Nations residential schools in Canada, Pourier felt compelled to share with someone besides his girlfriend what he had seen in Drexel Hall. He contacted an old friend named Tashina Banks Rama, who was serving as Executive Vice President of Red Cloud School. Together with eight others they retraced Pourier's steps into the basement where he said he recalled seeing the mounds. What they found was that during renovations made in 1997 a wall had been removed and a concrete slab had been poured over the dirt floor under new heating and ventilation ducts. After Banks Rama contacted Maka Black Elk, the school's director of Truth and Healing, Red Cloud's administration invited Marsha Small to search for burials under Drexel Hall and other places on campus. The Jesuits had put up $70,000 to finance her work. Small had misgivings that her investigation would be seen by some people as an attempt by the Church to whitewash its past by appearing to be transparent. On the other hand she was intrigued by the fact that both the tribe and the Church supported bringing her to Red Cloud. "You should know who you're dealing with here," Small remembered thinking about the Jesuits when she got the first email from the school. "Because I hate you."[17]

Arriving at the school in May 2022 her first step was meeting in the gymnasium with the community to explain how ground penetrating radar works, what it can reveal, and what it cannot prove. She shared the floor with her partner, Jarrod Burks, an Ohio archaeologist who conducts surveys for the Defense POW/MIA Accounting Agency in its effort to recover the remains of missing soldiers. The technology, they explained, shows disturbances in the soil that might indicate a burial—or tree roots. After the meeting people took turns pushing Small's ground-penetrating radar device across the lawn in front of Drexel Hall. No anomalies were detected under the lawn nor at an empty field on which a cultural center is slated to be built. And then she and Burks and their crew moved the device to the basement under Drexel Hall. After an afternoon of scanning an area the size of a parking space she announced that she had found two anomalies that might be graves.

The voices of the growing divisions in the Oglala community regarding the school got louder during Small's visit. Among the thousand or so practicing Catholics on the reservation, whose population is 20,000, some older people have fond memories of their time as boarding students, are grateful for the education they received, and resent the accusation that Holy Rosary hid the deaths of their classmates. "So sure, you're going to find bones," a woman at a community meeting said, "but they're going to be of pigs and chickens and there's going to be garbage. But that's all you're going to find."[18] Some younger people want the Jesuits and nuns removed from the reservation immediately along with every other Christian missionary, and the school turned over to the tribe, among other demands. In the middle ground between these extremes are school administrators who are Oglala and working to reconcile Red Cloud's past with its present as not only one of the best private high schools in South Dakota, preparing 98 percent of its graduates to go on to college, but the largest employer on the Pine Ridge Reservation.

Dusty Lee Nelson called the school's truth and healing efforts a "charade." She said this effort by Red Cloud's administration and the Catholic Church to pursue their own investigation is the opposite of transparency. "It's all about mitigating damage control." She is a mentor to the local chapter of the International Indigenous Youth Council, a vocal activist group that was forged during year-long protests against the Dakota Access Pipeline sixty miles north of Red Cloud on the Standing Rock Reservation. While Marsha Small was on campus three men sang the American Indian Movement song while members of the Youth Council rode horses around the school's new church and a sign they had propped there against a wall. "We are the grandchildren of the Lakota you could not remove," it said. One of them burned a copy of the eleventh and fifteenth-century Vatican decrees constituting the Doctrine of Discovery.

At meetings of the tribal council the Youth Council presented a list of demands that ranged from monetary reparations to the renaming of the school's sports teams, the Crusaders (who regularly play teams from the Pine Ridge School, the Thorpes). They also demanded that GPR be used to scan the entire campus. And they insisted that the reservation ban all churches and missionaries, including the Jesuits at Red Cloud School. If that were to happen it would not be the tribe's first expulsion. In July 2022 the Oglala council voted to ban Matthew Monfore, the White Christian founder of the so-called Jesus is King Mission, accusing him of spreading hate-filled pamphlets on the reservation that "demonizes the Lakota culture and faith," according to a letter from tribal president Kevin Killer. The vote came in response to the posting of Monfore's pamphlets by the Youth Council on their Facebook page. "If your life does not bring exclusive glory to Jesus alone, it is not from God," he wrote. "Native teachings are of the spirit of the antichrist." He compared *Tunkshila*, the Lakota word for the Creator, to a corrupt and unjust demon, described Nicholas Black Elk, a Lakota medicine man, as a racist, and called Leonard Crow Dog, a spiritual leader, a "drunk." Widespread anger at Monfore's insults was fueled by the photo published of Pope Francis wearing a Native headdress during his apology for the Church's role in Canada's First Nations boarding schools. [19]

After lunch on the day of Small's visit a gathering of community members, school administrators, journalists, and Jesuits was standing in a wide circle on a campus lawn when a pair of huge black SUVs pulled into a nearby parking lot. The crowd gasped when they saw who it was emerging from one of the vehicles. This was Bryan Newland, the U.S. Assistant Secretary of the Interior for Indian Affairs, which had released the first volume of the Federal Indian Boarding School Initiative a week earlier. Newland, who is an attorney and the former tribal president of the Bay Mills Indian Community (Ojibwe) in Michigan, is leading the federal investigation of the boarding school era. His surprise visit was reported by Crystal Echo Hawk (Pawnee) and Lashay Wesley (Choctaw) in one of their *American Genocide* podcasts. "For the first time we as the United States Federal Government are acknowledging what we did with these boarding schools and why they existed," Newland told the gathering. "The boarding schools were part of a twin policy of taking land from Indian people and assimilating Indian people. The thought was that Indian people wouldn't need so much land if we were all assimilated. As part of that process there was a deliberate choice to target Indian children to carry this out. Because they thought it would be cheaper and safer." He said the fact that he was speaking in English instead of his Native language was a testament to the devastating success of that policy.

Following his remarks he was approached by Alex White Plume, an Army veteran and a famous farmer whose crop of industrial hemp was destroyed by federal drug agents in 2002, although the fiber was and still is legally sold across the U.S., and was growing in the soil of the reservation, which is a sovereign nation. Serving as interim tribal chairman in 2006 White Plume advocated for the exclusive use of the Lakota language at government meetings because "we created all these problems by using the English language." Speaking nevertheless in English to Newland he said: "We're not going to go healing until genocide is addressed by the United States government . . . I would like you to go out across Indian country and tell them about genocide—use that word genocide. The Pope just met with people in Alaska and he didn't mention genocide. He's trying to do a cheap apology. I'm not going to accept no cheap apology." Crystal Echo Hawk told her podcast audience that the federal government will likely not describe what the boarding schools did to Native Americans was genocide. "They cannot make that admission because there's a whole legal framework that the United States would have to commit itself to."[20]

After the meeting on the lawn Small and Burks moved their equipment to the basement under Drexel Hall and spent an afternoon scanning a space the size of a studio apartment. Later, after they had analyzed their data, they informed the school that they had found two anomalies that might be graves. There was only one way to find out: remove a section of concrete floor and excavate the soil underneath.

Chapter Six

CUSTER HAD IT COMING

T he theatrical activism of the Pine Ridge Youth Council is rooted in a Native American protest that began sixty years ago. In 1963 the government shut down its notorious Alcatraz Federal Penitentiary, designated the island as "excess federal property," and transferred it from the Department of Justice to the General Services Administration. A year later five Lakota men filed a claim for Alcatraz hoping to transform the former prison into an American Indian museum and a college focusing on Native studies. The U.S. Attorney General argued that the group's claim had no merit. The Lakota responded by landing on the island, pounding stakes in the ground and claiming all twenty-two acres for the tribe. They brought along their lawyer and some news people. Among the Lakota was Walter Means and his twenty-four-year-old son, Russell, who would lead another occupation nine years later that drew international attention.

According to their loose interpretation of the 1868 Fort Laramie Treaty they said the Sioux Nation was legally permitted to take possession of unused, retired, excess, or surplus Federal property, words that don't appear in the treaty. However, they said because they were "civilized human beings" they would be willing to compensate the government 47 cents per acre—the same ludicrous amount the Indian Claims Commission had awarded California tribes in 1964 for the theft of their land. They said the Coast Guard could keep its lighthouse—they didn't want it. They pitched a green tent on the parade ground and filled it with provisions for a long stay in order to guard their claims. When the warden was summoned from his weekend on the mainland he threatened to arrest everyone for trespassing. And he implied that he and his six-man garrison were ready to use force. On the advice of their attorney the Lakota retreated four hours after landing. But the prison remained an emotionally charged target of Native American activism; for one reason, Indians had been incarcerated on the Rock as far back as 1873, the most infamous example being those nineteen Hopi leaders in the mid-1890s after refusing to send their pueblo's children to a government boarding school.

The Indians would return. On November 9, 1969, the Canadian owner of a $4 million yacht named *Monte Cristo* volunteered to ferry fifty Indians from Fisherman's Wharf across the one-and-a-quarter-mile stretch of San Francisco Bay to Alcatraz. Their intent was to make a symbolic gesture by sailing around the island and claiming it. After the *Monte Cristo* circled twice and fired its cannons five men decided to take the gesture a step further and actually set foot on Alcatraz. But because the boat was too big to dock the men jumped into the water and swam the last hundred yards to shore, where they declared ownership of the island for their organization, the Indians of All Tribes, by virtue of the Doctrine of Discovery. The Coast Guard removed them fifteen minutes later and they were returned to San Francisco. Later in the day fourteen Native Americans returned to the island and spent the night.

Their leaders included a Shoshone woman named LaNada Means, the first Native American enrolled in the University of California at Berkeley, and a Mohawk student at San Francisco State named Richard Oakes. Means had been frequently expelled from boarding schools and reservation schools for complaining about abusive teachers. She moved to the Bay Area in 1965. Oakes had worked as a steel worker and a bartender before enrolling in college. The group left Alcatraz the next day with the realization that Alcatraz had become a war cry among the thousands of urban

Indians in the Bay Area who had been persuaded to abandon their reservations by the 1956 Indian Relocation Act, which promised them training and job placement. To muster support for a much longer and larger takeover of the island Oakes and Means recruited Native American students from UCLA and other California campuses.

On November 20, 1969, the denizens of an artsy Sausalito watering hole called the No Name Bar made two large boats available to the Indians of All Tribes. At 2 A.M. some ninety Native Americans representing twenty tribes, including thirty women and six children, cast off from the Sausalito docks and headed the four miles across the Bay toward Alcatraz, eluding an ineffectual Coast Guard blockade. The island's only security guard, who was manning the guard shack on the main dock, had been expecting the invasion. He radioed a message. "Mayday! Mayday! The Indians have landed!"[1] Indians of All Tribes was a force that would grow at its height to almost 400 and included Indigenous people from all over the Americas. They moved into the warden's home and the apartment houses where some seventy guards had once lived with their families. They ignored government demands that they leave and spray-painted "Red Power" and "Custer Had It Coming" on the buildings, which were deteriorating from the constant spray of salt water. One of the first to arrive, LaNada Means hammered home the demand for complete Native American control of the island in order to build a cultural center that included Native American Studies, a spiritual center, an ecology center, and a museum. She had been married to Ted Means, Russell's brother. Their two-year-old son came ashore with his mother during the first wave.

The occupiers elected a governing council that oversaw the operations of the island's clinic, kitchen, and media department. For the children they set up a nursery and an elementary school. A security force patrolled the shoreline to guard against intruders. A Dakota Santee named John Trudell hosted an island news program called *Radio Free Alcatraz* that was broadcast by FM stations in Berkeley, Los Angeles, and New York. The occupiers published a newsletter called *Rock Talk*. They issued what they called the Alcatraz Proclamation.

We, the native Americans, re-claim the land known as Alcatraz Island in the name of all American Indians by right of discovery. We wish to be fair and honorable in our dealings with the Caucasian inhabitants of this land, and hereby offer the following treaty: We will purchase said Alcatraz Island for $24 in glass beads and red cloth, a precedent set by the white man's purchase of a similar island about 300 years ago. We know that $24 in trade goods for these sixteen acres is more than was paid when Manhattan Island was sold, but we know that land values have risen over the years. Our offer of $1.24 per acre is greater than the 47 cents per acre the white men are now paying the California Indians for their land. . . . We will give to the inhabitants of this land a portion of that land for their own, to be held in trust by the American Indian Government for as long as the sun shall rise and the rivers go down to the sea—to be administered by the Bureau of Caucasian Affairs (BCA). We will further guide the inhabitants in the proper way of living. We will offer them our religion, our education, our life-ways, in order to help them achieve our level of civilization and thus raise them and all their white brothers up from their savage and unhappy state.

The occupation of Alcatraz was a cause célèbre that attracted both celebrities and opportunists. Grace Thorpe, the daughter of Jim Thorpe, Olympic gold medalist and Carlisle's most famous student, convinced a number of celebrities to visit the island and publicize their support for the occupation, including Marlon Brando, Jonathan Winters, Buffy Sainte-Marie, and Dick Gregory. Jane Fonda helped arrange television interviews for Means to drum up support for Native American causes. The rock band Creedence Clearwater Revival bought the occupiers a $125,000 boat called the *Clearwater*.[2] Counterfeit Native Americans now called Pretendians tried to exploit the occupation to line their pockets. Hippies were finally banned from spending the night at Alcatraz when they began showing up in droves, sponging off Native food supplies and leaving messes. Nineteen months after Indians of All Nations seized control of Alcatraz Federal marshals removed the last fifteen men, women, and children. Everyone else had either left to go back to college or had grown tired of the unsanitary conditions that were caused when the General Services Administration cut off water and electricity to the island.

Although the seizure of Alcatraz didn't transfer its ownership to Native Americans it inspired Indians to occupy more than seventy other government facilities across the U.S., including a six-day takeover of the Bureau of Indian Affairs building in Washington, D.C. Just before the 1972 Presidential Election some 500 members and supporters of the burgeoning American Indian Movement (AIM) traveled in a caravan across America they dubbed the Trail of Broken Treaties. They intended to present Federal officials a proclamation called the Twenty Points, which demanded that the government recognize Native American sovereignty and the restoration of Indigenous rights, including freedom of religion, the return of 110 million acres of stolen land, the repeal of the termination laws and the restoration of terminated tribes. After a group of them were attacked by guards wielding clubs at the four-story BIA building a few blocks from the White House they barricaded themselves inside and unfurled a banner that read "Native American Embassy." Then they began reading documents that incriminated the BIA as a leading coconspirator in the plot against Native America. To end the siege the Nixon administration granted the protesters immunity for the damage they did to the building and paid their way home. But it rejected the demands made in the Twenty Points.

However, Nixon was opposed to the Eisenhower-era policies that allowed the Federal government to steal more than three million acres of tribal lands by terminating or attempting to terminate sixty Indian reservations and negating the legal status of tribes as sovereign nations. Pressured by his administration, Congress repealed the 1954 Termination Act, returned sovereignty to the Menominee of Wisconsin, returned much of Mt. Adams in Washington State to the Yakima Nation, and Blue Lake to the Taos Pueblo people in New Mexico. In one of the largest land claims settlements in U.S. history forty million acres were returned to Alaska

Natives, who were also paid more than a billion dollars in reparations. And, in line with his conservative distrust of Big Government, Nixon supported legislation that offered tribes control over their own operations and programs. While the occupation of Alcatraz, the BIA building, and other Federal facilities raised public awareness of Native issues during the civil rights agitation of the 1960s, and the early 1970s opposition to the Vietnam War, the Red Power movement continued to grow. One consequence was the occupation of Wounded Knee.

On the night of February 27, 1973, some 300 Oglala and other tribal people drove in a 54-vehicle caravan from a community hall outside the Pine Ridge Reservation to the town of Pine Ridge and on to the unincorporated hamlet of Wounded Knee fourteen miles north. They seized control of the Sacred Heart Catholic Church and marched the pastor to the choir loft after tying his hands behind his back. The pastor was a Jesuit who had worked at Holy Rosary Mission. They also seized the Wounded Knee Museum and Gildersleeve's Trading Post, where tourists could buy western knickknacks and postcards with images of the victims of the U.S. Seventh Calvary's December 1890 massacre of 300 men, women, and children, whose frozen bodies the soldiers dumped in a trench a few yards from where the church would stand.

The occupiers demanded that the U.S. government finally honor its treaty obligations, notably the Ft. Laramie Treaty, which promised that the Black Hills would be set aside for exclusive use by the Sioux people. They also demanded an investigation of the Oglala tribal Chairman, Richard Wilson, who ruled the reservation with a paramilitary force of thugs called the Guardians of the Oglala Nation—the GOONs. At a meeting of the tribal council a week earlier Wilson's opponents accused him of giving his friends and relatives plum jobs, harassing and terrorizing his enemies, and using tribal funds for his personal use. "There's nothing in tribal law against nepotism," Wilson responded while complaining that it was difficult to get anything done "when you're being harassed by the village idiot." The meeting had been delayed until Wilson and his supporters on the council showed the gathering of 500 people a film called *Anarchy U.S.A.*, which claimed that the civil rights movement was being exploited by a world-wide communist conspiracy planning to take over the United States. A motion to impeach Wilson failed after he waived his right to a waiting period and demanded an immediate hearing, knowing his opponents on the council were not prepared to proceed and would not have swung the vote even if they forced the issue. They walked out and the charges against him were dropped.

In 1973 Pine Ridge was a police state, a 2,500-square-mile prairie ghetto ruled by a corrupt autocrat and his vigilantes. The per capita income was about $5,500 in today's currency. Most people lived in tents, tarpaper shacks, rusting trailers, or abandoned cars without electricity or running water. Unemployment and underemployment hovered around 70 percent. The rates of suicide, alcoholism, and infant mortality were several times higher than the national average. Only two businesses were owned by Natives. The largest factory, which made dolls and moccasins, was owned by a southern corporation. The shopping center in Pine Ridge was owned by Ideal Markets Corporation and the service station was owned by Huskie Oil. What profits were earned never stayed on the reservation. [3]

The community meetings that followed Wilson's aborted impeachment reflected the deep division between traditional, conservative Oglala people and supporters of the tribal council. Some of the old chiefs and elders along with representatives of Native civil rights groups called for a wider protest. They decided to ask for help from the American Indian Movement, a controversial decision because of AIM's in-your-face tactics. For example, on February 6, after an Oglala man had been stabbed through the heart in Buffalo Gap, South Dakota, by a White service station owner, AIM organized a force of 200 to demand that the charge of manslaughter be upgraded to murder. After they were met by riot police at the courthouse in Custer they burned down the Chamber of Commerce. AIM leaders Dennis Banks, Russell Means, and Clyde Bellecourt jumped at the chance to challenge Wilson, whose enmity toward the organization and Means in particular was widely known. In 1972 he had ordered Means off the reservation, although he owned a home there and was a tribal member.

And Wilson's cronies passed an ordinance forbidding gatherings of five or more Oglalas without permission from the tribal council.

Reacting to the occupation of Wounded Knee, authorities set up roadblocks several miles from the village and arrested Native people trying to leave. A combined force of FBI agents, BIA police, and federal marshals in their matching baby blue "Major Tom" jumpsuits manned the roadblocks. Wilson's Goon Squad set up its own roadblocks after he learned that lawyers would be allowed past the government's checkpoints. White ranchers wandered the backroads, claiming they were there to hunt rabbits. The U.S. arsenal would include snipers, a helicopter named "Snoopy," and armored personnel carriers equipped with .50-caliber machine guns. The occupiers, who were armed with hunting rifles and handguns, set up their own barricades with trenches and burned vehicles. On the second day of the siege the occupiers fired warning shots at airplanes with photographers on board, although journalists were allowed into the village on foot. There was also a brief firefight between the occupiers and government vehicles that had driven within a quarter mile of the village, the first salvo of what would be almost daily gunfire from both sides. Wider violence on the part of the government was likely averted because of the dozen people it called "hostages" who remained at Wounded Knee after the takeover. They didn't want to abandon their homes even after Senator George McGovern offered them safe passage during his meeting with AIM leaders on March 1. Means told a CBS reporter that the government can "Either negotiate with us for meaningful results, positive results, or you're going to have to kill us, and here at Wounded Knee is where it's going to have to happen."[4]

Seventy-one days after it began, the occupation of Wounded Knee ended. Law enforcement had killed two Native American men, fired half a million rounds, launched flares that started grass fires, and buzzed the village with a pair of low-flying Phantom jets. At least a dozen people on both sides were wounded including a U.S. marshal who was left paralyzed from the waist down after being shot by an unknown combatant. For their part in the occupation Dennis Banks and Russell Means were arrested and charged with conspiracy and assault. Defended by William Kunstler, the attorney for the Chicago Seven, in 1974 they were found not guilty. The judge accused the prosecution of aggravated misconduct. That same year Means ran against Richard Wilson for tribal chairman and lost a close election which the U.S. Commission on Civil Rights reported was "permeated with fraud." The economic and political conditions at Pine Ridge continued to deteriorate throughout the 1970s. One grim statistic was the murder rate—almost six times the national average. Many of the victims were opponents of Wilson and his Goon Squad.

The occupations of Alcatraz, the BIA building, and Wounded Knee ignited political action across Indian Country that drew international attention to the failure of the U.S. to abide by its treaty promises and compelled lawmakers to address some of the injustices. "People across the world didn't even know we still existed," AIM activist and Cheyenne River Sioux member Marcella Gilbert said. "They thought John Wayne killed us all."[5] In 1978 AIM organized a demonstration it called "The Longest Walk." Starting on Alcatraz, which had been reimagined as a Federal recreation area that was becoming a major tourist attraction, twenty-four Native Americans walked across the United States to Washington, D.C. By the time they got there they were joined by some 3,000 supporters, who marched through the streets to the beat of a drum. Over the next week they staged rallies at the Supreme Court, Congress, the FBI building, and the Capitol to bring attention to a set of eleven bills that would repeal Indian treaties and erode Native water, fishing, and hunting rights on Indian lands. One of their graphic gestures was the raising of tipis on the Mall. AIM organizers knew that the bills had little chance of passing but because the legislation represented a racist backlash they demanded a response. Congress not only rejected these measures, it passed two pieces of legislation that year aimed at correcting the assault on Native cultures. The American Indian Religious Freedom Act guaranteed Indigenous people the right to practice Native forms of worship and access to sacred sites such as the Medicine Wheel in Wyoming and the Sweet Grass Hills in Montana. The Indian Child Welfare Act was intended to ensure that Native American kids were raised by their own families. It was passed in response to the large number of children removed from their families by ignorant, misguided public and private agencies and placed in White foster homes.

The Longest Walk was repeated in 2008 by activists concerned about environmental damage on Indigenous lands caused by corporate exploitation of natural resources. The organizers issued a statement called the "Manifesto of Change" that outlines a threat to the San Francisco Peaks in Arizona, an extinct volcano revered as a sacred site by thirteen tribal nations, including the Navajo and the Hopi. In 2002 the U.S. Forest Service granted a permit for the construction of a fifteen-mile pipeline from Flagstaff to a ski facility in the Peaks called Arizona Snowbowl to transport reclaimed sewage water to the resort. The water is converted into snow and sprayed on the slopes. A study revealed that the water contains human and veterinary antibiotics, caffeine, codeine, oral contraceptives, and other hormones, steroids, anti-seizure medication, solvents, disinfectants, flame retardants, moth and mosquito repellants, and wood preservatives. Legal challenges to the scheme have failed repeatedly in court. In 2022 thirteen tribes in the region joined forces to challenge the ski resort's plan for a massive expansion.[6]

A year later another protest against a pipeline brought together the largest political gathering of Native Americans since the treaty councils in the mid-nineteenth century. Thousands of people from 280 tribes joined young members of the Dakota and Lakota Nations, who live on the Standing Rock Reservation straddling the border between North and South Dakota. They warned that the underground pipeline, which was designed to transport crude oil from the Bakken field in North Dakota to the Midwest, threatened tribal water supplies, burial grounds, and cultural sites. The original plan had the pipeline crossing under the Missouri River upstream from Bismarck, the state's capitol. But protests from local officials worried about the city's water supply forced the pipeline's builders to cross under the river somewhere else. The best place, they decided, was 1,500 feet from the boundary of an Indian reservation, a boundary the tribe never agreed to, on land it never ceded.[7]

Calling themselves "water protectors" the activists set up camps and prepared for a long campaign of resistance. Hundreds of activists were injured by local law enforcement and private security forces, who attacked them with water cannons, sound cannons, tear gas, rubber bullets, concussion grenades, and dogs. Some of the 525 protesters arrested by the Morton County Sheriff's office were thrown into cages resembling dog kennels built on a concrete floor and lacking any bedding or furniture. Numbers were drawn on the arms of some detainees, authorities admitted, but only in order to keep track of their belongings, they said.[8] The Obama administration halted construction in 2016 but a month later the incoming president reversed that order. Donald Trump invested at least $500,000 in Energy Transfer Partners, the pipeline's owner, and another $500,000 in Phillips 66, which would have a 25 percent stake in the Dakota Access project. The corporation's CEO donated $100,000 to Trump's 2016 campaign. Not surprisingly, despite massive protests and numerous lawsuits, the Federal government allowed the pipeline project to move forward. It was completed in April 2017—including a section laid under Lake Oahu, the tribe's source of water. The pipeline began pumping oil in June. During its first six months of operation it leaked five times. In 2020 a Federal judge revoked Energy Transfer's permit to drill under Lake Oahu until the Army Corps of Engineers prepares a full environmental analysis. That report was released in September 2023 but made no recommendations whether the pipeline should be shut down or not. The judge said that the company's abysmal safety record "does not inspire confidence." An appeal by Energy Transfer was rejected by the Supreme Court in 2022. Meanwhile the pipeline continued to pump oil, although its owners had no permit.

From the occupation of Alcatraz to the Indigenous Youth Council protest at Red Cloud, Native American activists have made it clear that they have no intention of melting down in America's melting pot. But there are different approaches to the challenge of remaining distinctly Piegan, Lakota, or Diné. The daughters of the men who founded the American Indian Movement in 1968 personify two of these paths. One of them is working within the system and the other is working to dismantle that system. They were interviewed during Marsha Small's first visit to Red Cloud by Crystal Echo Hawk and Lashay Wesley for their *American Genocide* podcast.[9] Tashina Banks Rama said that her father, Dennis Banks, who died in 2017, told her that it was his generation's job "to go and beat these doors down and fight our way into these institutions and have native people be heard and recognized. It's your generation and the next generation's job to walk into these institutions and work them from the inside with the same mission." As a Red Cloud School administrator, Banks Rama said she's able to advocate for change "at the table" when dealing with the Jesuits and Church officials who operate the institution. The school, which enrolls more than 500 Lakota students, announced in July 2023 that it's changing its name to Maȟpíya Lúta (Red Cloud in Lakota). This is in keeping with its Lakota language curriculum and immersion program. Sierra Concha, Banks Rama's daughter and the school's literacy project coordinator, said that this work is important "because we're reclaiming not only our language but our Indigenous knowledge systems—things that come with language and are tied to every part of our identity like songs, prayers, and stories. Our language is the very core of our being and who we are as unique Indigenous people."[10]

Ensuring that Lakota remains a living language has become pivotal in the struggle to combat assimilation; fewer than 2,000 of the 200,000 Lakota people living in 2021 were fluent speakers. The boarding school era is responsible in part for the decline of Native fluency in not only Lakota but Siksiká, 'Ōlelo Hawai'i, Tlingit, Cherokee and many other Indigenous languages. Concha's grandmother was sent to Holy Rosary as a child as was her mother. When he was five years old Dennis Banks was forced to attend the Pipestone Indian Training School in Minnesota, where he spent as much time running away back home to his Ojibwe family as sitting in a class. According to his account he was beaten every time the school caught him.[11]

Banks Rama sent all ten of her children to Red Cloud in her effort to give them the sort of hybrid education that might allow them to function successfully in both cultures. "Now we have native policy makers, legislators, lawyers, and business people—people who understand the system," she said. "Tribes have a better understanding of their sovereignty now and how to assert their sovereignty when dealing with the federal government."[12]

One of these Oglala leaders is Tatewin Means, the daughter of AIM founder Russell Means, who died in 2012. She served as the attorney general for the Oglala tribe and ran unsuccessfully for South Dakota attorney general in 2018. She is now the chief executive of the Thunder Valley Community Development Corporation, which has built solar-powered homes in its small community near the reservation town of Porcupine. The nonprofit is also focusing on worker training, an immersion program in the Lakota language for kids, and food sovereignty, a system in which the people whose labor produces food also control how it's distributed, as opposed to the for-profit system imposed by corporations. In the *American Genocide* podcast Means told Echo Hawk and Wesley that she wants the churches removed from Pine Ridge, especially the Catholic Church running Red Cloud School. "These churches still have that paternalistic ethic that they know best. That they are doing us a favor by taking our children and saving them from us . . . The answer isn't more of the colonizer oppressor system the answer is more investment into our traditional lifeways like our language, like our food sovereignty." She said at Thunder Valley "we are as close as possible to how our ancestors lived and interacted with one another. That we are able to truly shed those influences of colonization. That includes Christian influences. That would have no part of our community. That we could drive through this land base and not see a church. That's a part of my liberation dream." She said, however, that it's very hard to hold the Church accountable because they "have people protecting them." Some Native people, she said, are staunch advocates of the Church. "They will tell the Jesuits 'Don't leave. We need you.'"

Although Means and Banks don't agree about what role if any the Church should play at Red Cloud they are united in their position that it must pay financial reparations to the Lakota. "What does reparations look like?" Banks Rama asked. "Is it money? Absolutely it's money. But it's also other things—mental health, wellness, spiritual health." Means said that reparations "could go to immersion programs, could go to food sovereignty programs, to building our energy infrastructure." If they truly care about our people, she said, what's the issue? "Or do they only love us if we're going to be Christians?"

The Youth Council and others at Pine Ridge believe that there are more graves on or near the campus of Red Cloud than the Jesuits are revealing. Maka Black Elk, director of the school's Truth and Healing Initiative—disputes this allegation. "We have no reason to believe that there are any graves outside of the cemetery. The narrative out there from some of our naysayers is that this is a crime scene and that there's bodies everywhere with no evidence of that whatsoever . . . It speaks to the mistrust that some members of the community have for this institution." People also want to know how much land the Church owns on the reservation, how much tribal trust and treaty money the Federal government paid Holy Rosary to assimilate Oglala children, and how much Church properties are worth. And most importantly, they want to know how many children died at Holy Rosary, and from what causes. Like the staff at most Indian boarding schools the Catholics kept exhaustive records. But these documents are stored in the archives of the Bureau of Catholic Indian Missions at Marquette University, a Jesuit institution in Milwaukee, Wisconsin, 850 miles east of Red Cloud.

A reporter from *Indian Country Today* spent hours in these dusty old repositories searching for information. Mary Annette Pember, a citizen of the Red Cliff Band of Ojibwe in Wisconsin, learned that although there is a ton of old papers in the collection some of these documents are heavily redacted with black marker. And there are other documents that Church officials refuse to let the public see. Marquette's archivist told her that sealing these records was not an attempt to protect the Church but rather an effort to protect the privacy of certain individuals. Pember said that the privacy claim has been an obstacle for researchers. She wants access to the quarterly reports sent by the boarding schools to the Bureau of Catholic Missions beginning in 1900, records that would reveal the names of the children enrolled. Federal boarding schools such as Carlisle have made this information available to anyone searching online. Pember said that by cross-referencing names with death records it would be possible to determine if someone was buried at Red Cloud without a grave marker. (The Indian Boarding School Truth and Healing Commission Bill would give the Federal government the power to subpoena the Church for its records.)

However, in searching through unrestricted diaries and correspondence Pember found references to twenty children who died at Holy Rosary, only ten of whom were named. The causes of their deaths are not listed. These were Ignez Blackface, Sophia Bush, Lawrence Clifford, Harley Cook, Clara Klondalario, Ellen Shangro, Rosa Red Elk, Louisa White, Clara Yellow Bear, and Zora Ironteeth, who died in 1917 at the age of seven. The gravesite of only one child—Zora—is marked on an old map of the cemetery at Red Cloud. But Pember could not find any marker in the spot where the records said Zora was laid to rest. Had there ever been one it likely weathered away, she speculates, especially if it had been made of wood. But she has established one fact: at Red Cloud there is at least one unmarked grave of a child.[13]

In October 2022 Marsha Small returned to Red Cloud to excavate the basement under Drexel Hall where she, Jarrod Burks and their crew had detected anomalies the previous May. The first step was to remove the floor by cutting it into sections with a water-cooled concrete saw and carrying the sections up and out of the building by hand. A week later they were joined by Burks and three assistants along with tribal police detectives and two FBI agents who had worked with tribal authorities on previous cases (the FBI is responsible for investigating federal crimes committed on some 200 Indian reservations.) "I'm scared," she told a reporter from *Wired* magazine. "I'm scared we're gonna find something, and I'm scared we're not gonna find something. Because if we don't find something, they'll say the church bought us off." Small's crew removed a shallow layer of sandy gravel, and then marked off sixteen one-square-meter squares in the exposed dirt.

The squares were excavated in succeeding depths of about eight inches down to about three feet under the surface of the original concrete floor. The soil was ladled into buckets and taken outside to a large tent, where workers sifted it through screens. They found the bones of rodents and bones larger than those of a human that were likely bison or livestock deposited before Drexel Hall was built. But they did not find any human bones or evidence that the ground had harbored graves. Small and Burks concluded that construction debris accounted for the first anomaly and the second one was due to the burrows of rodents.[14] Had Pourier been mistaken about what he had seen? The excavated room is shown on a schematic drawn for the 1997 renovation of Drexel Hall marked with the word "Graveyard." Banks Rama said the label referred to an old, now-discarded Halloween tradition at Red Cloud, whose decorations were stored in the basement.

After the findings were published the school again insisted that it was concealing nothing. "The report affirms that no evidence of graves existed in the soil and that there was no evidence of graves ever having been removed," the administration stated on the school's website. "Maȟpíya Lúta continues its commitment to pursuing all avenues of truth-seeking." But Small would not dismiss the possibility that children had been buried under Drexel Hall. "What I see on the horizon is that community rising up against that church. And if they do it right, they'll kick 'em out. Then they'll bring me in, or they'll bring somebody else in, and we'll find bodies. They still have that breath of fire."[15]

Chapter Seven

THE LORD'S VINEYARD

While Mount Rushmore's carved heads stared at Donald Trump, he told a campaign rally on the eve of Independence Day in 2020 that "Angry mobs are trying to tear down statues of our founders, deface our most sacred memorials, and unleash a wave of violent crime in our cities." As the crowd chanted "USA! USA! USA!" and "Four more years!" he announced that federal agents had arrested one of the four men who tried to topple the bronze statue of Andrew Jackson near the White House during protests following the murder of George Floyd by Minneapolis police. Trump did not mention that Jackson was a slave owner who orchestrated the 1830 Indian Removal Act, which directed the U.S. Army to evict 60,000 Indigenous people from their homelands in the Southeast and force-march the survivors to Oklahoma. Or that a week after his inauguration he had hung a portrait of Jackson in the Oval Office.

Trump's public adoration of Old Hickory was only one of the insults to Native Americans his presence in the Black Hills represented. His sycophant, South Dakota Governor Kristi Noem, wanted to appease business owners who feast on the Rushmore tourist trade by pressing the National Park Service to issue South Dakota a permit for a massive fireworks show on the mountain following Trump's speech. Citing water contamination and wildfire risks to the ponderosa forest the agency had refused to issue any such permit since 2009. Noem enlisted Trump's help in pressuring the Park Service, which finally caved. Trump dismissed concerns about forest fires. "What can burn?" he asked. "It's stone."[1]

After the Park Service reinstated the ban in 2021 Noem sued Interior Secretary Deb Haaland. But the 8th Circuit Court of Appeals sided with Haaland. A month after the event Trump tweeted that adding his face to the four U.S. presidents depicted on Mt. Rushmore would be "a good idea."[2] Protesters who used vans to block a road to Trump's event argued that for Native Americans the best idea regarding the faces on Mount Rushmore would be to remove them. For one reason, they were carved by Gutzon Borglum, a notorious admirer of the Ku Klux Klan who once said: "I would not trust an Indian, off-hand, 9 out of 10, where I would not trust a white man 1 out of 10."[3]

During an interview Nick Tilsen, a member of the Oglala Lakota Nation and founder of the Thunder Valley Community Development Corporation at Pine Ridge, told a Lower Brule member and university professor named Nick Estes that "What South Dakota and the National Park Service call 'a shrine to democracy' is actually an international symbol of white supremacy."[4] Tilsen was arrested at the roadblock along with twenty other activists after police in riot gear backed by Air National Guardsmen fired pepper balls at them and carted them off in handcuffs as Trump supporters yelled: "Go back to where you came from!" An Oglala Lakota member named Freddie Longworth yelled at the police. "Respect our right to exist or expect our resistance," a slogan that was beginning to gain traction across Indian Country. "RespectExpect" was spray-painted in 2021 on Trump's beloved statue of Andrew Jackson.

Tribal leaders believe that Trump's visit was retaliation for Native America's tenacious decade-long opposition to the Keystone XL pipeline, a project that was finally abandoned in 2021 by Canadian-owned TC Energy. And they saw Trump's speech before a crowd of 7,500 unmasked partisans during the height of the COVID-19 pandemic as retribution against the Pine Ridge and Cheyenne River reservations for barring out-siders in an effort to halt the spread of the virus, which had been ravaging the Navajo Reservation, among others. Noem threatened to sue the tribes for the checkpoints they set up on state and federal highways. But knowing she would lose in court she backed down.[5] Harold Frazier, chairman of the Cheyenne River Sioux Tribe, accused Trump of "putting our tribal mem-bers at risk to stage a photo op at one of our most sacred sites."[6]

Protesters who used vans to block a road to the event for three hours car-ried signs that said "You are on stolen land" and "Honor the treaties."[7] These were references to the 1851 Horse Creek Treaty, which established a home-land for the Sioux and seven other tribes on a vast swath of land across what would become five Plains states. Because the treaty was broken soon after it was signed sporadic violence culminating in Red Cloud's War compelled the U.S. to negotiate the 1868 Fort Laramie Treaty, which created the Great Sioux Reservation. The Sioux were granted sole possession of *He Sapa*, the Lakota name for the Black Hills, and were promised that non-Indians would not be allowed to trespass. After Custer was killed at the Battle of Greasy Grass Congress retaliated by passing a law in 1877 that confiscated the Black Hills, confined the Dakota, Lakota, and Nakota people to the reservation and opened *He Sapa* to a flood of miners who would eventually extract gold worth almost 100 billion dollars from ravaged earth.

In 1920 the tribe filed a lawsuit in the federal Court of Claims seeking compensation for the government's theft of the Black Hills. Finally, in 1980, the U.S. Supreme Court ruled that the "Sioux Nation of Indians" was entitled to $17.1 million plus interest, which in 2023 amounted to more than $2 billion, for the illegal taking of their land. "A more ripe and rank case of dishonorable dealings will never, in all probability, be found in our history" the Court concluded in its summation of the government's shameless plunder. Although that kind of money might address some of the lingering multi-generational ills caused by Indian boarding schools, the tribe doesn't want it. What it wants is the return of *He Sapa*. The slogan appears on T-shirts and posters across Indian Country. "The Black Hills are not for sale."

As the moment in 1889 approached when South Dakota would be declared one of the United States, the railroads, White settlers, and local businessmen looked at what remained of the Great Sioux Reservation and saw the opportunity to steal even more land. Policy makers in the nation's capital were no longer fearful of the armed resistance by the Sioux that resulted in the Indigenous triumphs of Red Cloud's War or what Whites called the Battle of the Little Big Horn. As a result, an 1889 bill passed by Congress without the consent of the Sioux Nation carved up their territory into six reservations—Cheyenne River, Crow Creek, Lower Brulé, Pine Ridge, Rosebud, and Standing Rock, each one the new home of the seven bands of the Sioux. This act of thievery reduced their land by more than nine million acres, an area the size of Connecticut, Massachusetts, and Rhode Island combined. While White residents greeted the centennial of South Dakota statehood with parties and speeches, including one by President George H. W. Bush in Sioux Falls congratulating his audience for building "a good state," Native American residents did not join in the festivities. "For American Indians what is there to celebrate?" asked *Lakota Times* editor Tim Giago. [8]

In May 2016 representatives from the Northern Arapaho and the Sicangu Lakota met with the U.S. Army to ask for the return of their children's remains from Carlisle. The next year the graves of three Northern Arapaho boys were excavated in the presence of family members. Like all of the reburials at the Carlisle cemetery the remains had been placed in wooden caskets, which had deteriorated over the course of almost a century. And because the remains themselves had laid in the ground for more than 150 years the gravesites were sifted through by hand instead of using mechanical equipment. The deceased included Little Chief, renamed Dickens by the school, the fourteen-year-old son of a chief named Sharp Nose. The second child was Horse, renamed Horace. The third gravesite was recorded as containing the remains of Little Plume, aged nine, renamed

Hayes Vanderbilt Friday. But Army Corps of Engineers archaeologists found instead the remains of two individuals. Based on an analysis of the bones it was determined that because of their ages and sex neither one was Little Plume. Millie Friday, a relative who was present at the exhumation with other family members, said that they all cried when they learned the news. "We went there to bring all of our children home, and now we're only bringing two." Friday said that as they left the cemetery she reached down and touched Little Plume's headstone. "We're going to come back and get you," she told him. Horse and Little Chief were reburied on the Wind River Reservation in Wyoming. Instead of a burial for Little Plume tribal members held a ceremony with a line of mounted horsemen making their way to the burial ground, and one riderless horse. But in 2018 after subsequent research revealed that his remains were in another grave, Little Plume was finally brought home to Wind River. Another Arapaho boy was repatriated to the reservation in September 2023. His student card listed him as thirteen-year-old Beau Niel, who died in 1880, the son of a chief named Old Crow. [9]

Other tribes found dealing with the Army a frustrating struggle. The Army argued that its policy regarding the repatriation of remains superseded the Native American Graves Protection and Repatriation Act (NAGPRA), which stipulated that if a direct descendent of the deceased cannot be determined the tribe can take custody of the remains. Officials demanded a signed affidavit from a child's closest living relative stating that he or she has no objection to disinterring their kin, a rigid policy that prohibits repatriation by the tribe if a living relative cannot be identified. The tribes argued that determining the closest blood relative of a child dead for almost 150 years would be difficult and in some cases impossible. After all, a person living in the nineteenth century who was fourteen years old or younger probably would not have left behind any descendants. And unlike the nuclear family responsible for child-rearing in White culture the Plains tribes typically considered raising children a communal function of the entire band or village. A member of the Sissiton-Wahpeton Oyate named Tamara St. John, who is a South Dakota state representative, told a reporter that the Army's policy was "something of a false front, and I feel resentment for it because it became an obstacle and has been delaying for us for years, but it's also something that created division and questioning."[10] (In 2024 the Winnebago Tribe of Nebraska sued the U.S. Army for refusing to release the remains of two Winnebago children who died and were buried at Carlisle in the late 1890s—Samuel Gilbert and Edward Hensley.)

But finally, after years of research St. John and others were able to track down people related to Amos La Framboise and Edward Upright. However, when their graves were excavated in September 2023 the only thing found remaining of Amos was part of his knee. And the name on his gravestone was misspelled as La Farmbois. "How careful and loving were you with our child when you dug him up from the Ashland Cemetery," St. John said, "and then dug him up again from another?" In Upright's grave were teeth, large bones, and his skull. After inviting the same Army officials they had quarreled with for years to observe their private ceremony, tribal representatives wrapped the caskets in buffalo robes and took them back home to the Lake Traverse Reservation. At sunrise they were placed on scaffolds, then spent two nights beginning at sundown in a tipi before being reburied. Amos was laid to rest next to his father.

The day before the boys were exhumed a family from the Puyallup Nation in Washington state gathered to witness the disinterment of Edward Spott, sixteen, who died of tuberculosis at Carlisle in 1896. After serving his five-year term he had enrolled at the Dickinson College prep school in the town of Carlisle. The Industrial School's student newspaper, the *Indian Helper*, wrote in 1895 about a theatrical production staged by the debating society in which Spott played Myles Standish, the head of the Plymouth Colony's militia who was notorious for his brutality against Native Americans. Spott's family was shocked when Army archaeologists determined that the bones they found in his grave were those of a female between sixteen and twenty-two years old. Spott is now listed as missing. The remains of the girl were reburied and will join the more than a dozen other burials of "unknown" children. Allysha Winburn, a forensic anthropologist who led the team analyzing these remains and those of four others—including Launy Shorty, Beau Niel, Amos La Framboise, and Edward Upright—promised that the search for Eddie Spott would continue.

In 2017 Kirby Metoxen was on a road trip with friends when they decided to take a detour to Carlisle. A tribal councilman serving Wisconsin's Oneida Nation, he had heard stories about the infamous school from his parents and tribal elders. As he wandered through the BIA cemetery he was surprised by some of the names on the gravestones. Here was Sophia Coulon, a prevalent last name among the Oneida. And here was Ophelia Powless, who shared her last name with Metoxen's grandmother. But the name that especially affected him was that of Jemima Metoxen, who died at the age of sixteen in 1904, stricken with spinal meningitis. Ophelia died in 1891 of pneumonia at the age of sixteen. Sophia, who died in 1893 of tuberculosis when she was eighteen, had been hired as a housekeeper by families in three states as part of Carlisle's outing program. "These children didn't ask to be here," Metoxen told a gathering of Native Americans. "How come nobody came to get these kids? It's forever changed me."

In 2019 he returned to Carlisle with the relatives of the girls who had requested that they be disinterred. Although he does not share a direct kinship with the girls, Metoxen said he was overwhelmed when he saw their bones. "It was like my own child. And the thought they were all by themselves, I couldn't get over thinking of a young child getting ready to go to the next world, alone, with no family." The girls were honored during the Oneida's annual powwow and were reburied two days later, Metoxen and Coulon at the Oneida Sacred Burial Grounds, and Powless at Holy Apostles Cemetery on the grounds of the Episcopal Church's oldest Indian mission. Henry Huff, who is related to Jemima Metoxen, said that bringing the girls home was a relief. "There's a warmness in your heart that they're back here by their family." [11]

Another Oneida child in the BIA cemetery was too young to be enrolled at Carlisle. This was Paul Wheelock, who died in 1900 at the age of ten months. The school reported that he "took a severe cold which settled in his throat and lungs, from which he slowly pined away." Paul was the son of Dennison Wheelock, a rare graduate of Carlisle who was appointed bandmaster of the famous Carlisle Indian Band, which performed at World Fairs and Presidential inaugurations. He met his future wife, a Chippewa named Louisa LaChapelle from the White Earth Reservation in northwestern Minnesota, while they were enrolled at Carlisle. Wheelock became a world-class coronet player and a composer who wrote *Suite Aboriginal*, a symphony in three movements—"Morning on the Plains," "The Lover's Song," and "The Dance of the Red Men." His symphony premiered at Carnegie Hall the year his son died. Wheelock became a lawyer at the age of forty who argued cases on behalf of Indian nations before the U.S. Supreme Court and the Court of Claims. He and Pratt became life-long friends who shared the belief that reservations and the BIA should be abolished, Indians should be granted full citizenship, and public schools should open their doors to the tribes. Wheelock's infant son was disinterred in 2022 as was another Oneida boy, Frank Green, who died in an accident at the age of fifteen. Their families took their remains back to the Oneida Nation's reservation in Wisconsin for reburial in Holy Apostles cemetery.[12]

On a June day in 1898 Green watched mesmerized as hundreds of Indians, cowboys, soldiers, and horses thundered around the show grounds in the town of Carlisle reenacting stagecoach robberies, the Pony Express and Indian attacks on settlers and wagon trains. Featured in Buffalo Bill's Wild West spectacle was sharpshooting Annie Oakley. But what captivated Green was the troupe of wild Plains warriors, most of them Lakota, their faces painted, dressed in buckskin and feathers, clothing his classmates lost when they arrived at Carlisle along with their long hair and their freedom to speak their own languages. "A spectacle such as this has never been witnessed in Carlisle," the *Carlisle Sentinel* gushed. The students and staff of the Indian School were the guests of honor invited by Bill Cody, who rode at the head of the parade that wound through the streets of town while thousands of people watched, awestruck. Although Pratt attended the show he was opposed to Cody's exploitation of Indians and his reinforcement of Native culture, which, in his opinion, failed to prepare them for lives as White replicas. Author and activist Vine Deloria Jr. had a different opinion of Native Americans in Cody's show. "Playing Indian," he wrote, "was how they refused to abandon their culture. Perhaps they realized in the deepest sense, that even a caricature of their youth was preferable to a complete surrender to the homogenization that was overtaking American society."[13] The show provided a space to be Indian and avoid meddling from missionaries, teachers, agents, humanitarians, and politicians.[14]

After the matinee performance some 100 of the Indian men were invited to the school for dinner. They arrived in their Native clothes, speaking their own tongues, their hair long. No doubt painfully reminded of home, Green and a friend snuck away from the school grounds to watch the evening performance of the show. Afterward his friend went back to school and Green stowed away on the midnight train taking Cody's spectacle to its next gig in Huntington, Pennsylvania. It was at least the fifth time he would run away from Carlisle. Six months earlier he had been arrested by a police detective at the train station in Harrisburg, twenty miles east of the school. According to conflicting reports Green either fell from the train and died instantly. Or as he was walking along the tracks he tried to grab onto a passing freight, was thrown under the wheels, and cut to pieces, according to one report. "The poor boy has been a disturbing element for some time," the *Indian Helper* editorialized. "Few tears were shed for his loss." The *Carlisle Gazette* described him as "wayward and incorrigible." In a letter to the Commissioner of Indian Affairs Pratt described Green as a thief and "an exceptionally bad boy." If Green had lived only a week longer he would have learned that Carlisle had lost patience with him and was arranging to ship him back to Wisconsin.

Green wasn't the only Carlisle student whose life was altered after watching the Wild West show. In 1912 a twenty-one-year-old Hidatsa from Elbowoods, North Dakota, named Lifts His Arm—renamed Charles Packineau by the school—ran away to attend one of Cody's performances in Harrisburg. (Elbowoods had been the headquarters of the Fort Berthold Reservation before it and a dozen other Native towns were inundated in the 1950s by Lake Sakakawea, which was created by Garrison Dam. Elbowoods was forced to move its cemetery.) After the show Lifts His Arm hopped a freight after deciding he wanted to go back to North Dakota. But he only got a hundred miles closer to home. The next morning his corpse was discovered sprawled beside the tracks. His mangled body was identified by his name engraved on a pocketknife. Described as a model student with "good moral character and good disposition" he had been subjected to training in Carlisle's "Plumbing and Steam Fitting Department." His remains were returned to the reservation on a freight train. He had run away from Carlisle with four other boys. Two of them returned to school and the other two were hired by the show.[15]

St. Paul, Alaska, is one of the most remote villages in America. It lies on a forty-three-square-mile volcanic island in the Bering Sea 300 miles west of the Alaskan mainland and 500 miles east of Siberia. The population in 2024 numbered about 400 people, almost all of them Unangax̂ (Aleut) Native Americans. Although the island of St. Paul offers a harbor and docks for small fishing boats most people get there and back by a direct flight on a prop plane from Anchorage. The tourists who pay around $1,000 for a round-trip ticket are drawn to the place because of its wildlife—whales, arctic foxes, herds of reindeer, a half million fur seals, and more than 300 species of resident and migrating birds.

On a July day in 2021 most of the people in town had gathered at the island's airport to wait for a plane. But it wasn't tourists they were there to greet. Returning home at last was a Unangax̂ girl named Sophia Tetoff. One of a dozen half-siblings, she had been orphaned in 1895 at the age of eight. She and her ten-year-old sister Irene were put on board the USS *Bear*—a forerunner of the Coast Guard's ice-breaking fleet in the Arctic—and shipped to the Jesse Lee Home on the island of Unalaska in the Aleutian chain. This was a two-story Methodist boarding school that looked like a barn. Sheldon Jackson, a Presbyterian minister and head of colonial education in the territory, echoed Richard Pratt's assimilationist ideology when he ordered teachers to forbid Native Alaskan student to speak their own languages or read from books written in these languages. "It is the purpose of the government in establishing schools in Alaska," he wrote, "to train up English speaking American citizens. You will therefore teach in English and give special prominence to instruction in the English language . . . your teaching should be pervaded by the spirit of the Bible." The ban, which was still in force when Alaska became a state in 1959, is credited by some critics for the fading of twenty Native languages. Jackson had established a string of contract schools for Natives in Alaska paid for by the federal government and administered by various Christian denominations. In 1885 a Tlingit family accused him of holding its children against their will at the Presbyterian boarding school he founded seven years earlier in Sitka, Alaska. A court ruled in favor of the family, ordered the children released and barred Jackson from claiming custody of Native children. While he was attempting to erase Native culture he collected some 5,000 Native Alaskan ethnographic items now "owned" by Princeton University and an Alaska museum. [16]

Three years after the Tetoff sisters arrived at the Jesse Lee Home, Irene died there of tuberculosis. In 1901 Sophia was shipped off to Carlisle on a trip by steamer and rail that took eighteen days. In Port Townsend, Washington, the petite twelve-year-old stared up at the telegraph wires strung above the street. "O my!" she cried. "What for do they have their clothes lines so high?"[17] Eight months after entering Carlisle she was outed to work as a servant for a White family in New Jersey. Over the next three years she was outed four more times, her forced labor benefitting White families in three different states. In 1905 during her stint at the Kavenaugh household in Kennett Square, Pennsylvania, she got sick and was returned to Carlisle. After wasting away with tuberculosis for a year in the school hospital she died at the age of seventeen.

The school did not notify the people on St. Paul Island that one of their own was dead. A lost child, Sofia was not mentioned in the tribe's records. But a Tlingit elder searching Carlisle's cemetery for Alaska Natives came across her headstone and contacted Lauren Peters, a former flight officer for Atlantic Coast Airlines and an advisor on the board overseeing the Native

American Graves Protection and Repatriation Act. Tetoff, she told him, was her family name. The name on Sophia's grave marker was misspelled as "Tatoff" and her tribal affiliation was recorded there as "Chuskon," a word someone made up. After the Army agreed to disinter her great aunt Peters and her son flew from their home in California to Carlisle for a ceremony marking the transfer of Sophia from her grave into a simple wooden casket. They wrapped her bones in a fur seal pelt "to put her to bed in her box," Peters said. In the custom of the military Sophia's grave marker has been destroyed and the plot replanted with grass. She was reburied near family members in St. Paul's Russian Orthodox cemetery, a relic of the days when Alaska was a colony of the Russians, who forced the Unangax̂ into slavery to hunt seals for their fur. Her casket was draped with gold cloth and inscribed with phrases written in her first language.[18]

In July 2021 members of the Sicangu Youth Council and their chaperones drove in a caravan through the main gate of the Carlisle Barracks on their way to a ceremony during which they would accept the remains of nine Rosebud students. Like all visitors eighteen years or older they were required to produce a photo ID and submit to a criminal history check before the authorities issued them a pass. The children, who ranged in age from eleven to eighteen, were buried in the school's cemetery between 1880 and 1886. In addition to Knocks Off and Little Girl these included a son and a daughter of chiefs—Strikes First, renamed Dennis, the twelve-year-old son of a chief named Blue Tomahawk, who fought during the annihilation of the Seventh Cavalry at the Battle of the Greasy Grass, and Take the Tail, renamed Lucy, the eleven-year-old daughter of Pretty Eagle. For members of the Youth Council, who organized the caravan, this day was the culmination of six years of lobbying the Army to release long-lost members to their tribe. Asia Black Bull, twenty-one, said the Council's success represented a triumph for all of Indian Country. "As Indigenous people, we've all been standing up," she said. "We've all been rising. We're a failed system of what the U.S. tried to do, to annihilate us. We're still here."[19]

Defined by per capita income, members of the Oceti Sakowin Oyate—the Sioux Nation—have been among the poorest people in America for decades. However, when a thirty-eight-year-old Flemish Jesuit named Pierre-Jean De Smet happened to meet with some Yankton Sioux in 1839 on the Vermillion River in what is now South Dakota, the Oceti Sakowin Oyate was one of the wealthiest populations in America. While the territory east of the Mississippi was filling with landless immigrants, the denizens of urban slums, and impoverished slaves, the Lakota, Dakota, and Nakota ruled 250,000 square miles stretching south from Canada to Nebraska, and west from Minnesota to Wyoming. Their bison-based economy was vibrantly successful.

De Smet was a curiosity. Dressed in a black robe and sporting a crucifix, unlike any White man the Sioux had ever met he wanted nothing from them—not women, horses, furs, or land. He didn't try to sell them whiskey or guns. And he was the rare White man who came in peace. Stories across the Northern Plains of meetings with De Smet would be told for many years. Because he set the bar for the Catholic missionaries who followed him west his story is instructive in understanding the theory and practice of Indian boarding schools established by the government and Christian denominations. During his half century on the frontier he logged 180,000 miles traveling from tribe to tribe. And to raise money for what he envisioned as a federation of Catholic Indians united by a web of missions he made numerus trips to the East Coast plus nineteen crossings of the Atlantic to Europe. The missions he founded included St. Joseph among the Potawatomie in Iowa, St. Mary and St. Ignatius among the Salish in Montana, and Sacred Heart among the Sahaptin (Coeur d'Alenes) in Idaho. He was also instrumental in the establishment of St. Peter's among the Blackfeet, fearlessly venturing among what he called the "most treacherous and wily set of savages among all the nations of the American desert, in whose words no reliance can be placed." To facilitate his goal of converting masses of Indigenous people to Catholicism he acted as a peacemaker, believing that an Indian at war was an Indian too busy to baptize. As a testament to the supernatural power Native Americans believed he possessed he never lost his scalp.

De Smet had sailed from Europe to America in 1821. In America he accompanied a dozen other Flemish Jesuits to a tobacco plantation near Washington, D.C., called White Marsh Manor. It was one of five Maryland plantations owned by the Society of Jesus and operated with the labor of Black slaves and tenant farmers. While studying philosophy and theology as a novitiate on his way to becoming a brother in the Society of Jesus and eventually a priest, De Smet was learning two other things. First, White Marsh was going broke and, second, Catholics were not popular in Protestant America. After the Jesuits were thrown out of several European countries during the 1700s for meddling in politics, in 1814 the Vatican rescinded its agreement to stand by these banishments and brought the order back to life, a resurgence Thomas Jefferson described as "a retrograde step from light toward darkness."

But John Calhoun, James Monroe's secretary of war, saw a way to use them. He had been approached in early 1823 by the Bishop of Louisiana with a scheme to start a school for Indians on a 200-acre farm owned by his vast diocese. It was located near Florissant, Missouri, an old Creole village fifteen miles northwest of St. Louis. Acting on his authority as the head of Indian Affairs, Calhoun agreed to pay Jesuits $200 a year apiece to build and operate this school and promised some additional money for construction projects. An avowed advocate of slavery, Calhoun figured that exploiting priests and ministers might be a cheap way to pacify the savages before they caused any more trouble for his government. The Catholics wouldn't ask for more money because they knew he would contract instead with Protestants, who had already gobbled up much of the yearly $10,000 allotted by the government under the 1819 Civilization Fund Act. Calhoun's offer came just as the Church had decided to cut its losses in Maryland by shutting down White Marsh Manor and evicting the Jesuits.

In May 1823 De Smet stood around with the others watching as slaves piled their belongings onto horse-drawn wagons. He would not miss White

Marsh. His purpose in coming to America was to have a grand adventure while saving the souls of savages. So far he hadn't even seen an Indian. And studying Socrates and Thomas Aquinas while watching slaves weed the tobacco was hardly *History of the Expedition under the Command of Captains Lewis and Clark*, which he had read feverishly at boarding school in Ghent. When everything was packed the entourage set forth on its way to its first stop—Baltimore. The two priests walked behind the wagons in the first row, followed by the three brothers, and De Smet and the five other novitiates in the third rank. Bringing up the rear were the slaves. These were three married couples—Thomas and Mary Brown, Isaac and Susanna Hawkins, and Moses and Nancy Queen. They had been forced to abandon their children and siblings, knowing they would probably never see them again.

In Baltimore they turned west and entered the Cumberland Road, the macadam artery built by the federal government stretching 280 miles across the Allegheny Mountains to Wheeling, Virginia on the Ohio River. At night they slept in sheds or begged lodging from the few Catholic families they passed along the way. When they got to the river eighteen days later the Jesuits didn't have enough money to book passage for themselves or their freight on a steamer so they bought a pair of flatboats and lashed them together. They packed their slaves, horses, and baggage onto one of these floating slabs and occupied the other, separating themselves from the slaves and the animals with a wall. They commanded the slaves to cook meals for them.

Because an Ohio flatboat had no keel, which could strand the vessel on one of the sunken sandbars, it was nearly impossible to navigate. As the flotilla drifted and careened along the big, treacherous river it slammed into driftwood, got tangled in low-hanging trees and was blown this way and that by gusty winds. At one point it sideswiped a steamboat. Most everyone on board except for De Smet, whose aquatic youth prepared him for this, figured that they would drown. Finally, at Shawneetown, Illinois, they docked. They sold the horses and the flatboats and used the money to put their trunks and boxes on a steamboat bound for St. Louis.

Then they set out on the Shawneetown Trail across the tall-grass prairies of southern Illinois. To the few travelers they passed, this pilgrimage must have been a bizarre sight indeed. Here were men in long black robes and wide-rimmed black hats. One of them, De Smet, was obese, carrying 220 pounds on his five-foot-seven-inch frame. And here were people with black skin dressed in rough canvas, their eyes downcast as they avoided the stares of strangers. Slogging through mud and drenched by spring rains for eight days, the priests force-marched their entourage 140 miles to the ferry that would take them across the Mississippi to St. Louis. After a few days rest they resumed their march to Florissant and the shacks they would call St. Stanislaus novitiate.

The following year, 1824, the Jesuits opened Saint Francis Regis Seminary, the first federally funded Catholic boarding school for Indians in the United States. This marked the beginning of a century of collaboration between the Vatican and D.C. to assimilate Indians into White society. The first students were two Sauk boys, six and eight years old. Chiefs from the Iowa tribe seventy miles west had agreed to enroll five of their boys, but on the way east two of them got sick and were returned home. At Florissant the other three children began wailing miserably as their parents prepared to abandon them to these weird men wearing long black robes. One of the Jesuits played a flute, trying to pacify them. It didn't work. That night the boys escaped and ran for five miles before the Jesuits could chase them down on horses.

Federal money arrived a year later, provided by the Civilization Fund Act of 1819. The law was clearly a violation of the clause in the First Amendment intended to put a wall between church and state. But because Indians were regarded as foreign nationals there were no serious legal objections. Over the next seven years the Seminary received the equivalent in today's currency of $100,000. The Church spent this taxpayer money to teach Indians how to speak English so the Jesuits could use them as guides and interpreters as they infiltrated the western tribes. And the boys were required to work several hours a day as farmers and stockmen in order to feed their masters. In an 1825 letter from Rev. Charles F. Van Quickenborne, who was in charge of the seminary, he wrote that the Native American boys "all wept when the hoe was put into their hands for the first time." The educational theory and practice the Jesuits put in place at Florissant would lay the foundation for the hundreds of government and denominational Indian boarding schools to come. Forced labor and corporal punishment were common. In an 1832 letter written to another Jesuit by Brother John O'Connor, who worked at the school, O'Connor described watching Jesuits "tie the hands of the Indian scholars like so many felons and take them to be cruelly scourged on the naked back in the open air under his own eyes." He adds that their hands "were stretched in the form of a cross fastened to a tree and a post." De Smet verified this account, writing that a dozen boys left the school with "the stripes of cowhide on their back." Several of them ran away because of the "horror" and "displeasure" of watching a "Priest of the Society beating to blood their companions." Seven years after it was founded the seminary for obvious reasons had failed to attract or conscript enough Indian children to convince the government that it was worth the money, and in the funding was cut off.

During the failed St. Regis experiment De Smet was ordained a priest. After the school closed he was appointed treasurer of St. Louis University, which the Jesuits began operating in 1829 using the forced labor of at least sixteen slaves imported from their plantations in Maryland (Missouri had been admitted to the Union as a slave state in 1821.) By 1831 at least twenty-six people were held in slavery by the Jesuits. Most of them labored on the farm in Florissant. But according to a Jesuit history, "enslaved people were transferred back and forth between Florissant and Saint Louis. In addition to those they owned, Jesuits, local bishops and clergy, and other religious orders often lent or hired out their enslaved laborers to one another or to other slaveholders, much like they might have lent or borrowed a piece of equipment."[20] He also taught English to some forty White adolescent and adult students. Just as it had been at White Marsh this wasn't the duty he had signed up for. In 1833 he returned to Europe for four years, where he raised money and recruited more Jesuits. But his craving for adventure and the "divine romance" of converting savages compelled him to return.

In 1838 his burning ambition finally won him an assignment to establish his own mission, which would be called St. Joseph. He traveled up the Missouri River on a steamboat to what is now Council Bluffs, Iowa, where he was given a chilly reception by 2,000 Potawatomi Indians, despite the fact that their chief, a Mohawk-Irish Métis named Billy Caldwell, had been raised a Catholic and had invited the Jesuits to try their luck. Still, De Smet was excited to finally come face to face with the objects of his desire. "I had not seen so imposing a sight nor such fine-looking Indians in America," he wrote. "The Iowas are beggars compared to these."

De Smet spent his days at St. Joseph trying to teach Catholicism to people who didn't speak English and whose language he found indecipherable. He drew maps of the area and visited the huts of sick Indians children, pretending to treat them by rubbing a little camphor on their bodies and then secretly baptizing them with water he sprinkled from a vial. But he quickly grasped that converting the Potawatomi would be difficult because of their "superstitious practices and prejudices," their tradition of polygamy, and their tendency to become "melancholy and morose" if they spent more than a couple of months in one place. Plus, their shamans wielded more spiritual power than the Jesuits because for one reason, many of their herbal treatments for disease and injury actually worked. For De Smet the most imposing obstacle was the tribe's addiction to whiskey brought upriver by unscrupulous White traders. The physical life at St. Josephs was equally challenging. Bears and wolves carried off the chickens, swarms of mosquitos and biting flies breeding along the Missouri plagued De Smet during the summer. For his Indians, more menacing than threats from the natural world were other human beings, especially the Sioux, who resented the incursion of tribes herded by the U.S. government into their territory.

After Santee Sioux raiders killed two Potawatomi men in 1839, De Smet boarded a steamboat and headed 135 miles up the river determined to broker a peace between the tribes. His choice of vessels was stupid. This was the SS *St. Peter*, the American Fur Company side-wheeler whose passengers spread smallpox all along the Upper Missouri in 1837 as it made its annual voyage to Fort Union on the Montana-North Dakota border.

The epidemic killed at least 20,000 Indians and eliminated some bands entirely. De Smet, who wrote long letters about every detail of his days, no matter how boring, casually mentioned that Indians along the river were avoiding the *St. Peter*.

In May 1839 De Smet arrived among the Yankton Sioux at the mouth of the Vermillion River in what is now South Dakota. They entertained him with a dance and a venison feast. He was too fat to sit on his buffalo robe like the Indians did, on their haunches with their knees drawn up. The chiefs promised to keep the peace, but they had no intention of doing so permanently. Believing he had accomplished something De Smet returned downstream in a long, narrow canoe with a pair of pilots. The peace he believed he brokered was a delusion. Not long after De Smet returned to St. Josephs the Santee Sioux attacked a band of Potawatomis. In September he would meet with two men from the Rocky Mountains who would present him with the opportunity to change direction yet again.

Pierre Gaucher and Ignace La Mousse were Iroquois Indians who had converted to Catholicism. They were among a crew from the Northeast who had been recruited as trappers by the Hudson's Bay Company and sent to what is now western Montana. They settled among the Salish Indians in Red Willow Valley—what is now called the Bitterroot Valley—after being driven from the Northern Plains by the Blackfeet in the 1870s, where they eventually settled among the Salish Indians and intermarried. The Salish had been driven out of buffalo country by the Blackfeet and ravaged by European diseases such as measles and smallpox and were desperate for help. Gathered around the campfires with their wives and in-laws the Iroquois spoke about white men in long black robes who seemed to have a direct line to a supernatural power. The Salish were willing to try anything to restore their health and hunting grounds and jumped at the Iroquois' offer to travel west to find one of these white shamans and bring him back.

Although De Smet described these men as "good" Iroquois he was thinking about a favorite story of martyr-crazy Jesuits involving some "bad" Iroquois. In the 1640s they were alleged to have tortured, murdered, and eaten six French Black Robes in Canada. When Gaucher and La Mousse pleaded in French for the Jesuits to visit the Salish, De Smet penned a letter to his superior in St. Louis urging him to comply with their request and sent them with it down the Missouri. Soon after their visit De Smet finally had to admit that St. Joseph's was a failure. He blamed liquor. "What can we do in the midst of 2,000 drunks?" he wrote, before heading back to St. Louis in February 1840.

Meanwhile, the Iroquois had met with the bishop of St. Louis, who agreed to supply the Salish with a Black Robe. The man he chose to travel the 1,600 miles to Montana was Pierre-Jean De Smet. After a reconnaissance mission in 1840 and De Smet returned west the next year with two other Jesuits. In 1841, financed by cash from a fundraising trip to New Orleans, De Smet and two other Jesuits founded St. Mary's Mission in the Red Willow Valley. He called their venture a "reduction," referring to the *reduccione* system established in the 1600s by Spanish Jesuits in South America that plucked native people from their villages and force them to work in walled compounds. Before anything else the priests cut down a swath of cottonwood and erected a cross. Then they built a few low, crude shacks, one of which was their church. But the goal of St. Mary's wasn't quality construction, it was the replacement of native spirituality with Christianity, and bison hunting with vegetable gardening. The Jesuits were keenly aware that Presbyterian and Methodist missionaries had been sniffing around tribes in the Pacific Northwest. In fact, in 1834 an uncle and nephew team of Methodists had tried their luck with the Salish. But because they didn't fit the Iroquois' description of the Black Robes in either appearance or practice they were rebuffed and soon moved on to look for another place to harvest souls in Indian Country. This bitter competition in the Lord's Vineyard would influence the development of the boarding school system throughout its existence. De Smet reported to his superiors in 1845 that "Protestant ministers of doubtful morals had traversed the country defaming Black Robes." While Protestant missionaries sought to turn Indians into confected, god-fearing, English-speaking White people with jobs and houses the Jesuits were more interested in Christian Indians—at least in the beginning of the Indian boarding school era—whether they retained their language, clothing, and industry or not.

De Smet's primary goal was to add the trappings of Catholicism to Salish religious practice, not a difficult task because the form of their rituals was not much different than those of the Church. Hymns were added to native songs, the symbolic purification symbolized by the smoke from burning incense was added to the cleansing smoke of smoldering sweetgrass, and prayers to Jesus and God were added to supplications offered to guardian spirits and the Great Spirit. For the Salish the most potent Christian liturgy was baptism. Although no more than words and water, the exorcism of sin represented by the practice echoed the physical and spiritual cleansing offered by the sweat lodge and the dousing in a cold stream that followed a righteous sweat. The difference was that the Salish didn't believe in sin and had no use for the concepts of heaven and hell. While praising the Salish for their honesty, politeness, hospitality, and amiable natures, he dismissed their native spirituality because it wasn't directed by the Roman Catholic's "one, true Church." He never bothered to learn more than a smattering of Salish words and was contemptuously ignorant of other Native tongues, one of the many reasons he failed to achieve his dream of founding a mission among the Sioux.

Although the Salish added some Catholic rituals to their lives they were uninterested in Christian morality and balked when the Jesuits demanded that they abandon their old ways. De Smet railed against polygamy, choosing to ignore the fact that a man who could attract multiple wives was respected for his prowess and was often a highly skilled hunter who needed more than one woman to process the game he brought home, a team who shared the hunter's wealth. He was bewildered by the high rate of divorce among Indians, who "often part for the most frivolous reasons." He found the elaborate ceremonies surrounding the smoking of the pipe laughable, failing to understand that this ritual established a line of communication between human beings and the spirit world. And he was horrified by the "barbarous custom of abandoning the old and the sick pitilessly to the ferocious beasts of the desert, as soon as they begin to be in the way in their hunting expeditions." De Smet further meddled in Salish culture by attempting to wean the Indians from gambling, polygamy, and bison hunting, insisting that they learn how to be farmers and carpenters. At St. Mary's he convinced Salish shamans to throw their medicine bundles into a hole and abandon what he called their "superstitions." But his biggest mistake with the Salish was his attempt to convert their enemies.

In 1846 he embarked on a foray into bison country intending to convert the Blackfeet or at least chalk up a few baptisms, convince them to leave his beloved Christian Salish in peace and consider uniting with them in alliance. For decades the Blackfeet had slaughtered Salish who ventured onto the prairie to hunt and had boldly invaded Salish territory in the Rocky Mountains to steal their women and horses. The Blackfeet he met with were not interested in Christianity but they believed that the recent success of the Salish in battle was due to some kind of "great medicine" the Black Robes had shared with them, a power the Blackfeet could use to take more scalps and steal more horses. The Salish believed that De Smet had betrayed them by sharing this force with their enemies.

In 1850 the Red Willow Salish finally rejected De Smet and his promises about Christianity. Referring to the traders, wolfers, and trappers seeping into Red Willow, the Indians confronted the Jesuits on what would be the final Easter they celebrated at St. Mary's. "You told us the religion of the whites would make us better men, yet the whites we see are worse than we are." Some Salish believed that because the Jesuits could not make a living anywhere else they had come west to sponge off the tribe. After one of the Jesuits failed to heal a dying tribal member other Salish spread the rumor that the Black Robes were trying to kill them off so they could steal their land. Faced with increasing hostility the Jesuits abandoned St. Mary's and leased it for $250 to a White trader named Major John Owen, even though the mission was built on Salish land. After they left, their church was burned to the ground by an unknown arsonist. De Smet tried his luck again in 1854, when he founded St. Ignatius Mission sixty miles north of St. Mary's. The objects of his spiritual fervor this time were other Salish-speaking tribes.

Despite his failure at St. Mary's De Smet had captured the attention of the U.S. government. In 1857 a pair of Indian agents, Cumming and Vaughan, suggested that the Jesuits establish a permanent mission to serve as a colonial outpost where the Blackfeet could be "Christianized." The Blackfeet called themselves The Lords of the Plains. They were enemies of anyone who ventured into what they claimed as their territory. They not only fought against the Salish, but with the Crow, the Assiniboine, and the Shoshone. Knowing this, the agents figured that it would be cheaper and far less dangerous to pacify the Blackfeet with Christianity than to attempt to exterminate them in battle, especially if it were European Jesuits such as De Smet and not American bureaucrats doing the pacification. De Smet lobbied the Vatican for a mission among the Blackfeet and was rewarded with the establishment of St. Peter's in 1859. It would be forced to move three times before its final iteration under the Bird Tail.

In 1851 De Smet met for the second time with the Sioux to plead for peace. This time he was serving the United States government in its campaign to pacify the Northern Plains tribes, which were increasingly unhappy with the waves of White settlers crossing Indian land. Families on their way to farm in Oregon, prospectors heading to California for the gold, and Mormons fleeing to Utah with their cattle were exploiting food and fuel claimed by Indians. Violence was inevitable. In 1846 De Smet had been relieved of his duties as a missionary because the Vatican believed he exaggerated his stories of converting legions of Indians, and that he made promises to them the Church could not keep. He was transferred back to St. Louis University, where he was assigned to raise funds and distribute them to the missions among the western tribes. He found the work monotonous and frustrating, the same old thing day after day as he tried to put money in all the hands reaching out for it. So when he was asked by the superintendent of Indian affairs to attend a peace conference bringing together White agents and Plains tribes De Smet jumped at the chance.

In September 10,000 Native people gathered at Horse Creek in what is now western Nebraska to hear the United States promise that the Indians could keep all their land if they allowed settlers to pass safely through it. Each tribe would get $50,000 a year in goods for fifty years if they would allow the government to build forts and roads and stop fighting with one another. For eleven days De Smet used his reputation as a colonist whose word they could trust to convince the chiefs to put their marks on what would be known as the Horse Creek Treaty. Twenty-one of them signed for the Indian nations, which included the Sioux, Cheyenne, Crow, Arapaho, Assiniboine, Mandan, Gros Ventre, and Arikara. Some Métis people asked for a land allotment as well, but didn't get anything, despite De Smet's argument that land was "the sole means of preserving union among all those wandering and scattered families, which become every year more and more numerous." Always eager to prepare Indian souls for a White heaven he baptized more than 1,100 natives, most of them children. And because he knew more about the geography of the Northern Plains than any other colonist he was pressed into service drawing a map showing which tribe would be assigned to which territory (although the Blackfeet did not attend the conference they were relegated to a hunk of what is now Montana northwest of Crow land). It's likely that without De Smet the government would have failed to make a deal and the inevitable White invasion of the Plains would have stalled.

Despite De Smet's efforts to co-opt the Indians into compliance, the treaty soon disintegrated. Congress reduced the terms of the U.S. commitment to supply annuities from fifty years to ten. A number of payments never materialized or were delivered to some tribes and not others. By 1851 the 50,000 settlers heading every year to the West Coast were sapping Indigenous resources the government had promised to protect. They killed increasingly scarce bison and game, and their cattle devoured grass. The tribes began fighting with each other over hunting grounds, most notably incursions by the Sioux into Crow land, which finally forced the Absaroka to retreat north and west. In 1854 near Fort Laramie, Wyoming a Sicangu Lakota warrior killed a stray cow owned by Mormons traveling on the Oregon Trail. In violation of the Horse Creek Treaty twenty-nine soldiers under the command of a hot-headed second lieutenant named John Grattan forced their way into a camp of some 5,000 Lakota, intending to arrest the man. It would be Grattan's first and last encounter with the Lakota. A nervous solder fired a shot, hitting an Indian. Led by Red Cloud, warriors killed Grattan and eleven of his soldiers. The other eighteen fled on foot but would not get very far. They were chased down and killed by warriors led by Spotted Tail.

In 1868 De Smet was back at the bargaining table with the Sioux Nation for a third time. Now a tool of the federal government, he had been asked by the Secretary of the Interior to convince Sitting Bull to sign the Fort Laramie Treaty. In June of that year, suffering from kidney disease, the old Jesuit sat in the sweltering heat on the banks of the Powder River in Montana with the famous Hunkpapa chief, eighty other war chiefs and Black Moon, a leader of the Miniconju band of Lakota. Five thousand Sioux witnessed the meeting. De Smet told them through his interpreter that what God wanted was peace among His children. Because peace was pleasing to Him the Powder River chiefs should sign the treaty, which he said would get them what they wanted. What Sitting Bull wanted was no more forts on the Bozeman Trail, no more gold miners trespassing on tribal land, and no more reservations. Because of their adamant distrust of the government he and Black Moon refused to sign the treaty and never felt obligated by its provisions. Eight years later they stood together at the Little Big Horn when Custer was killed. But reflecting the decentralized organization of Sioux leadership, Red Cloud, Spotted Tail, and other chiefs reluctantly decided to give peace another chance.[21]

Chapter Eight

THE LONG WALK

U nder U.S. President Grant's 1868 Peace Policy, which paid Christian missionaries to indoctrinate Native people, the Navajo Reservation was awarded to the Presbyterians. That same year they established a mission and a school at Fort Defiance just north of Window Rock in what is now Arizona. But the Diné (Navajo) people had no use for them and the missionaries abandoned their effort two years later. They moved to the Phoenix area and tried to sell their wares to Mexicans. Next up to bat in the early 1890s were the Baptists, Methodists, and Episcopalians, of which all three denominations at least temporarily abandoned their campaigns. Neither in school nor in church did the Diné embrace any Christian messages about Jesus, private property, monogamy, or individualism. A Baptist minister and his wife wrote that the Navajo possessed "scarcily any more knowledge of the laws of our government or the laws of God than the people of Afganistan." A Methodist missionary wrote that "no heathen country of which I read is more heathenish than these Navajo." Their religious practices, he continued, "show them to be entirely ignorant of God, and the light of Christianity."[1] A Presbyterian minister described the site of the mission he had been ordered to establish as nothing more than "sagebrush and rattlesnakes."[2]

During the 1800s, Diné government operated by consensus. Most decisions were made by matrilineal clans whose members were bound together by kinship ties. Although there were leaders—both men and women—who achieved their status through their speaking ability, knowledge of rituals, or ownership of sheep and horses, they could influence these decisions but they were not empowered to speak for all Diné or tell others what to do. A mother owned the dwelling, called a hogan, shared ownership with her husband of the livestock and the garden, and was often the head of her clan. She also owned the loom she used to weave wool into rugs, which by 1900 she sold to tourists. This decentralized, egalitarian organization—in one degree or another common to many tribal nations—was something the male-dominated and hierarchical Spanish and later the Americans found hard to understand. Their common refrain was, *who's in charge, here?* Diné spirituality revolved, and still revolves, around an intricate pantheon of gods, including the sun and the moon. And daily life was guided by a complex philosophy called *Hózhó*, which informs both a lifestyle and a state of mind. Hózhó emphasizes that "humans have the ability to be self-empowered through responsible thought, speech, and behavior. Likewise, Hózhó acknowledges that humans can self-destruct by thinking, speaking, and behaving irresponsibly."[3]

Despite the failures and false starts of the Protestants, in 1895 Joseph Stephan, the director of the Bureau of Catholic Indian Missions, approached Katharine Drexel with the idea of establishing a presence among the Navajo. She paid approximately $365,000 (in the currency of 2024) for a 240-acre ranch in an area known as La Cienega Amarilla, a mile outside the western border of the reservation. None of the male Catholic orders Stephan approached to staff the new venture were much interested until Drexel visited the Cincinnati province of Franciscans and twisted arms. Finally, in 1898, three Franciscan fathers arrived at the La Cienega mission, which she had christened St. Michael's. They would soon learn why the Protestants found their efforts to convert the Diné a waste of time.

First, simply finding them was a challenge. Although there were as many as 25,000 seminomadic Diné spread across a reservation the size of West

Virginia they were often on the move, herding their sheep from one grazing patch to another. There were no trains and only a few rough trails. While their economy was based on gardens and sheep they also engaged in raids on other tribes, including the Utes and the Pueblo people, to take food, material goods, and captives, which they sold. They had never been defeated by the U.S. Army, but there had been frequent skirmishes with the colonizers during the decade before the Civil War. This included an attack by 2,000 warriors against the army garrison stationed at Fort Defiance, which the military repelled with cannon fire. After Confederate troops advanced into New Mexico during the Civil War the U.S. used the incursion as an excuse to move the Diné into camps, ostensibly for their own protection. The Indian agent warned them that if they didn't comply they would be treated as enemies. After rebel forces were driven out of the territory the Diné continued raiding settlers and other tribes. Finally, in 1863 Colonel Kit Carson was ordered to demand the surrender of the Navajo. When none of them showed up he directed a scorched earth campaign to destroy their economy, murder them, and drive them into submission.

Between 1863 and 1866 9,000 Diné were marched at gunpoint in some fifty groups to a forty-square-mile internment camp called Bosque Redondo in what is now New Mexico. The government intended to turn them into sedentary farmers whose children would be coerced into BIA schools and converted to Christianity. Some 200 died on what they called The Long Walk, which ranged in distance between 250 to 450 miles, depending on which route from Fort Defiance the army chose for each removal. In 1868 the so-called Navajo wars ended when Manuelito and other Diné leaders put their mark on a contract similar to the Fort Laramie Treaty of 1868. Under its terms the Navajo would cease raiding settlers, would not attack wagon trains or railroads, and would agree to send their children to schools provided by the government. The government promised to give the tribe seeds, 15,000 sheep and goats, 500 head of cattle, some money, and 160 acres of land for each family. The Navajo Reservation would consist of some 5,500 square miles but excluded some of the best land for farming and grazing, which had been confiscated by White settlers during the Bosque

Redondo internment. In June 1868 some 8,000 Diné men, women and children began the long walk home in a column that stretched for ten miles and included 2,000 sheep and 1,000 horses. This was one of the rare occasions when the government allowed a tribe to return to its ancestral homeland after being removed. The government, of course, never completely lived up to its promise to supply the tribe with subsidies. While the Long Walk cemented ties between formerly separated bands it magnified the distrust and animosity the Diné felt for American colonists.

The other major problem for the missionaries was the issue of *Diné bizaad*, the Navajo's difficult, unwritten tongue. This is a tone language in which the pitch of a word can change its meaning. It also includes several consonants not found in English, and the verb is spoken at the end of the sentence. Because it was considered impolite to address someone by their name (because names have special powers), a fourth pronoun case was used, as opposed to the three cases used in English. Although some Diné spoke Spanish very few of them knew any English. So the Franciscans saw that to harvest souls and recruit students they would have to learn Diné bizaad. To that end they set out to devise a written version of the language. With the help of two interpreters the priests plowed through *Webster's Dictionary of the American Language* and a Montgomery Ward mail-order catalog, assigning a code they fabricated to items the two cultures shared in common.[4] They would later publish a Navajo dictionary and a vocabulary, printed and bound at St. Michael's. The books, the printing press, and their salaries were paid for by Drexel. In the 1940s one of priests released a four-volume treatise titled *Learning Navajo*.[5]

Their immediate tasks, however, were constructing buildings, planting a garden, and digging a well. A structure of a thousand square feet, whose original owner had envisioned it as a trading post, was remodeled so it could be used as the mission. The interior adobe walls were plastered, chimneys built, and the single room was divided into six rooms. In 1899 the mission opened a day school that was initially housed in a log cabin. Filling it with students was the next hurdle. Diné elders believed that government boarding schools rendered their children unfit for life on the reservation.

In 1882 a prominent war chief named Manuelito agreed to send to the Carlisle Indian Industrial School his sons—Manuelito Chiquito, twenty, and Manuelito Chonihis, fifteen—and a nephew the school renamed Tom Torlino. Nine months after the younger son arrived in Pennsylvania he died of tuberculosis. Enraged, his father demanded that all dozen Diné children sent to Carlisle be returned immediately. Pratt consented to send only the older brother home. But he died seven days after arriving in Arizona, also of tuberculosis. [6]

Most tribal parents hated the three government schools on the reservation as much as they hated Carlisle. Children were taken from their families and kept in these institutions for months or even years. The most loathsome of these was the Bureau of Indian Affairs boarding school at Fort Defiance eight miles north of St. Michael's. Parents believed that the teachers and administrators were hostile or indifferent to their children and cared nothing about Diné culture or language. And after a diphtheria outbreak they worried about the health of their sons and daughters. Tensions between the government and the tribe hit a boiling point in 1902 near an imposing red sandstone monolith called Round Rock. The government's over-zealous Indian field agent had called for a meeting of Diné at a trading post in the area so he could order them to give up their children to the Fort Defiance school, which was sixty miles south. He showed up with two interpreters and a contingent of tribal police. Some fifty Diné, led by a war chief named Black Horse, had assembled to tell the agent that his people had no intention of surrendering their kids. If push came to shove they had hidden their rifles a quarter-mile away. When the agent ignored Black Horse's demands he tried pleading, but the agent was adamant. At a signal from Black Horse "the Agent was surrounded by the Indians, who took hold of him, threw him to the ground, trampled upon him, broke his nose, and made him a sad and sorrowful sight." [7] One of the Diné had drawn his knife and another his axe but because of the crush of men surrounding the fallen agent they couldn't get close enough to finish the job. Finally, the police came to the rescue. Barricaded inside the trading post they spent the night waiting for the Diné to make their next move. The next morning they accepted the agent's apology. He was reprimanded by the BIA and replaced with another agent. Not a single child from Black Horse's band ever stepped foot inside the Fort Defiance school, which operated until 1959, when it was closed because of fire hazards in its dormitories.

After the 1879 arrival of the first railroad in Arizona the border towns around the reservation began to fill with Americans, compelling the Diné to interact with them. Drexel met with tribal members to convince them that their children would be safe at St. Michael's, and would be provided the curriculum that families wanted, including training in harness making, carpentry, wagon construction, shoemaking, and silver smithing. Of course, there would also be arithmetic, English language instruction, geography, U.S. history, and indoctrination in Christianity. She laid on a feast and attended Diné ceremonies, even going so far as eating peyote during a nine-day healing ritual called the Mountain Chant. Because the government boarding schools had angered them by taking away their children Drexel promised the parents that they could visit their kids at St. Michael's any time they wanted, and the mission would provide accommodations for the visitors and hay for their horses.[8] She also invited several children and their families to visit St. Catherine's Mission, a boarding school she opened in Santa Fe in 1886 and staffed with nuns from the order she founded, the Sisters of the Blessed Sacrament.

For members of the Franciscan order, St. Michael's was not their first rodeo in Navajoland. Beginning in the 1540s waves of Spanish soldiers, settlers, and friars flooded into what is now New Mexico and Arizona, killing and enslaving Pueblo people, a collective term for several tribes that included the Hopi, Taos, Acoma, and Zuni. Attempting to suppress Native spirituality, the Franciscans outlawed the Kachina rituals of the Pueblo, and burned prayer sticks, effigies, and the masks worn by dancers during these ceremonies. In 1680 the Pueblos revolted, driving the Spanish south along the Rio Grande River toward Mexico, and capturing Santa Fe, the largest village in the region. During the fighting 400 colonists and twenty-one priests were killed. The Spaniards returned in force twelve years later, and by the year 1700 colonists, missionaries, and soldiers had subdued the

Pueblo people. The Franciscans made a few attempts to convert the Diné after the rebellion, but until the establishment of St. Michel's in 1898 they had no success setting up a permanent mission.

It's not known what the Franciscans at St. Michael's learned from the 1680 Pueblo Rebellion, if anything, but they were determined to avoid alienating the Diné by trying to force Catholicism down their throats. After studying the language they "preached in Navajo, instructed the children in the Navajo language, wrote catechisms in Navajo, translated parts of the Bible into Navajo, and used the Navajo language on a daily basis when interacting with the Navajos, many of whom did not understand English."[9] Co-opting Diné spirituality required that in order to understand the religion they would have to understand the language. The Diné, for example, had no linguistic equivalents for Catholic concepts such as "the Soul, Supreme Being, Responsibility, Sin, Punishment, Reward, Eternity, Heaven, Hell and a host of others."[10] Unlike the government campaigns at Carlisle, Haskell, and Chemawa to erase Native culture the Franciscans missionaries were fishing for souls, not simulated Americans. They soon learned that they would have little or no success converting the adults, so they concentrated on the children.

In 1902 a boarding school at St. Michael's was opened to replace the failed day school. The Franciscans reasoned that because parents were required to transport their children to and from the classroom, which because of the distances took more time than they were willing spend, a school where the children were fed, clothed, and sheltered for relatively long periods would be more appealing. A dozen Sisters of the Blessed Sacrament traveled from their "motherhouse" near Philadelphia to staff it. Before they arrived workers hurriedly built a roof over the five rooms in the adobe house the nuns would occupy and spread Rough On Rats arsenic throughout the buildings at St. Michael's to poison the burgeoning rodent population. In November workers covered a Studebaker farm wagon with a canopy and hooked up a team of horses to it. Then an American friar name Anselm Webber and his interpreter set forth to bring back the first shipment of Diné children to St. Michael's. Since arriving in Arizona in 1898 Webber had spent much of his time in the saddle trying to convince the tribe to send its sons and daughters to the Mission. Because he had been given vague assurances from people living in the Red Rock area ninety miles north of St. Michael's he decided to cast his first line there. He had eight days to go before the boarding school opened. Like the foolhardy Ursulines who freighted that wagon load of Piegan girls through the snow to St. Peter's Mission the same year, Webber cared more about saving the souls of native children than he did about their physical safety. November low temperatures in the desert routinely dropped below freezing and blizzards could hit at any moment. The Diné he finally met with agreed to enroll some of their children at St. Michael's after Webber made it clear that the decision was theirs to make, not the government's. And he agreed to let parents and relatives accompany him and his "precious cargo" to the Mission. Finally, he packed twenty-one children into his prairie schooner. They climbed a snowy mountain pass so steep the children were unloaded and made to walk. Then they crossed an ice sheet and were caught in the open desert during a blizzard. Four days after leaving their homes in Red Rock the children arrived at St. Michael's "half-frozen."

Like the arrival of Piegan children at St. Peter's, what greeted the Diné at St. Michael's was a stone fortress. Constructed of red sandstone blocks quarried nearby, it was three stories tall with dormers inserted in its hipped roof. Two wings were separated by a corridor. On one side was the dining hall for children, another dining hall for their families when they visited, a kitchen, a bakery, a coal house, and the boys' dormitory with bathrooms. The shorter wing housed the girls' dormitory, classrooms, a chapel, an infirmary, a laundry, and a sewing room. Drexel had paid a Minneapolis contractor the equivalent of $2.5 million to construct this building in the unadorned neoclassical style popular at the turn of the century. During the school's first year fifty-six Diné children were enrolled, thirty-six of them boys. The curriculum was the standard boarding school dogma holding that what was best for Indians was a half day of academics and a half day of work and "industrial" training five days a week.

In the mornings the nuns taught aspects of the English language to grades one through four, with some perfunctory science, U.S. history, geography, and music thrown in. Since these women had little or no training as teachers, and lectured in English to children who did not speak English, it's unlikely their students learned much of anything. When it was time for lessons in Christianity the Franciscan friars who spoke Diné bizaad came to the classroom to teach from a Catholic catechism they had translated into Diné bizaad. This featured simplistic questions and answers intended to be memorized, such as: "What is the chief end of man? To glorify God and enjoy Him forever!" Unlike the odious government schools such as the one at Fort Defiance, St. Michael's allowed the children to speak with one another in their native tongue. After lunch the girls were shown how to perform the tasks of the domestic servants White Americans hoped they would become. This included cooking, baking, sewing, house cleaning, and laundering. St. Michael's was unique for including traditional Diné rug weaving in its program. And a Diné woman was brought in to teach the girls how to weave baskets, although both of these were skills girls learned from their mothers and grandmothers.

After lunch the boys were shown how to make shoes. And because they were expected to become sedentary farmers who sold crops they were also shown how to plant, cultivate, irrigate, and harvest the Euro-American way. But the Diné, like many tribes from the Southwest to the Northeast, had been growing "The Three Sisters" for thousands of years. This nutritious and spiritually charged trio was beans, maize, and squash grown as companions close to one another in the same plot. The beans were planted at the base of the maize stalks, which provided a trellis for their vines. The nitrogen fixed by the roots of the beans fertilized the soil, nurturing the squash, which shaded the corn and the beans with its large leaves. Some tribes also planted a fourth sister—sunflowers—to distract pests and attract pollinators. Differing from the Protestant missions, the school year at St. Michael's ran from November through August in order to allow children to help out with the annual late summer harvest.

In 1903 a St. Michael's nun named Sister Angelista reported to the Commissioner of Indian Affairs that her Navajo children were "generally morally good, cheerful and industrious." She wrote that they are "intellectually above the average Indian," and if they could speak English they could be as accomplished in the classroom as White children. Because they are "great mimics," she continued "care should be taken to place before them the highest ideals if we wish to make of them good Americans."[11] Enrollment at St. Michael's increased to ninety-four in 1905, 125 in 1908 and 157 in 1910. The school added grade five and a sort of preschool grade for beginners. The nuns added dress-making to the girls' curriculum and showed them how to cook White American food along with lessons in table-setting and serving. Although the school's capacity was 150, in 1915 there were 154 children enrolled. Two years later enrollment grew to 200, leading to overcrowding. The following year Drexel provided money to construct a new building and expand the boys' dormitory. By 1907 she had spent $4.6 million in today's currency on buildings, salaries and supplies for the Mission, and would continue to pump money into the conversion campaign.

Because of the school's perceived inroads among the Diné the Protestants decided to get back in the game. In 1901 the Presbyterians began sniffing around for a site where they could establish a Mission and a school. A businessman named John Lorenzo Hubbell urged them to locate near his trading post outside the village of Ganado twenty-five miles west of St. Michael's. Offering the Christians a piece of his own land, he figured that the school and medical facility they intended to build would benefit his family and employees and attract more people to the area, which would be good for business. Hubbell had tried to convince the Franciscans to build their Mission at Ganado, but the site they chose for St. Michael's had better water and grazing resources. The Interior Department awarded the Presbyterians 160 acres of Diné land, and a site two miles north of Hubbell's Trading Post was selected for the new Mission.

They hired a young minister and his wife, Charles and Alice Bierkemper, as missionaries. Their attempts at evangelizing the Diné had mixed results. An old woman Bierkemper was trying to convert was warned by her relatives that if she joined his church they would poison her. She had listened so much to White people, they said, that their "devil had gotten into her." A minister who joined the Ganado mission in 1914 wrote that "Preaching to the Navajo is like preaching to a jackrabbit. You first have to run him down, talk to him, turn him loose, then pray that you may someday find him again."[12] Like most Protestant missionaries the Presbyterians believed that the Diné were depraved because they spoke an unintelligible language, wore strange clothes, ate strange food, engaged in heathen rites, and were doomed to damnation because they had not accepted the Gospel.[13] They were so certain that tribal people existed in unredeemed degradation that they denounced all native practices without ever examining them.[14] "Navahoes are a religious people," one missionary allowed, "albeit their religion is false."[15] Unlike the Franciscans at St. Michael's the Presbyterians made little effort to speak Diné bizaad, which hampered their conversion campaign. Yet they remained militant in their efforts to erase Diné spirituality, economy, and culture as soon as possible. This is in contrast to the theory and practice at St. Michael's, which emphasized that the conversion of the Diné to Catholicism was the first and highest goal and would eventually lead to their incorporation into Euro-America society. In 2024, however, less than three percent of enrolled members of the Navajo Nation identify as Catholics.

A few families allowed their children to sit in on the classes Alice Bierkemper offered. As an inducement she showed them how to use her sewing machine. By 1910 her school boasted twenty students. Two years later the Ganado mission opened a boarding school, enrolling ten Diné boys and twenty girls, who slept on separate floors in the dormitory building. Using the prevailing Indian school template they attended class in the church five mornings a week and worked in the fields and household during the afternoons. Meanwhile, the childless Bierkempers adopted a Diné orphan boy, cut his hair, dressed him in little sailor suits, taught him English, and trotted him out to impress visitors with the child's remarkable transformation.

In 1912, after they were transferred for unknown reasons to Washington State, the Presbyterians replaced them with Clarence Platt and his wife. During the year of their arrival half of the students at Ganado were hospitalized. Fearing that their children would catch one of the prevailing reservation diseases such as trachoma, tuberculosis, or measles they were not allowed to play with Diné children. By 1912 trachoma among tribes in the Southwest had become epidemic. The disease was transmitted at Indian schools by flies and through the shared use of towels. A doctor reported that "It has been the bringing together in close contact in the schools of children with the disease who under the old system of tribal life led a more or less isolated existence and consequently were less likely to give the disease to others."[16] Public health authorities determined that at least one-quarter of the Diné population was afflicted with what at the time was called "Indian sore eye." Of the 121 children examined in 1912 at St. Michael's boarding school seventeen were found to be suffering from the disease.[17]

Trachoma is caused by the *Chlamydia trachomatis* bacterium, which produces granular bumps on the inside of the eyelid that can scar the cornea and cause blindness. It is most common in hot, dry climates such as that of the Southwest. The Navajo began suffering from the disease only after they were confined to the reservation, and it became epidemic largely because the government crowded Native children into unhealthy classrooms and dormitories. Some of the treatments for the disease were gruesome. One was called grattage, after the French word for scratching. The bumps were scraped off the inner eyelid in a painful, bloody procedure made only marginally more bearable by the eventual application of topical cocaine. Another method was to scour the eye with copper sulphate, a caustic chemical also called blue stone. These tortures were abandoned when the antibacterial drug sulfanilamide was introduced by a doctor in 1938.

In 1913 health authorities reported that more than 8 percent of the Navajo were infected with tuberculosis, and 5 percent of their children in boarding schools, a relatively low figure reflecting the fact that tubercular children were excluded from these institutions (in the coming decades, however, the disease would become rampant). However, one Arizona boarding school reported that a third of its students who left school after coming down with TB were dead from the disease within a decade. It was widely believed until the 1930s that Indians "are far more susceptible to tuberculosis than are the White races of mankind." This supremacist notion was rooted in the belief that Caucasian bodies and Indigenous bodies were somehow different organisms. By mid-century that belief had been totally debunked by medical workers, who cited unsanitary water supplies, bad diet, and general poverty as the underlying conditions that lead to TB epidemics. "Tuberculosis is simply a contagious disease," a team of epidemiologists concluded in 1947. "Wherever it is permitted to exist, it spreads to all races of people."[18]

However, that enlightenment did nothing to improve the staggering health problems among the Diné. On the Navajo Reservation in 1947 the death rate from tuberculosis was ten times that of the general population of the United States.[19] In the 1950s two new antibiotics, streptomycin and isoniazid, were used to neutralize Mycobacterium tuberculosis, the TB bacterium. As the drugs became more widely available the epidemic was slowed considerably.

A Diné woman named Annie Dodge Wauneka was also instrumental in the campaign against TB. In 1918 at the age of eight she was sent away to the BIA boarding school at Fort Defiance. That was the year the reservation and the whole planet were besieged by influenza. Although she came down with a mild case many of her classmates died. During her fourth-grade year the school became infested with trachoma. In an effort to quarantine the malady the government sent children free of infection to other schools, which in turn sent their infected children to Fort Defiance. She was moved to nearby St. Michael's, where four years earlier Anselm Webber had avoided a single case of influenza in his school by allowing no one in and no one out (although the third and final wave of the disease in 1919 struck down a number of children). It's unknown if she was influenced by the lessons in Christianity the nuns taught, but she became a practicing Catholic later in life as well as beginning each day with the Diné ritual of prayer and a sprinkling of corn pollen. Beginning in the sixth grade, she was shipped to the Albuquerque Indian School in New Mexico, where she left after the eleventh grade. She married, gave birth to nine children, and earned a college degree from the University of Arizona in public health.

She honed her political skills while accompanying her influential father, Henry Chee Dodge, to meetings of the Navajo Business Council, which in 1922 had elected him as its first chairman. In 1951 she became one of the first women elected to the council. She devoted her significant energy to the fight against TB by encouraging tribal people who got sick to get medical treatment and to stay in the hospital until they were cured. This was a struggle because the Diné were leery of White medicine and hospital stays that kept them away from their gardens and livestock. She approached the problem by suggesting that while doctors were treating them with antibiotics traditional medicine makers could administer their herbal remedies, as well. She traveled ceaselessly from one side of the reservation to the other, dressed in traditional Diné clothing, including a colorful shawl and silver jewelry. Her efforts paid off. By 1970 tuberculosis infections had fallen 35 percent. She is credited with saving the lives of 2,000 TB patients. And she convinced 20,000 Diné to get screened for the disease. In 1963 President Kennedy chose her to receive the Congressional Medal of Freedom.[20]

—⁓—

Although the Church of Jesus Christ of Latter-day Saints (LDS) never established a boarding school on Dinétah (the Navajo Nation) it pursued Diné souls as avidly as any of the other denominations. Mormons recruited Navajo children, baptized them, placed them in foster homes, and enrolled them not in reservation boarding or day schools, but in White public schools. During the summer they were returned to their biological families. The Mormons called their campaign the Lamanite Placement Program. According to the LDS origin story, in 600 B.C.E. three Hebrew families sailed to America, where their descendants were divided into tribes and went their separate ways. The *Book of Mormon* holds that there are two types of Indian—Nephites, who are light-skinned and civilized, and Lamanites, who are "idle, savage, and bloodthirsty." God cursed the Lamanites with dark skin, but LDS doctrine maintained that by assimilating Indian children into Mormon culture and religion they could be "lightened," and their curse lifted.

Contact between Mormons and the Diné began in the 1860s with traders exchanging goods and Diné raiders stealing livestock from relatively bountiful Mormon farms in southern Utah. After relations improved the Mormons established a trading post on the Colorado River, bringing material benefits to the Navajo but also angering them because they located it on Diné territory without their permission. During the mid-1850s it was common for Mormons to buy Indian children from Mexican traders and Indigenous raiders, who had kept them as slaves. These bound children supplied the Mormons with free labor and were legally trapped as indentured servants for twenty years. Some of them were exchanged as gifts. Indian slavery in Utah was not abolished until 1862.

In 1875 the first Navajo converted to the LDS faith, but the Mormons were more interested in doing business with the Diné than converting them. They suspended their half-hearted proselytizing at the end of the nineteenth century, and it wasn't until 1942 that they established another Mormon mission. Based in Gallup, New Mexico, near the reservation's border, it offered classes in LDS religion, farming, and housekeeping. In 1947 a seventeen-year-old Diné girl named Helen John moved into an LDS household in Utah, which Mormons believe was the unofficial beginning of the Lamanite Placement Program. The official beginning came in 1954 when the church formally adopted the campaign and began sending swarms of missionaries and paid recruiters into Dinétah to sell parents and children on the benefits of living with White families, promising the Navajo "educational, spiritual, social, and cultural opportunities" they couldn't find on the reservation. Middle-class Mormon families who fostered Native children paid for their food, clothing, medical care, and school expenses. It's estimated that between 1947 and 2000 some 50,000 children from sixty tribes were "placed," most of them Diné. Some 5,000 Native children were living in Mormon homes in 1972.

Every autumn students were bused to processing centers in Utah and surrounding states, where they were fed, bathed, disinfected, and examined by medical personnel before being introduced to their foster families, who took them home and immersed them in Mormon culture and religion. Some of them were baptized in the LDS faith before they got on the bus, and some of them after they got off the bus. "Host families would joke that children came with wet hair," said Jessie Embry, a research professor at the LDS-owned Brigham Young University. "There are other stories about children not even knowing they were being baptized. The missionaries said, 'Come with me and I'll buy you a hamburger,' and then they were baptized." LDS leaders considered the program a success. Spencer Kimball, the chairman of the LDS Committee on Indian Relationships, claimed that the skin of Indians who had been placed were becoming lighter. "The day of the Lamanites is nigh," he wrote. "For years they have been growing delightsome, and they are now becoming white and delightsome, as they were promised . . . These young members of the Church are changing to whiteness and to delightsomeness." Kimball was fond of telling a story about a Navajo mother and father and their sixteen-year-old daughter, who had been "placed" in a Mormon family. It was evident, he said, that the girl "was several shades lighter than her parents—on the same reservation, in the same hogan, subject to the same sun and wind and weather." It wasn't until 2013 that the LDS church renounced this twaddle.[21] Many Native people believe that the program benefitted them. Children learned English and developed skills in classes that were not available on the reservations. And families struggling to make ends meet had one less mouth to feed. Joann Black, a Diné member, was placed with her first foster family in June 1973. She said she "loved being on placement" because she found opportunities she couldn't find on the reservation. "Being on the reservation is way different than being raised in the Anglo community. They have piano lessons, dance lessons, and things like that for their kids. But in our culture, we were lucky enough if we got to join a sport."[22] Most of the 500 Native students attending Brigham Young University in 1978 had been placed in Mormon households. According to a 1966 BIA press release, "One little, two little, three little Indians—and 206 more—are brightening the homes and lives of 172 American families, mostly non-Indians, who have taken the Indian waifs as their own."

In 2016 two Diné siblings who had been placed in Mormon homes filed suit against the LDS Church in Window Rock District Court on the Navajo Nation. They alleged that members of these families had sexually abused them. The brother, named in the suit as "RJ," was placed when he was ten years old and was removed from the household after he reported the abuse to missionaries. He was placed in one home and then another and claims he was abused in each one. His sister, named "MM" in the suit, said when she was eleven years old she was raped by an adult man, a friend of her foster family. During her junior and senior years she was placed with her brother in a home where she said in court documents that their foster father sexually molested her. According to the *Independent* newspaper, "'RJ' and 'MM' agreed the circumstances of their large family posed further difficulties. Their father was an alcoholic, 'RJ' said, and their 'desperately poor' mother put at least five of her twelve children in the placement program with the hope that they would get a good education and have a good life. According to 'RJ' and 'MM,' four of the children were abused in the program."[23]

A Diné boy identified as "X" recounted in legal filings that when he was in the fourth grade two men in ties and short-sleeved white shirts came to his parent's home on the Navajo Reservation in New Mexico. Speaking English, they convinced the family to enroll "X" in the Lamanite Placement Program. Because he spoke only Diné bizaad, he couldn't understand what was happening when he was sent to local LDS classes and baptized as a Mormon. The bus traveling from New Mexico to Utah was full of crying, screaming children. He was placed for two years in a Mormon home, and then transferred to another household, where he was treated like a servant while the couple's own children played games. Over time he was slapped, beaten, pushed down stairs, and whipped with a belt. The husband began sexually abusing him and threatened him with violence if "X" told the wife. When "X" appealed for help from a caseworker and a Boy Scout leader he was ignored.[24]

In 2018 "X" and more than a dozen other Diné who had sued the LDS church for sexual abuse accepted cash payments and signed nondisclosure agreements. But one woman refused to settle. Identified in a newspaper account as Bízhíníth baá—her Diné name—she claimed in court documents that when she was twelve years old her foster father raped her "three or four times a week." She appealed for help from a local leader of the LDS Relief Society but she was scolded, slapped, and warned to say nothing.[25] When she was sixty-five years old the church sent her a check but she returned it, claiming she intended to proceed with her lawsuit in order to hold the church publicly accountable. In 2019 the church countersued, arguing that she had agreed to settle, which she denied, saying that "a conversation with my husband is not a conversation with me." The church sought a resolution of the dispute in a Utah court, but her attorney maintained that the matter could only be resolved in a Navajo court.[26]

As Native-run schools improved in the 1970s and tribes began asserting their sovereignty, a rising chorus of voices in Indian Country accused the churches of acting like adoption agencies and demanded that missionary foster programs cease. At Congressional hearings called to hear testimony about the proposed 1978 Indian Child Welfare Act (ICWA) politicians learned that Indian children were placed away from their families at a rate twenty times that of non-Indian children. And that 85 percent of all Native children in foster care were living in non-Indian homes, even when they had fit and willing relatives.[27] White child welfare workers didn't understand that in many Indigenous societies children are raised by an extended family of parents, aunts, uncles, and grandparents. They saw a single woman struggling to care for her children and appealed to a state court to order the child removed. Many Native students in the program returned to their reservations in the summer feeling like they were outsiders. "There was a great deal of anger, a great deal of angst among Indian people about the Mormon Church's activities on the reservations that emerged during the development and passage of the Indian Child Welfare Act," according to attorney Bert Hirsch, who was the chief of staff for the Association of American Indian Affairs at the time. "They felt that their kids were being 'captured' and weren't being allowed to return to their families—not all of them, but enough that it became a big problem."

Because the church had labeled the program "educational placement" instead of "foster placement" it had lobbied against early drafts of the ICWA that would have required the church to follow federal law. At the hearings LDS Social Services Commissioner Harold C. Brown was asked about the refusal of the church to inform families where their children had been placed. He replied that the church would have "difficulties" in notifying the tribes as to the whereabouts of their children because tribes "would not know what to do with the information if it came." Finally, he added, Mormon parents had "a right to privacy and confidentiality." He was repeatedly heckled and booed during the proceedings by Native people.[28] President Jimmy Carter signed the ICWA in November 1978. It guaranteed that tribal courts would have complete jurisdiction over any custody proceedings involving Native children living on reservations. And it stipulated that if the tribal court decided a child should be removed from a home, preference for placement would be given to the extended family, another reservation family or at last resort a family on a different reservation. While this was a victory for tribal nations and reinforced the existing sovereignty of tribal courts, the law was passed only after Congress granted the LDS Church an exemption for its placement program. The sponsor of the bill, Senator James Abourezk of South Dakota, said that without exempting the church the strong Mormon lobby would have defeated the measure.[29]

In 2016 a Diné baby was taken from his mother after Texas child welfare authorities accused her of using drugs, and given to a White, Christian evangelical couple named Chad and Jennifer Brackeen. Citing the ICWA the Navajo Nation intervened and sought to place the child with a Diné family. A Texas judge agreed, but after the Brackeens appealed the decision the Diné family terminated the adoption process and the couple adopted the child. The tribe intervened again when the couple tried to adopt the boy's sister, as well. The Brackeens, two other foster couples and three states filed suit in federal court to overturn the ICWA on the grounds of racial discrimination. After a Texas district judge struck down the law, attacking the sovereignty of tribal nations, the case wound its way to the Supreme Court. On June 15, 2023, in a major victory for tribal rights, the Court in *Haaland v. Brackeen* upheld every aspect of the ICWA. The decision was 7 to 2, with Clarence Thomas and Samuel Alito dissenting. The boy is still living with the Brackeens, who are his legal guardians. In 2023 the couple was preparing to head back to court to legally adopt the girl.

Although the last Native children placed in foster homes graduated from high school in 2000, marking the end of the Lamanite Placement Program, and despite a plague of lawsuits, the LDS Church got some of what it wanted from the Diné. In 2024 about 20 percent of all enrolled tribal members identify as Mormons. And in 2024 there were twenty Mormon churches on the Navajo Nation.

During the boarding school era there were thirty schools operating on the Navajo Reservation and the smaller Hopi Reservation, whose territory is surrounded by that of Dinétah. The BIA schools were operated more like internment camps than learning institutions. In January 2023 a former student at the Kayenta Indian School named June Marie Wauneka shared her experiences there with Secretary of the Interior Haaland and Arizona Governor Katie Hobbs. The meeting was reported in the *Arizona Republic* by Arlyssa Becenti, a Diné journalist. "We had our hair cut," Wauneka said (a common surname among the Diné). "My grandma had taught us to have long hair and take care of it but it was cut off and that was the biggest thing that I thought was wrong," Wauneka said, remembering the day she and her three sisters arrived at Kayenta. "We couldn't talk Navajo to each other. We were forbidden to say Navajo words, and when we did, they got the soap and washed out our mouths." After she was bullied, forced to eat foreign food such as sauerkraut, and yelled at by dormitory supervisors, she and some friends ran away. "They found us and brought us back. The last time we ran away we were punished. They had us stand in line, put out our hands and they wanted to know who was the one that planned to run away. We all stood there and didn't want to tell on one another. We stood there and they had a big, long ruler and kept on hitting our hands." As the other students started to weep, Wauneka recalled, they were told to sit down. But she stood and took the whippings until her hands bled. "I said 'I can do this. I can take this. Pretty soon it was hurting so bad, the kids were saying 'Come on. Come on. Please sit down.' So finally I did."

Other former boarding school students shared their stories with Haaland. Marie Peterson lived with her family in a hogan in Black Mesa north of Phoenix. When she was eight or nine years old a BIA truck and a black police car with a white star painted on the door drove up. The Navajo cop informed the family in Diné bizaad that their children would be taken away to boarding school. "You have to put your fingerprints on this paper," he told Marie's parents. "If you refuse you will be arrested." Marie and her siblings were taken to the BIA's Albuquerque Indian School. Not long after arriving she was diagnosed with tuberculosis, and the diseased portion of her lung was removed. After she recuperated in a sanitarium for a year she and her siblings agreed to be relocated to the Chemawa Indian School in Oregon so they could be together again.

Along with his sister, Ernest Dick was sent to Chinle Boarding School on the reservation. "They said once we were in the building that's it, my parents didn't have control. It was very uncomfortable. When you talked in Navajo they washed your mouth out with yellow soap with a brush. But I still spoke Navajo." Dick said he hated the food, calling the peas they were fed "rabbit poop." The milk, he said, was usually spoiled, but they still had to drink it. There was no running water in the dorms. And because there were no toilets the children were forced to use buckets. In 1945 the Associated Press published a photo of Isabel Yazzie and Theresa Tully sleeping in a single tiny bed at Chinle. "Thirty-five Diné children sleep in a room intended for 10," the AP reported. "Sometimes as many as four are crowded into a single bed."[30]

Katharine Drexel. Photographer and date unknown. *Courtesy of Catholic Online.*

Louis Riel. Photo by William James Topley, circa 1875. *Courtesy of Library and Archives Canada.*

"Stagecoach Mary" Fields. Photographer and date unknown. *Courtesy Smithsonian National Postal Museum.*

General Richard Henry Pratt in full dress uniform with saber, 1899. Photo by John N. Choate. *Courtesy of the Cumberland County Historical Society, Carlisle, PA.*

Anthony Austin (right) and George Ell. Photo by John N. Choate, 1890. *Courtesy of the National Anthropological Archives, Smithsonian Institution.*

William Hazlett (standing) and Richard Sanderville. Photo by John N. Choate, 1891. *Courtesy of the National Anthropological Archives, Smithsonian Institution.*

(Above) To'Haali (Tom Torlino), a Diné student at Carlisle, photographed as he entered the school in 1882. (Facing page) Torlino as he appeared three years later. These images were published in John N. Choate's "Souvenir of the Carlisle Indian School." *Courtesy of the Cumberland County Historical Society.*

Richard Henry Pratt with twelve students soon after they arrived at Carlisle in 1882. Front row, left to right: Tom Torlino, George Williams, Manuelito Chonihis, Antoinette Williams, Charles Damon. Back row, left to right: Stailey Norcross, Manuelito Chiquito, Charlie, John Bitzclay (died in 1883), Francisco, Saahtlie (George Watchman), Benjamin Damon. Seated on the bandstand is Richard Pratt. Photo by John N. Choate. *Courtesy of the Cumberland County Historical Society.*

A studio photograph taken of the Diné group who entered Carlisle in 1882 after some time at the school. Two young boys seated in front: left, Charles Damon; right, George Williams. Front row, seated, left to right: Manuelito Chonihis, Charlie, Tom Torlino, Manuelito Chiquito, Antoinette Williams. Back row, standing, left to right, Saahtlie (George Watchman), Benjamin Damon, Francisco, Stailey Norcross. Photo by John N. Choate. *Courtesy of the Cumberland County Historical Society.*

Brockey (Charles Buck) and Spyna Devereaux. Photographer and date unknown. *Courtesy of the National Archives and Records Administration.*

The unwilling poster boy for Carlisle was a Diné man named Tom Torlino. When he arrived at the school in 1882 he was photographed in a studio setting wearing a traditional Navajo shoulder blanket, earrings, a necklace of silver regalia, and long, wild hair. Photographed again three years later, he was wearing a suit and tie and his hair was cropped and parted on one side. According to historians Barbara Landis and Richard Tritt of the Cumberland County Historical Society the lighting was manipulated to make his dark skin look much paler. Richard Pratt used these before-and-after images as propaganda to convince America that with the kind of education students such as Torlino were getting at Carlisle they could literally blend into White society. Torlino, whose Diné name was To'Haali, returned to Coyote Canyon in Dinétah and resumed his life as a sheep and cattle rancher, a racehorse breeder, and an influential medicine maker. According to the Sharlot Hall Museum in Arizona, when his uncle, Chief Manuelito, needed a letter written, he dictated it to Torlino. When Manuelito wanted help from the U.S. Army Corps of Engineers to design a water system for Coyote Canyon, Torlino was the go-between. Despite the damage done to the Diné and most other tribes during the boarding school era, the campaign to absorb Native people into Euro-American culture was a failure.

Now, some 150 years after Richard Pratt began crusading to eliminate Indian reservations, the Navajo Nation's land base has not shrunk, it has grown considerably. The 1868 Treaty of Bosque Redondo established a 5,200-square-mile rectangle, but as the population of the Diné climbed, between 1868 and 1934 there were fourteen additions to their territory created mostly by the executive orders of several U.S. Presidents. These annexations increased the size of the reservation to 27,000 square miles spread across Arizona, New Mexico, and Utah, spanning two time zones, making it in terms of territory the largest reservation in the U.S. And its more than 400,000 enrolled members make the Diné the most populous of the 574 federally recognized tribes. On the national level America's Native population in 2024 was twenty-five times greater than it was in 1860. So much for the expectation of nineteenth-century settlers that the Indian would soon be extinct.

Chapter Nine

BLACKFEET WARRIOR

The release of the Interior Department's investigation of Native American boarding schools turned up the volume on conversations about reparations. These range from easily resolved disputes regarding the facts and fictions of history to demands for massive transfers of wealth and power. For example, some of New York City's 110,000 tribal people want the Christopher Columbus statue in the middle of Columbus Circle removed, citing the fact that in recent years dozens of such monuments to this murderous slave-trader have been pulled down across the Western Hemisphere. The struggle for recognition of the tribes as sovereign nations resulted in the 2020 U.S. Supreme Court ruling that because a large portion of eastern Oklahoma lies on the reservation of the Muscogee Nation only the tribe and the federal government—not the state—have jurisdiction over such matters as criminal prosecutions of Natives for capital offenses. However, the most far-reaching of the demands for restitutions are about land. The eight tribes of the Oceti Sakowin Oyate in South Dakota still adamantly refuse to accept payment for the Black Hills awarded them by the U.S. Supreme Court in 1980, a settlement gathering compound interest that was worth more than $2 billion in 2023. The Hills were never for sale, the tribes argue, and have alarmed the descendants of White settlers by demanding that the land—including Mount Rushmore—be returned to the Sioux Nation. And tribal people across the United States are eyeing the Vatican's global real estate holdings, so vast Church authorities themselves have no idea what or how much they own.

Challenging the entrenched power structure takes tenacity, courage, and role models, especially for minority people. One Blackfeet woman whose life is an inspiration to others working to make governments accountable was a petite, soft-spoken warrior named Elouise Pepion Cobell. Given the Siksiká name Inokesquetee saki or Yellowbird Woman, she was born in 1945 on the reservation, to a family of eight children raised by Polite Pépion and Catherine Dubray, a Métis couple descended from fur traders and freight haulers. Although shy and quiet, Elouise was the great-grand daughter of Mountain Chief, a legendary Blackfeet leader who fought the Crows and the Kootenai and attended numerous late nineteenth century treaty negotiations in Washington, D.C. She grew up without electricity or indoor plumbing at the family's small cattle ranch, where she would live most of her life on land allotted to her grandfather along Blacktail Creek near the southern border of the reservation thirty miles east of Glacier Park.

Her parents had heard the horror stories about Indian boarding schools and vowed to educate her in some other way. The government's Cut Bank Boarding School on the reservation was especially notorious. A 1950 report from the Association on American Indian Affairs characterized the institution as "a little worse than a good prison" that should be closed down. The Association's director said he was "shocked and repelled" by the place, calling it and other boarding schools in the region "islands of education neglect."[1] So the family joined with their neighbors and built a one-room schoolhouse. When Polite led her inside during class one day four-year-old Elouise sat down at a desk and refused to leave until he promised he would bring her back the next morning. She had an early aptitude for numbers. That skill would serve her well as she devoted her adult life to successfully bringing one of the largest class action lawsuits in American history.

After she graduated from high school she studied accounting at Great Falls Commercial College, then enrolled in the business school at the University of Montana in Missoula. During summer breaks she interned as a clerk at the Bureau of Indian Affairs office back on the Blackfeet Reservation, where she witnessed the rude treatment tribal members got when they inquired about their trust accounts. "People would come in and try to get information, and they'd just make them sit out in hard, old wooden chairs," she told a reporter. "I had no idea at that point that it was their own money."[2] She had grown up hearing complaints from her parents and neighbors about their trust payments—some years a small check might come in the mail, and some years nothing. And when money did arrive it was rarely accompanied by any explanation, much less a financial statement.[3]

The money, she would learn, was deposited in the accounts of Native American property owners whose land was leased to petroleum, timber, agricultural, and mineral extraction companies. The lucrative leases that to this day generate revenue from oil and natural gas fields across much of Indian Country, including the Blackfeet Reservation, complicate federal efforts to reduce greenhouse gases at the same time atoning for its anti-Indigenous policies of the past. The Individual Indian Trust was established in 1887 as part of the Dawes Act, which allotted communal reservation land to individuals and allowed the sale of "surplus" land to settlers and speculators, resulting in the reduction of the tribal land base from 140 million acres to 50 million. Some of the money generated by these leases was used to finance Indian boarding schools, which further disrupted the social fabric of Indigenous families. As the allotment owners died their heirs were given the allotments. Over the course of several generations these transfers often resulted in "fractional" reservation land owned by many people. For example, some 1,200 Lac Courte Oreilles (Chippewa) people in Wisconsin own pieces of one small parcel. As Cobell drove across the reservation she passed oil wells, cattle herds, lumber trucks, and fields of alfalfa enriching people who weren't Native Americans. According to the Montana Cadastral, an online portal that identifies the ownership of every parcel in the state, most of this 2,200-square mile expanse of prairie and forest is still held in trust for Blackfeet people by the Interior Department. Historically, most tribal members who own land allotments don't live on the land. For example, in 1922, ten years after the Blackfeet Reservation was allotted, only 500 of the 3,000 enrolled members lived on their acreage. After Cobell turned eighteen she asked the BIA for an accounting of her own Individual Indian Money (IMM). This is an interest-yielding bank account managed by the Department of the Interior for a person with money or other assets held in trust by the federal government. Officials refused, telling her she wasn't capable of reading a financial statement.

So she decided to become an accountant. But before she could earn her degree she dropped out of college when her mother was diagnosed with cancer. After Catherine Dubray died Cobell moved to Seattle and worked as an accountant for a television station. She met a Blackfeet man named Alvin Cobell, who was a commercial fisherman in Alaska. They married and had a son. In 1971 they agreed to come back and help Polite Pépion work the ranch. Five years later the Blackfeet Nation hired her as its treasurer. In her office at tribal headquarters in Browning she discovered that the records were, as she put it, "in total chaos," the books supplying more questions than answers. Why, for example, was money leaving the tribe's account when she was the only official authorized to write checks? Why was a man reaping payments from an oil lease he hadn't paid a cent for in a year? Why did Josephine Wild Gun receive less than $1,000 a year even although 7,000 acres of her family's land were leased out for grazing, oil, minerals, and timber? Why was the BIA sending trust account checks for eight cents? When Cobell wrote the Interior Department demanding explanations her letters were ignored. She was beginning to believe that federal officials behaved like shady brokers, treating Native Americans as if they were easy marks instead of clients. [4]

She focused on the tribe's tangled accounting and eventually brought some semblance of order to the books. In 1983, financial incompetence presented her with another opportunity to help her people when the U.S. comptroller of currency declared that the sixty-seven-year-old First

National Bank of Browning was insolvent and shut it down. The bank, which had been founded by White businessmen, had issued a number of bad loans that borrowers could not pay back, resulting in a depletion of its operating capital. The Federal Deposit Insurance Company stepped in and refunded depositors most of the money tied up in frozen accounts. But meanwhile, because the reservation no longer had a bank it soon turned into a currency desert. People were driving thirty miles or more during the winter to cash checks in towns outside the reservation, where they also began doing their shopping. Browning merchants reported that sales in their stores had been cut in half. Tribal officials arranged a short-term remedy. A Wells Fargo armored car loaded with money supplied by a Great Falls bank made regular deliveries north to Browning so reservation people could cash their checks closer to home. [5]

State and tribal officials pleaded for another bank to take the place of the failed institution but got no offers. That's when Cobell went back to school to study banking after deciding that it was time for her tribe to own its own bank. In 1987 the Blackfeet National Bank opened its doors with assets of $1 million. The first national bank located on a reservation and the first bank in history owned by a Native American tribe, it was overseen by a five-member board of directors that included Cobell. In 2001 it was bought by what would be called the Native American National Bank. Opening its first branch in Browning, where it is still the only bank on the reservation, it held assets of $25 million deposited by two dozen tribes and Alaska native corporations. After its main offices were opened in Denver, by 2007 it held assets of $86 million, including $2 million deposited by the Democratic Party ahead of its convention the next year in that city.[6]

Cobell never gave up her obsession with the government's mishandling of Indian trust funds. She was encouraged in 1992 when Congress issued a blistering report about the BIA's incompetence and corruption titled "Misplaced Trust." But for two years the BIA dragged its heels, its opacity prompting Congress to pass the American Indian Trust Fund Management Reform Act. Paul Homan was the trustee appointed to investigate the estimated 300,000 accounts the government maintains for individual Native Americans and an additional 1,500 accounts it holds for 280 tribes, containing assets totaling $2.9 billion. Of the 238,000 individual trusts his team located, 50,000 had no addresses, which meant the money never left the Treasury. Some 16,000 accounts were verified by no documents whatsoever, and 118,000 were missing critical documents. The BIA holds 45,600 accounts for individuals whose "whereabouts are unknown" and $21.7 million is held ostensibly for minors, but all the individuals documented are eighteen years or older. The government has no idea who owns funds belonging to 21,000 dead individuals. Some 128,000 accounts are not identified by either a Social Security number or a tax identification number, registrations required on all commercial bank accounts. The BIA is not capable of managing the trust accounts, Homan said. He shared the opinion of numerous surveys that have rated BIA the most inept of Washington's bureaucracies. "Without any question, this is the worst I've seen as a banker and as an auditor," he told a reporter from the *Washington Post*. "Simply put, we cannot account for their money." He proposed stripping the accounts from the BIA and turning them over to a new agency patterned on the Federal Home Loan Bank. But when his plan was squashed by the Clinton Administration he resigned.[7]

In 1996 Cobell traveled to Washington, D.C., to meet with U.S. Attorney General Janet Reno, who was still taking heat for ordering the assault on the 1993 Branch Davidian compound in Texas that killed eighty civilians, including twenty-one children. But when Cobell arrived at the Justice Department she was fobbed off on one of Reno's underlings. After a decade of pleading with the federal government this was the last straw, she decided. She began arranging meetings with lawyers. One of these was a banking attorney named Dennis Gingold, who arrived at a meeting with Cobell and officials from the Interior Department believing he would be discussing finance and banks with Americans from India. After he listened to Cobell's stories about BIA trusts he turned to the bureaucrats. "I can't believe you guys haven't been sued." He later told a reporter that "Regulators would never allow this to go on at a bank. A bank would be shut down."[8]

Four months after Reno snubbed Cobell she and Gingold filed a
class action lawsuit in D.C.'s U.S. District Court initially titled *Cobell v.
Babbitt* (the Secretary of the Interior at the time). She was the lead plaintiff and Gingold the lead attorney pressing their case against the Interior
and Treasury departments on behalf of 300,000 Native Americans and
tribes. At this point they were not seeking cash, just clarity. The demands
for a financial settlement would come in the next round. The judge was a
conservative Texan named Royce Lamberth appointed by Ronald Reagan
but noted for the fairness of his rulings. Three years later he found Babbitt
and other bureaucrats in contempt and fined them $600,000 for failing
to produce records ordered by the court. "The federal government here
did not just stub its toe," Lamberth wrote during the contempt trial. "It
abused the rights of the plaintiffs to obtain these trust documents, and it
engaged in a shocking pattern of deception of the court. I have never seen
more egregious misconduct by the federal government."[9] What documents
that did exist were kept in rat-infested warehouses across the country. BIA
officials had shredded 162 boxes of papers. It soon became clear that the
government could not present the papers Lamberth demanded. After he
learned that the BIA's computer system was so permeable hackers could
set up fake trust accounts he ordered its website shut down. Finally, in
1999 the court ruled for the plaintiffs. Lamberth wrote that "the beneficiaries of this trust did not voluntarily choose to have their lands taken
from them; they did not willingly relinquish pervasive control of their
money to the United States. The United States imposed this trust on the
Indian people. As the government concedes, the purpose of the IIM
trust was to deprive plaintiffs' ancestors of their native lands and rid the
nation of their tribal identity." The next phase of Cobell's lawsuit was
determining how much money the government would have to pay. The
plaintiffs' pretrial estimates ranged as high as $176 billion. The defendants
claimed that at most the figure would be in the low millions. Not willing
to pay out *anything* and ignoring the fact that it wasn't the government's
money to begin with, the Interior and Treasury departments assigned an
army of 100 lawyers to the case.

In 1997 Cobell got one of the most surprising phone calls of her life when she learned that the MacArthur Foundation had awarded her a $310,000 "genius grant" given to Americans who demonstrate "extraordinary originality and dedication in their creative pursuits and a marked capacity for self-direction." Remembering the BIA officials who dismissed her questions about their accounting, Cobell later joked to a reporter from *Mother Jones* magazine how she had made the leap from "dumb Indian" to "genius" in one lifetime. A Santa Fe financier and arts patron named J. Patrick Lannan read about Cobell's grant and arranged to meet her at the Glacier Park Lodge. The Lannan Foundation he founded in 1989 awards money to "exceptional contemporary artists, writers, and activists," according to the organization's website, and is especially interested in Native American causes. She told him that what was needed to uncover the truth about Indian trust lands was money to hire accountants. He called her later to offer $1 million. The Foundation's contribution to Cobell's cause would eventually top $4 million with an additional $3 million provided as a loan.

Collaborating with accountants from three other tribes, she began to follow the path of Native American money into the U.S. Treasury's general fund, what the department calls "America's checkbook." Its checks are used to finance anything from military support for Saddam Hussein's forces against Iran during the late 1980s to the corporate welfare scheme known as farm subsidies. "One administration after another treated the trusts as slush funds," she told a reporter. "It didn't matter to them that it was Indians' money." Her lawsuit persisted through four administrations and against four named defendants, Secretaries of the Interior Bruce Babbitt, then Gale Norton, Dirk Kempthorne, and finally Ken Salazar. In 2009, after fighting nearly three decades for justice, Cobell prevailed. The class she represented was awarded $3.4 billion for three purposes—a $1.4 billion cash payment to some 300,000 trust account holders, $1.9 million to buy fractionized allotments from willing sellers and return the land to communal ownership, and $60 million to establish the Cobell Educational Scholarship Fund. Although *Mother Jones* adroitly called the settlement an "accounting coup" these figures represent a fraction of what was likely skimmed from

Indian trust accounts. But Cobell and her lawsuit partners decided not to appeal the ruling, knowing that many poverty-stricken reservation people were desperate. She spent another two years lobbying Congress to approve the appropriation, which Barack Obama signed into law in June 2011. She was sitting in the front row at the signing ceremony when he cited her as the central force compelling the government "to make things right." In 2012 the Treasury Department began sending beneficiaries their checks, most of them payments of $1,000. In 2013 the Department of the Interior initiated the land consolidation program ordered by the court, announcing at the end of the process a decade later that it had bought 3 million acres of fractionized allotments—a territory the size of Connecticut—from more than 123,000 individuals in fifteen states, and restored the land to tribal ownership.

But Eloise Cobell did not live to see these modest reparations. In October 2011 she died of ovarian cancer. As the tribal radio station paid tribute to her with an all-day broadcast of songs by Elvis Presley, her favorite singer, a line of vehicles two miles long followed the white hearse bearing her casket across the Blackfeet Reservation, first to the Browning High School auditorium, where an overflow crowd listened to eulogies and stories, and then to the Cobell ranch on Blacktail Creek, where she was buried. She was honored by her tribe, which designated her as a warrior, and she was posthumously awarded the Congressional Medal of Freedom. At the Department of the Interior the flags were flown at half-staff.

American Indian Hall on the campus of Montana State University in Bozeman is a striking ensemble of curved spaces that reflect the architecture of the tipi and the arrangement of tipis in a village. "The power of the World always works in circles," Oglala spiritual leader Black Elk said, "and everything tries to be round." A portion of the three-level, 31,000-square-foot building is covered by an enormous steel eagle feather. Inspired by the Sun Dance, the most profound of the communal rituals practiced by Plains

Indians, the building is powered largely by solar panels. Financed by $20 million in private donations, American Indian Hall was designed to house the Native American Studies program and serve as a meeting place and a home away from home for Native students, who account for some 800 of the school's 2024 enrollment of 16,000. At a 2018 ceremony featuring the surprise announcement that construction of the Hall would soon begin, MSU President Waded Cruzado issued what is now a standard acknowledgment recited by officials before the start of public meetings. "This very land on which we stand today is aboriginal land," she said, "once a cherished home to several American Indian tribes."[10]

What she failed to mention is that not only was MSU built on Native American land, but the school is still being *financed* by Native American territory. Since its founding in 1893 MSU has taken two steady and significant streams of revenue generated by Montana territory stolen from the Blackfeet, Crow, Nez Perce, Ojibwe, and Confederated Salish and Kootenai. One stream is a permanent endowment created by the interest earned on money paid by settlers for a portion of this land. The other stream is cash raised by leasing the remaining properties mostly for timber harvesting and cabin sites. The scheme that created MSU was embedded in the Morrill Act, named after the Vermont senator who sponsored the bill. Signed by Abraham Lincoln in 1862, the law was intended to establish schools that teach agriculture, engineering, and military "science" to working class students at a time when higher education was confined to the genteel study of the classics. Reserve Officers Training Corps program is still required for a school to keep its land-grant status. A 2020 study titled *Land-Grab Universities* that was published in *High Country News* illuminates the transfer of almost 11 million acres of aboriginal land from the federal government to the states, an act of thievery masquerading as a donation. The report's award-winning authors, a lecturer in American History at the University of Cambridge named Robert Lee, and the publication's associate editor, Tristan Ahtone, compiled an extensive database recording the GPS coordinates of 80,000 parcels of Morrill land, plus the identities of the Native American inhabitants or caretakers of this land, and an accounting of the money raised from the sale of much of this territory between 1862 and the early twentieth century. As the authors explained, "We reconstructed approximately 10.7 million acres taken from nearly 250 tribes, bands and communities through over 160 violence-backed land cessions, a legal term for the giving up of territory."[11]

The fifty-two so-called "land-grant" colleges established by the Morrill Act are almost all public institutions such as the University of Florida, Oklahoma State, and Berkeley. The Federal government awarded the states between 90,000 and 990,000 acres depending on the size of their congressional delegation. Montana got the minimum allotment, which was ceded from the sixteenth and thirty-sixth sections in every thirty-six-square mile township in the state. When the territory was admitted to the Union in 1889 MSU received an additional 50,000 federal acres. Eastern states without enough federal land within their borders were issued vouchers called scrip that allowed them to choose acreage from anywhere in the United States. For example, Cornell, an Ivy League school that along with the Massachusetts Institute of Technology are the only private land-grant universities, got the largest allocation and used a quarter of its scrip to purchase tracts in California's San Joaquin Valley, which now produces 25 percent of America's food. It also scooped up valuable timber land in Wisconsin. By 1914 the school had sold all of its Morrill acres, creating an endowment of $180 million in today's dollars. That year Montana State University boasted an endowment of what in today's currency was $30 million, the second largest fund behind Cornell's. MSU, which still owns 63,000 acres of its original allotment, reaped almost $520,000 from interest earned in 2022 on the principle its land sales created. Washington State University still owns 80 percent of its original allotment, for which it paid zero dollars to four tribes whose land was seized and $2,700 to six other tribes for lands that earned WSU $4.5 million in 2019, largely from timber sales.

Native American land sold to endow colleges includes the ground under the Directors Guild on LA's Sunset Boulevard, a military cemetery and Discovery Park in Seattle, a motel in Tucson, cornfields in Nebraska, and a Walmart Supercenter in Missoula, which was taken from the Pend d'Oreille, Salish, and Kootenai and added to the endowment of Texas A&M. An 1855 treaty guaranteed these Montana tribes protection from Blackfeet raiders and $12,000 worth of goods such as blankets, flannel, rice, and coffee if they would give up their territory in the Bitterroot Valley and move north to the Flathead Reservation. Although the treaty was finally approved by Congress five years later, the Blackfeet continued to steal their horses and women, and most of the annuities never arrived. In 1888 the Blackfeet and the Gros Ventres split $548 in goods in exchange for 15 million acres spread across northern Montana. MSU was awarded 8,400 acres, which the school sold for the equivalent of $2.2 million. Many other tribes fared even worse when dealing with demands that they give up their land. "To extinguish Indigenous title to land siphoned through the Morrill Act, the United States paid less than $400,000," *High Country News* reported. "But in truth, it often paid nothing at all. Not a single dollar was paid for more than a quarter of the parcels that supplied the grants—land confiscated through outright seizure or by treaties that were never ratified by the federal government. In 2023 more than 500,000 acres taken from tribal nations and given to land-grant colleges are still held in trust for at least twelve universities." In fiscal year 2019 alone, that acreage produced more than $5.4 million in revenue for these institutions.

After *Land-Grab Universities* was published Native Americans began asking for something more from these colleges than lip service. But by early 2024 land acknowledgments and other *mea culpa*s were largely the only responses they received. Cornell, which was awarded more than 987,000 acres of Native land spread across fifteen current states, issued a statement by Joel Malina, vice president of university relations. "Cornell acknowledges our central place in this history." The college, he said, is working "to build and maintain relationships with North American Indigenous Nations and communities," including establishing educational programs and "partnerships specifically geared to meeting the needs of Indigenous students." But by early 2024 the school's administration was still refusing to consider offering even minimal restitution in the form of tuition waivers to Native students. Kurt Anders Jordan, former director of the American Indian and Indigenous Studies Program at Cornell, assembled a team to dig deeper into the school's past, which found about 240 tribal communities across the United States and Canada that have been impacted by Cornell's grant. "If the university has gained and benefited so much, and tribes have lost so much, then what is the minimal thing that you could possibly do? And if you're committed to increasing the numbers of Indigenous students here at the institution, what would really catalyze that?"[12] Perhaps the motto of the school should be changed from *Cuiusvis hominis est errare* or "Anyone can err" to "Everything that makes me rich makes you poor." Without congressional intervention it appears unlikely that Cornell will concede the obvious restitution—the transfer of the interest earned by its land-grant endowment to Indigenous communities to buy back land from willing sellers. After all, the institution so loved Senator Justin Morrill that it named its first building after him, which was built in 1868 on land stolen from the Cayuga people. Still standing, Morrill Hall is a four-story bluestone slab so ugly a history professor in the 1860s said the only thing that could redeem it was dynamite.

In contrast, members of the 110 federally recognized tribes in California listed as residents of the state are eligible for free tuition to the ten schools of the University of California. In 2019 Governor Gavin Newsome apologized for what he said was the genocide of Native Americans. "California must reckon with our dark history. California Native American people suffered violence, discrimination and exploitation sanctioned by state government throughout its history." He was referencing what Peter Burnett, California's first governor, told the legislature in 1851. A war of extermination would be waged, he said, "until the Indian race becomes extinct." California's Indigenous people survived, although their way of life was later battered by three Indian boarding schools. In 1889 Katharine Drexel paid for eighty acres and materials to construct St. Boniface Indian Industrial School. In 1889 she paid $1.3 million in today's dollars for construction materials and eighty acres of land in Banning, eighty miles east of Los Angeles in an area ringed by Indian reservations such as the Morongo, Soboba, and Pala.

The bricks for what would be called Drexel Hall were made by Chinese laborers at a brickyard in town. Native American students were pressed into service constructing what was arguably the ugliest of Drexel's monuments to her obsession. During the school's sixty years of operation the Sisters of St. Joseph attempted to replace the languages, spirituality, and cultures of some 8,000 tribal children with English, Catholicism, and manual labor. The boys were assigned chores such as tending to the school's orchard and vineyard and milking the dairy cows. They pressed olives into oil and crushed grapes for wine, products sold to finance their assimilation. Girls added to the revenue stream by making candles. The school's printshop published a newspaper called *The Mission Indian*, in which a Franciscan Father named Benedict Hahn wrote that the early mission system imposed by Spanish colonizers had harmed Native people in southern California, injuries which he believed St. Boniface was working to heal.

Drexel Hall was damaged by an earthquake on Christmas Day 1899 that destroyed the business district of nearby San Jacinto and killed six elders of the Soboba Band of Luiseño Indians. Adding to the school's woes was the decision by the federal government to withdraw its contract. As she did at St. Peter's in Montana, Drexel stepped in to make up the deficit.[13] In 1974 Drexel Hall was deemed a fire hazard and demolished. What remains of the school is its cemetery. Time and vandals have weathered, destroyed, or moved some of the gravestones. After years of negotiating with the Morongo tribe, whose reservation lies less than a mile east, the city of Banning is planning a housing development that will surround the cemetery, which will be managed by the tribe. In 2006 a local Boy Scout working on a community project to earn his Eagle badge organized a brigade to clean up the trash that had been dumped on the burial ground over the years. He learned that more than eighty people were buried there, the last of them in 1941, although only sixteen of the burials are marked by gravestones. Ground penetrating radar detected a number of anomalies outside the cemetery fence that might be additional graves. At least twenty Indian students died at St. Boniface, mostly from tuberculosis.[14]

No state committed more acreage to land-grant colleges than Minnesota, and no Indigenous people lost more in the process than the Dakota. "Land-Grab Universities" documents that almost 830,000 acres ceded by the tribe to the United States fed the endowments of thirty-five land-grant universities. The state would furnish one out of every thirteen acres redistributed under the Morrill Act and would itself claim the most fertile parcels—which amounted to 145 square miles now spread across eighteen counties—to finance the University of Minnesota. This larceny was facilitated by two treaties forced in 1851 on the four bands of the Dakota, who relinquished twenty-four million acres in the present states of Minnesota, Iowa, and South Dakota. In exchange they were promised 12 cents an acre for land that was appraised at between $5 and $10 an acre. They didn't have much choice. By 1850, both the Sisseton and Wahpeton bands of Dakota were facing starvation. The bison and game animals at the center of their economy had been depleted and their meager crops could not make up the difference. Annuities would help them survive. And they knew that if they didn't sell the land the government would take it by force. The treaties confined the entire population of 8,000 Dakota to a strip of land twenty miles wide stretching 150 miles along the Minnesota River. Voicing the doctrine of the boarding school era whose beginning was still a decade in the future, government's negotiators outlined their goals in a report. "It was our constant aim to do what we could to break up the community system among the Indians, and cause them to recognize the individuality of property . . . If timely measures are taken for the proper location and management of these tribes, they may, at no distant period, become an intelligent and Christian people."[15]

By 1862 the tribes were reeling. Their corn crop was a failure and most of the game had disappeared. The government had confiscated half of their reservation and allowed it to be overrun by settlers. Most of the gold promised them was paid instead to corrupt fur traders for debts they claimed were owed them by the Indians. Desperate, the Dakota went to war. At the end of it five weeks later at least 500 settlers and soldiers were dead along with 75 to 100 warriors. Minnesota Governor Alexander Ramsey declared that the Dakota must be "exterminated or driven forever beyond the borders of the state." Congress canceled the treaties, dissolved the reservation, ordered that the Dakota be expelled from Minnesota, and force-marched some 1,600 noncombatants to a concentration camp surrounded by a stockade, where they would later be loaded onto steamboats and exiled to what is now South Dakota. In December 1862 the government executed thirty-eight warriors, the largest one-day mass hanging in U.S. history. [16]

In 1868 the state used its Morrill acres to endow the University of Minnesota. Originally a preparatory school in the Twin Cities, it went bankrupt in 1858 but was revived in 1867 with an endowment that was worth 250 times what the federal government claims it paid the Dakota, amounting to $500 million from sales and leases of the land. The University has five campuses, including one in Morris, which began as the Morris Industrial School for Indians. This was an off-reservation boarding school run by the Catholic Sisters of Mercy between 1887 and 1896. The Office of Indian Affairs assumed ownership in 1898 and closed it in 1909.

The campus offers free tuition to American tribal students, Alaska Natives and members of Canadian First Nations. An April 2023 a report issued by the Minnesota Indian Affairs Council and the University accused the school's founding board of regents of committing "genocide and ethnic cleansing of Indigenous peoples for financial gain, using the institution as a shell corporation through which to launder lands and resources." The Council has demanded that the University expand its tuition waivers for Native American students from the state's eleven tribes, hire more Native American faculty and give back some of the land it stole from the Dakota and Ojibwe people. [17] To ponder a response the administrators huddled in their offices at Morrill Hall, one of a dozen Morrill Halls on land-grant campuses across the U.S. In early 2024 the University was discussing the possibility of turning over the 3,400-acre Cloquet Forestry Center to the Fond du Lac band of Lake Superior Chippewa, whose reservation surrounds the Center.

By early 2024 the most that Montana State University offered Indigenous students in the way of reparations was a limited tuition waiver, which is offered by all the schools in the state's University System. To be eligible an applicant must be enrolled in one of Montana's twelve federally recognized tribes and must show proof of a "blood quantum" of at least 25 percent Indigenous. A bill introduced in the 2023 Montana legislative session by Jonathan Windy Boy (Chippewa Cree) would have eliminated this rule. The measure passed the House but was voted down by the Senate, where its Republican opponents said it would cost the Montana University System too much money. The schools also offer a waiver to out-of-state Native students by charging them the in-state rate for tuition. Meanwhile, over the last decade MSU has reaped more than $17 million from grazing, timber, and agricultural leases on some 260,000 surface and subsurface mineral acres held in trust for the school by the Montana Department of Natural Resources and Conservation.[18]

Progress toward compensating American tribes has been slow and challenging. The schools are reluctant to discuss giving land back because the politicians and bureaucrats who control the purse strings of these institutions would have to replace this revenue stream by raising taxes or tuition. And many of the tribes are in the process of formulating what it is they want from the federal government, the land-grant colleges, and the churches. "I don't think there is a one-size-fits-all policy of reparations for Indian tribes in the U.S.," said, Matthew Fletcher, a law professor at Michigan State University and a member of the Grand Traverse Band of Ottawa and Chippewa Indians in Michigan. "There are 574 federally recognized tribes. They are all unique and individual."[19]

In 1946 the federal government established a precedent for land reparations. The Indian Claims Commission Act was passed as a means of thanking the 44,000 tribal members who served in the armed forces during World War II, fighting in Europe and the Pacific. And more than 100,000 Indigenous people served the war effort on the home front by working in industry and agriculture. It might seem incongruous that they would support the foreign war of a nation that had mistreated them for centuries. But in a 2002 interview I asked Blackfeet author and novelist James Welch why so many of his tribe join the military. "The Blackfeet are warriors," he said. "And this is still our land." Paratrooper Ira Hamilton Hayes (Pima) was twenty-two when he joined five other Marines raising the American flag during the Battle of Iwo Jima, a moment captured by the most iconic photograph of the war. His story was told in *The Outsider*, a 1961 film starring Tony Curtis. U.S. forces finally prevailed at Iwo Jima against 20,000 Japanese soldiers entrenched on Mount Suribachi, a victory that would have been impossible without Diné "Code Talkers." They passed 800 messages between military units during the battle, baffling Japanese cryptographers, who had no way to reference what linguists consider the most difficult tongue to learn as a second language. Many of the almost 500 Marine Code Talkers who served in the Pacific were conscripted as children by Indian boarding schools. Chester Nez, for example, was enrolled in the BIA's Chinle School in Arizona, where President Chester Arthur's first name was forced on him, and he was prohibited from speaking Navajo.

After adjudicating their requests for reparations the Indian Claims Commission awarded $1.3 billion to 176 tribes and bands. Many Indigenous people wanted land, not money, but the government was unwilling to give back any of the territory it had stolen. Tribes that accepted the cash had to agree that they would not pursue further claims. The per capita payout was only $1,000, and much of this money was held in trust by the notoriously inept Bureau of Indian Affairs.

Indigenous families in America signed a waiver or put their mark or a thumbprint on a piece of paper in order to open school doors for their children. Some families were coerced into giving up their kids to White teachers, and others saw these institutions as the only hope for their survival. Paltry payments—if paid at all—were exchanged by the federal government for Native land along with promises to build educational institutions on the reservations. Sometimes the promises were kept, sometimes not. Because the schools run by the Bureau of Indians Affairs were dedicated to the forced assimilation of Native people and the erasure of their languages and cultures, often by brutal means, parents and guardians saw schools operated by religious denominations as less coercive. The government not only gave the churches land on which to build schools it paid them on a per capita basis for each student, a clear violation of the establishment clause in the First Amendment. But politicians and bureaucrats believed that the chief obstacle to assimilating Indians was their pagan beliefs, which could only be transformed by their conversion to Christianity. According to an 1886 report from the Commissioner of Indian Affairs converting heathens was "a work in which the Government cannot actively engage," but the government should provide "encouragement and cooperation" to missionaries. By 1899, however, Congress had phased out the awarding of contracts to church-run boarding schools, most of them Catholic. Opposition to the policy came from Protestants and their politicians, alarmed at the rising tide of Catholic immigration from eastern Europe and Italy. But because Katharine Drexel could not fund every Catholic boarding school the Church conceived a plan that would keep them in business.

Why not use the money held by the government in Native trust and treaty funds to pay the tuition of Indians? After the scheme became practice three Sicangu men from the Rosebud Reservation filed a lawsuit against the government that finally reached the Supreme Court in 1908. In *Reuben Quick Bear v. Leupp* the plaintiffs argued that the Fort Laramie Treaty of 1868 promised the children of the Great Sioux Nation an education paid for by the government. "The United States agreed that, for every thirty children of the said Sioux Tribe who can be induced or compelled to attend school," the treaty states, "a house shall be provided, and a teacher competent to teach the elementary branches of an English education shall be furnished, who will reside among said Indians, and faithfully discharge his or her duties as a teacher." Defense attorneys argued that the real plaintiff in the case was not the government but the Bureau of Catholic Indian Missions (BCIM), incorporated in 1894 to promote the Church's boarding school business. The Court ruled that mission schools could *ask* tribes to pay for the schooling of their children because denying Indians the right to use their money as they see fit would deprive them of their rights. Author and history professor Vine DeLoria Jr. (Lakota) said *Quick Bear* had nothing to do with the law or treaties but was basically a "payoff" to Catholics for supporting Theodore Roosevelt in the 1904 Presidential election.[20]

Starting in 1908 the administrators of mission schools were required to seek permission from parents before petitioning the BCIM for trust and treaty money. A report from a journalism project called Type Investigations published by *In These Times* found that the Church drained at least $36 million in 2023 dollars from these Native accounts.[21] A determination of the exact figure lies in the future because church and government boarding school records are scattered across the country in dusty boxes and battered filing cabinets. An effort has begun to find these records and digitize them so the information can be stored in a database and shared with researchers and families. The National Native American Boarding School Healing Coalition (NABS), a nonprofit organization, was awarded a federal grant to scan documents held in the libraries of two Philadelphia-area colleges. They include photos, financial records, letters, and administrative reports from at least nine Indian boarding schools across the U.S. that were operated from 1852 to 1945 by the Quakers. Although there are 20,000 pages in the two collections this figure represents a tiny fraction of the records it can be assumed were generated by at least 523 boarding schools across the U.S., including Alaska and Hawai'i.[22]

A large and important trove of documents is held by the Raynor Memorial Libraries at Marquette University, a Catholic institution in Milwaukee. These records were given to the school by the BCIM, to which all boarding schools run by Catholics sent regular reports. Requests by researchers to digitize these records have so far been rebuffed by the staff, who maintain that permission must come from the BCIM. Archivist Mark Thiel, who for decades until his retirement in 2021 was in charge of the Bureau's records, opposes digitization. NABS "is promoting a partisan agenda," he said. "I don't like the idea of combining the archives with a partisan agenda." Thiel dismissed as "tough love" the harsh conditions and corporal punishment common at the Church's Indian boarding schools. "When you're looking at something from a past era and you're applying contemporary standards, I think that there's a bias there," he told Mary Annette Pember, the reporter from *In These Times*. "I think you need to look at it from the lens of the past era." Thiel's remarks are a common refrain among conservative Christians and their political allies as they brace for the looming storm of demands from Native people for reparations.

What Thiel describes as a relic of the past is still very much part of the child-rearing practices of some Christians, who believe that corporal punishment is encouraged by a phrase from Scripture. However, "spare the rod, spoil the child" appears nowhere in either Testament. It was written by Samuel Butler in *Hudibras*, the mammoth 11,000-line satirical poem he published in three parts between 1663 and 1678. In the poem a Presbyterian knight named Hudibras argues frequently with his squire, a Puritan named Ralpho regarding the meaning of words. Although Butler was dismissive of Puritanism, the poem doesn't mock doctrine or theology. But both knight and squire are portrayed as incompetent buffoons. Sallying forth to confront his enemies, Hudibras has trouble getting on his horse and staying there. And the duo is regularly defeated in battle, often by women, most notably the village prostitute. Many Christians to this day argue that spanking their children is an effective teaching tool. A fundamentalist Protestant organization, for example, called Focus on the Family advises that "spanking can be an important time of connection." There is a spate of Christian parenting books that recommend assaulting children, including *Spanking: A Loving Discipline* to *Spank Your Child, PLEASE!* and *Lots of Love & A Spanking*. In *Don't Make Me Count to Three*, Ginger Hubbard advocates smacking both puppies and kids, including sick children and infants under twelve months old. "There are many adults," the author argues, "who could benefit from a good old fashioned whippin.'" Most of the Native Americans subjected to the harsh and physical abuse of boarding schools came from cultures that regarded corporal punishment as barbaric and counterproductive. This is not to say that their children were never punished. But the discipline was based on words or the silent treatment, and rarely was physical force employed.

—⁓—

How do you put a dollar figure on the ongoing trauma caused by Catholic boarding schools? That's a question the tribes will have to answer as more of the internal records of these eighty-seven institutions come to light. What is easier to quantify is the money skimmed from Indian trust and treaty funds. And land owned by the Catholic Church on Indian reservations has been and will continue to be a topic when the conversation turns to giving stolen wealth back to the tribes. As Ojibwe author and activist Winona LaDuke said, "The only compensation for land is land." Echoing that idea, in 2017 the Church gave the Sicangu 550 acres it had owned on the Rosebud Reservation since the nineteenth century. "We're out of the property business," the president of St. Francis Mission declared, "and we're out of a colonial approach to the work of mission."[23]

While that may be the case for the Jesuits at St. Francis, the U.S. Church as a whole is still very busy managing the revenue stream from its enormous real estate holdings, allowing it to weather substantial financial losses. These include the decline in tithings and donations resulting from the dwindling number of Americans who call themselves Catholics, and the more than $3 billion the Church has shelled out by the end of 2023 as a result of settling 3,000 sexual abuse lawsuits.[24] That figure would be much higher if not for the fact that thirty-six dioceses weaseled out of their liability by declaring bankruptcy, from which a dozen have emerged to start again. Financial losses as a result of closing churches and parochial schools during the COVID-19 pandemic were offset by the Payroll Protection Plan (PPP). An Associated Press investigation revealed that Catholic entities in the U.S. vigorously applied for PPP "loans" from the Small Business Administration and were granted between $1.4 billion and possibly more than $3.5 billion, federal money intended to rescue small companies that were shuttered because of the virus. Many millions of dollars went to dioceses that used bankruptcy to protect themselves from sexual abuse lawsuits. This bonanza made the Roman Catholic Church among the top beneficiaries of the government's pandemic welfare scheme. Although churches are tax-exempt and prohibited from seeking federal funds distributed by the Small Business Administration, Congress allowed nonprofits to apply for PPP loans as long as they abided by the SBA's "affiliation rule," which restricts recipients to those business entities with fewer than 500 employees. Many parishes exceed this cap, but the Church convinced the Trump administration to exempt religious organizations from the rule. Trying to fend off criticism of the government's clear violation of the First Amendment's establishment clause, Bishop Lawrence Persico of Erie, Pennsylvania, told *Forbes* magazine that "The separation of church and state does not mean that those motivated by their faith have no place in the public square."

Although very few of the dioceses issue financial statements "that would pass muster with a CPA," according to Jason Berry, a reporter who wrote the book *Render Unto Rome: The Secret Life of Money in the Catholic Church*, the U.S. Church is estimated to be worth as much as $30 billion. Even a fraction of this figure would go a long way toward financing the purchase of reservation land by tribal governments from willing non-Native sellers. That dollar figure pales in comparison to what the Roman Catholic Church owns across the rest of the planet. It is probably the wealthiest institution in the world. But no one knows for sure because its finances are a secret. It owns gold, jewels, cathedrals, oil wells, art, museums, farms, and forests. According to one estimate it owns 277,000 square miles of land, a territory the size of Texas. Another estimate places the number at 312,000 square miles. Even the Church has no idea of the true figure.

A young American cartographer from Connecticut decided to find out. In 2015 when she was twenty-five years old Molly Burhans began using sophisticated geographic information systems software to produce a visual representation of Church properties that is interactive—digital maps employing color, shape and line that respond to a user's questions. She soon learned that the data that would fuel such a project was almost nonexistent. The only maps showing Catholic holdings that she had been able to find were published in an old book entitled *Atlas Hierarchicus* and had not been updated since 1901. The boundaries of dioceses were hand-drawn guesstimates, and most of the information about real estate—schools, cathedrals, clergy residences, missions, etcetera—was so outdated it was of no use. She contacted parishes in Connecticut to ask about their real estate assets. "And what I found out was that none of them knew what they owned," Burhans told David Owen, writing about her in the *New Yorker* magazine. "Some of them didn't even have paper records." A devout Catholic and an environmentalist, her goal was to convince the Church to use its real estate to heal the planet and help the victims of bad economic management. If the Holy See had an accurate accounting of its land and how it was being used, she decided, informed decisions could be made about its effect on climate change, displaced populations, and deforestation. "You should put your environmental programs where they mean the most," she told Owen. "And if you don't understand the geographic context you can't do that."

She traveled to the Vatican to find someone in the Church's government who would let her examine its records and databases. When she met with two priests she asked them where they kept the Church's maps. They referred her to the Gallery of Maps, a wide, arched hallway the length of a football field lined on both sides with forty huge topographical frescoes depicting the Italian Peninsula. Painted in the sixteenth century, they are no more than 80 percent accurate. "Then I asked if I could speak to someone in their cartography department." The priests told her they didn't have one. Although the Church began losing track of its land holdings in the early 1900s Burhans and the institute she founded, called GoodLands, used Vatican statistics to produce 100 digital maps of the Roman Catholic empire, many of which were released to the public in 2019.

Following Burhans' lead I decided to compile a list of the Church's assets in my home county of Missoula, Montana, whose population in 2023 was 120,000 people, most of whom live in the City of Missoula. This task didn't require calling parish officials. According to the Montana Cadastral, which provides detailed information about private and public land ownership, the diocese owns eight churches in the county, three houses, ten acres of bare land, and a parochial school for grades K-12. The market value of these assets ranges as high as $50 million. That's not counting the thirty large and small stained glass windows adorning St. Francis Xavier Church in downtown Missoula. Although canon law prohibits their sale to an entity that is not another Catholic Church, they may be worth as much as $500,000. All of these properties are on land that belonged to the Salish, Kootenai, and Pend d'Oreilles people before they were swindled out of it by the 1855 Hellgate Treaty and moved to the Flathead Reservation, which lies four miles from Missoula's city limits. It would be a fitting gesture on Montana's part to offer ownership of Council Grove State Park to the tribes who were its original caretakers. A tranquil 187-acre expanse of parkland, riverbank, and forest eight miles downstream from Missoula, this is where the treaty was signed. A precedent exists for the return of Native land. In 2021 the 19,000-acre National Bison Range on the Flathead Reservation was transferred from the federal government to the Confederated Salish and Kootenai Tribes.[25]

The reservation was infected by two of the most notorious Indian boarding schools in the U.S. Ten years after Pierre-Jean De Smet and Adrianus Hoecken founded St. Ignatius Mission in 1854, an assimilation center for girls was opened there and staffed by the Sisters of Providence, who forced their conscripts to sew, keep house, and garden. In 1878 an industrial and agricultural boarding school for Indigenous boys was opened by the Jesuits to teach farm work, printing, and the mechanical trades. By 1892 there were 325 students enrolled at the two St. Ignatius schools. In 1941 the schools were combined into a coed facility that was operated by the Ursuline Sisters. By the 1950s corporal punishment and the sexual abuse of children at the Ursuline Academy were rampant. They were beaten with boards. Those who wet their beds were made to stand with the sheets over their heads until they dried. Others were fondled, penetrated, and raped. Runaways were common, and a string of fires was blamed on arson, one of which burned the boys' school to the ground in 1896.

In 2011, 500 former students at Indian boarding schools in Alaska and the Pacific Northwest won a $166 million settlement against the Oregon Province of the Society of Jesus, which had filed for bankruptcy protection in 2009. Among the plaintiffs were forty-five former students who accused priests and the nuns under their supervision at the Ursuline Academy of sexual and physical abuse. The accusations were unlike most other cases involving Catholic predators because the abusers included women. The most perverted of these was a German nun named Mother Superior Loyola. According to court documents she would take John Doe 1 to her bedroom and expose herself to him, forcing him to perform oral sex on her. John Doe 4 entered the Ursuline Academy/St. Ignatius Mission School at age six and left by age twelve. During this time, Mother Superior Loyola touched John Doe 4 inappropriately, including masturbation and progressing to intercourse. John Doe 8 was a boarding student at the school from 1957–1960. During this time he was forced to perform oral sex on Mother Superior Loyola in her bedroom. Brother Charlie sodomized the plaintiff on at least five occasions. Mother Superior Loyola would send him to perform chores at Father Balfe's house where the plaintiff would be sodomized and raped. [26]

Today tourists stop at St. Ignatius to gaze the red brick, gothic revival church that's the only edifice remaining of the Mission. The frescoes inside depict Madonna and Child as a Native woman with a papoose, and Christ as a chief in full headdress, displaying his heart wrapped in thorns. One of the plaintiffs in the case against the Ursuline Academy pointed to the church as he spoke with a reporter. "I want to be here," he said, "the day an earthquake brings this place down." [27]

Chapter Ten

THE VANISHING INDIAN
AND OTHER MYTHS

A mong the collection of art in the White House is a somber 1847
oil painting by Asher Brown Durand titled *The Indian's Vespers*. It
depicts an Indigenous man standing in a panoramic mountain landscape,
lifting his arms in prayer to the sun. That he is alone suggests he is one
of the last of his people. The sun is setting, symbolizing the eclipse of
Native life. Durand was a member of the Hudson River School, a group
of landscape artists whose themes centered on Euro-Americans discov-
ering "their" continent, exploring it, and settling their "new" land. In
Progress, Durand's 1853 painting, three Indigenous men look down from
a ruined forest on a scene that is both romantically pastoral and brutally
industrial. Passing through a mountainous landscape under an enormous
sky, a train makes its way toward a port town studded with belching
smokestacks and church steeples. The image is a representation of the
relentless march of "civilization" and industrialization as these forces
push aboriginal cultures out of the picture. Like that of many of his countrymen at the time, Durand's thinking about Indians was influenced by

The Last of the Mohicans, James Fenimore Cooper's 1826 adventure novel set during the 1757 French and Indian War. One of its main characters is the last chief of his tribe.

The story reflects the Myth of the Vanishing Indian, a lie settlers told one another to convince themselves that another myth was also true—Manifest Destiny, the notion that God ordained a White and Christian America to stretch from sea to shining sea. Belief in these fairy tales persists. One survey revealed that 40 percent of respondents don't think Indians still exist.[1] This is despite the fact that Indigenous people are taking larger roles in the media, on campus, in business, in politics, and in the arts. Organizations such as the Native American Bar Association and the American Indian Council of Architects and Engineers attest to the fact that they can be found in every profession, most visibly in film and television.

In 2021 during the first season of *Reservation Dogs* a critic for the *New York Times* wrote that "the series forgoes the usual reductive clichés about reservation life—the show is neither pitying, nor mysticizing—in favor of a nuanced and comic realism."[2] Streaming on FX, the show follows four teenagers living in a small town on the Muscogee Nation, a tribe that was force-marched in the 1830s during the Trail of Tears from their homeland in the Southeast to what is now Oklahoma. To finance their dream of escaping the reservation to live in LA they sell a delivery truck they've stolen and peddle meat pies. Its writers and directors are all Indigenous as are its stars. Its cocreator, Sterlin Harjo (Seminole), is a founding member of the comedy troupe, The 1491s. The series won numerous awards and was named one of the ten best television programs of 2021, 2022, and 2023 by the American Film Institute. Lily Gladstone appears in two episodes, portraying a medicine woman in touch with a dead ancestor who walked The Trail of Tears. Gladstone, who is Piegan and Nez Perce, grew up on the Blackfeet Reservation in Montana. She won the 2023 Golden Globe award for best actress in a drama for her role in Martin Scorsese's *Killers of the Flower Moon*. The film was adapted from a nonfiction investigation into the murders of wealthy Osage tribal members during the 1920s oil boom in Oklahoma. She was nominated for an Academy Award for the same role. There was widespread surprise that the Oscar went instead to Emma Stone for her role in *Poor Things*, a Frankenstein movie. Regardless, thousands of people from the Blackfeet Nation traveled from Canada and across the U.S. to honor Gladstone in Browning on a blustery March day in 2024. She was presented a "stand-up" headdress, a token of great respect unique to the Blackfeet Nation in which the feathers point toward the heavens. Presented by the Women's Stand-Up Headdress Society, this ceremonial icon is unlike that of the controversial "Lakota-style" headdress presented to Pope Francis, in which the feathers are swept backward. Gladstone also narrated *Bring Them Home*, a 2024 documentary that chronicles her tribe's efforts to return bison herds to the reservation.

Cast members from *Reservation Dogs* and Interior Secretary Haaland are among the many people who have sat down to dinner in Minneapolis at Owamni, which won the 2022 James Beard Foundation award for best new restaurant in America. The novelist Louise Erdrich (Chippewa), who owns a bookstore a couple miles away, is a repeat visitor. Located in a park near a waterfall on the Mississippi River, Owamni was started in 2021 by Sean Sherman (Oglala Lakota) and Dana Thompson, who is descended from Dakota people on her grandfather's side. The menu is introduced by a red neon sign inside the restaurant that says "You Are On Native Land." Entrees include smoked bison, braised elk, venison tartare, wild turkey, and duck sausage, accompanied by such other traditional Indigenous food as Three Sisters, wild rice, sweet potatoes, white beans, and duck eggs. Part of the preparation of the cuisine are traditional Indigenous methods to preserve food—smoking, drying, and fermenting. What is not on the menu are dishes whose ingredients were brought to the region by Europeans—pork, beef, chicken, sugar, wheat, and dairy. Owamni grew out of The Sioux Chef, a catering business Sherman and Thompson ran from a food truck called Tatanka Truck (the Sioux word for buffalo). In 2020 Sherman founded the Indigenous Food Lab, a training center that features dishes using only Native North American foods.[3]

Meanwhile, many reservations are food deserts where store-bought groceries are expensive and more often than not processed rather than fresh. To buy food at a grocery store on the vast Navajo Nation the typical resident must drive for three hours. There are only two grocery stores on the Blackfeet Reservation—which is the size of Delaware—both in the tribal seat of Browning. According to one study, the cost of a basket of selected items purchased at a grocery store in Montana is 23 percent higher on one of the state's seven reservations than it is off the reservation. Because of higher transportation costs and the comparative lack of marketing power smaller food stores can command, this sort of inequality occurs on many U.S. reservations. This has prompted tribal nations to embrace the goal of food sovereignty.[4] This involves establishing a supply chain that's produced on reservations independently of outside sources. It includes the development of bison herds, community gardens and greenhouses, reservation sales venues for farmers and ranchers, processing facilities, and the foraging of wild vegetables, fruits, and herbs.[5] According to the Intertribal Buffalo Council some eighty tribes in twenty states now manage more than 20,000 buffalo on a million acres of the 32 million acres of these tribal lands. And on many reservations communal gardens have been established. For example, there are eight of them on the Flathead Reservation.

Along with food sovereignty the revitalization of Native languages is another critical aspect of the campaign to restore tribal hegemony. Teaching children to speak these ancient tongues is part of the curriculum on some twenty reservations. For example, the Cuts Wood School for the Blackfeet uses immersion techniques to teach Siksiká to children from kindergarten through the eighth grade. Beginning in 1976 the Arapaho Language Lab on the Wind River Reservation in Wyoming began taking steps toward language preservation by holding classes in *Hinóno'eitíít*. The New Kituwah Academy and the Cherokee Immersion School operated by the Cherokee Nation in Oklahoma are working toward an ambitious goal: seeing to it that in fifty years at least 80 percent of tribal members will be fluent.

While Indigenous Americans have not vanished, what *have* disappeared are the boarding schools that tried to erase their cultures.[6] On a bright autumn Sunday my wife, Kitty, and I decided to visit the ruins of one. We drove our pickup the hundred miles from our place downstream from Missoula to the Continental Divide. Twenty miles on the eastern side we turned right on Highway 287, then a few miles later onto Birdtail Creek Road. Although it wasn't identified by any sign, we guessed that the muddy track we turned onto next was Mission Road. I put the truck into four-wheel drive and we began climbing into what geologists call the Adel Mountain volcanic field. There was no other traffic, no evidence that anyone else had passed this way recently, and not a house in sight. As the treacherous road doglegged, dropped, and rose again over the Birdtail Divide we talked about turning around and taking the other route, which was far less challenging. But there was no safe place to turn around. After a long descent we finally arrived at St. Peter's Mission. Or what was left of it. The two massive stone buildings that had housed the boys' and the girls' schools collapsed after they caught on fire. The boys' school was reduced to a field of rubble. Remnants of walls at the girl's school were still standing, as was the two-story "Opera House" built by the Ursulines. Painted red, it had been serving as a cattle barn for the ranch family who now owned it. But because it was unstable and could fall over at any moment they moved out their cattle and stopped going inside.

One of my earlier trips to this surreal place was on the day after the World Trade Center was destroyed. I had driven the safer route, past a Minuteman missile silo where military police glared at me as I passed by them on the gravel road. My father had worked as a quality control inspector who examined this very silo. My reason for visiting back then was a search for family history and had nothing to do with Indian boarding schools. Like most Americans who aren't Native, at the time I had no idea what these establishments were and what they tried to do. This is in spite of the fact that my great-grandfather, Thomas Moran, became the caretaker at St. Peter's after the Jesuits fled the place in 1866 because of hostilities between settlers and the Blackfeet Nation. He had stayed on after the priests returned in 1874, donating his labor and resources to them and the Ursulines. He spent the rest of his life on his homestead two miles from the Mission. My grandfather was born there, as was my mother.

Under Skull Butte we walked across a field to the little whitewashed log church which Moran helped build in 1878. Inside were a few pews, a modest altar, and the sort of iconography common to Catholic churches—statues of St. Peter and the Madonna and Child. The church is still occasionally used. In 2022 a professional violinist named Megan Karls played several pieces in the style of traditional Métis fiddling for a gathering of Métis people from the area. One of these was Alisa Herodes, whose grandmother had attended Mount Angela Institute, the girls' school at St. Peter's. "She told me she was forced there by horse and buggy," Herodes said. After Karl's performance, Herodes continued, "There wasn't a dry eye in the bunch. It was so powerful, hearing that music."[7]

When I was five or six years old my mother brought me to this church. The Mass was in a funny language she said was Latin. I liked the smoke and the smell of burning incense. On one wall was a portrait of a blonde, blue-eyed Jesus displaying his bleeding and burning heart, wrapped in thorns. I stared at Him, trying to make Him blink. Kitty and I walked up a rise to the Mission's cemetery. Moran's white marble headstone was one of the most prominent of the weathered old grave markers. There were a few recent burials marked by gravestones and flowers. And curiously, mourners had paid tribute to their dead with bright red, blue, and yellow glass insulators. These had once been attached to utility poles and are coveted by some collectors of antiques. I wondered if the deceased had been collectors.

What was most profound about the cemetery were sixty small white wooden crosses spread across this grassy hill above Mission Creek. These had not been here when I visited my great-grandfather's grave in 2001. The place was so quiet, for a moment I thought I had lost my hearing. Then Kitty, who had wandered to the other side of the cemetery, called me to come look at something she had found. It was a heavy metal sign with raised, cast letters. "In memory of all who were buried here," it said. "The white crosses mark the many unmarked graves beginning the year of 1866." I learned later that as many as ninety Native children had been buried here. I thought about Nancy Bird and the abrupt way the nuns had recorded her passing. Was she here? Like her dead classmates the records held by the diocese don't list names, only the dates of their deaths.

NOTES

Preface

1   Bill Vaughn, "The Snow on the Sweetgrass," *Outside*, October 2002,
www.outsideonline.com/adventure-travel/destinations/north-america
/snow-sweetgrass/.

Chapter One: Childhood's End

1   Joy SpearChief-Morris and Willow Fiddler, "Chief Littlechild's
Headdress Gift to Pope Francis Carries Heavy Significance," *Globe
and Mail*, posted July 26, 2022, at www.theglobeandmail.com/canada
/article-chief-littlechilds-headdress-gift-to-pope-francis-carries-heavy/.

2   This was a reference to the brand-new orange shirt worn by six-
year-old Phyllis Webstad on her first day at a residential school in
Williams Lake, British Columbia in 1976. The shirt, which was a gift
from her grandmother, was taken from her by school officials, took
and never returned. September 30 of each year in Canada is designated
Orange Shirt Day, marking the time of year when government agents
would take First Nations children from their families and put them in
residential schools.

3   Ian Austin, "The Vanished Indigenous Children in Canada," *New York
Times*, June 12, 2021, A6.

4   Jacques Rouillard, "In Kamloops, Not One Body Has Been Found,"
Dorchester Review, posted January 11, 2022, at dorchesterreview.ca
/blogs/news/in-kamloops-not-one-body-has-been-found.

5   Tristan Hopper, "The Graves Were Never a Secret: Why So Many
Residential School Cemeteries Remain Unmarked," *National Post*,
posted June 2, 2021, at nationalpost.com/news/canada/the-graves
-were-never-a-secret-why-so-many-residential-school-cemeteries
-remain-unmarked.

6   K. J. McCusker, "Genocide Deniers Ask: Where Are the Bodies of
the Residential Schoolchildren?" *Toronto Star*, posted January 28,
2022, posted at thestar.com/opinion/contributors/genocide-deniers
-ask-where-are-the-bodies-of-the-residential-schoolchildren/article
_bc6f9789-dcd1-55d0-a5fe-c1815bc5b284.html.

7   Stephen Cook, "Current and Former Alexis Nakota Sioux Chiefs
        Reflect on Papal Visit," *CBC News*, posted July 24, 2022, at www
        .cbc.ca/news/canada/edmonton/current-and-former-alexis-nakota
        -sioux-chiefs-reflect-on-papal-visit-1.6528073. In a 2002 interview I
        conducted with Blackfeet writer James Welch he said quietly: "Even
        back when I was a kid the Catholic boarding schools didn't allow
        us to speak Blackfeet or perform traditional religious ceremonies."
        To me, this was a surprise. Like most non-Indigenous Americans I
        knew nothing about the role of the Church in subjugating Indians.
8   Jason Warick, "Advocates Shocked by Catholic List Claiming
        $28M of 'In-Kind' Help for Residential School Survivors," CBC
        News, posted October 3, 2021, at cbc.ca/news/canada/saskatoon
        /irssa-log-catholic-in-kind-services-1.6197450.
9   Nicole Winfield, "Vatican Rejects Doctrine that Fueled Centuries
        of Colonialism," Associated Press, posted March 30, 2023, at
        apnews.com/article/vatican-Indigenous-papal-bulls-pope-francis
        -062e39ce5f7594a81bb80d0417b.
10   Kiowa writer N. Scott Momaday coined the phrase in his 1968
        Pulitzer-winning novel, *House Made of Dawn*.
11   Kayla Bruch, "Sixties Scoop Survivor Speaks Her Truth: 'I'm Not
        Going to Hide It,'" *City News Everywhere*, posted July 4, 2021, at
        calgary.citynews.ca/2021/07/04/60s-scoop-survivor-speaks-her-truth
        -im-not-going-to-hide-it/.
12   Jeff Welsch, "Northern Cheyenne Woman's Search for Indigenous
        Children's Remains Taking on New Significance," *Billings Gazette*,
        July 11, 2021, 1.
13   Helen Andrews, "Stirring Up Hatred Against Indian Boarding
        Schools," *American Conservative*, July 13, 2022, posted online
        at www.theamericanconservative.com/stirring-up-hatred-against
        -indian-boarding-schools/.
14   Committee on Labor and Public Welfare, *Indian Education: A National
        Tragedy—A National Challenge*, S. Rep. No. 91-501 at 42 (1969).
15   Karin Brulliard, "Lily Gladstone Made History. The Blackfeet Nation
        Found a Champion," *Washington Post*, January 27, 2024.

Chapter Two: The Interpreters

1   Genevieve McBride, *The Bird Tail* (New York: Vantage Press, 1974), 98.
2   Ibid., 98–99.
3   Wilfred P. Schoenberg, "Historic St. Peter's Mission: Landmark of
        the Jesuits and the Ursulines among the Blackfeet," *Montana: The
        Magazine of Western History* 11, no. 1 (Winter 1961): 72.

4   Richard Henry Pratt, *Battlefield and Classroom* (Norman: University of
        Oklahoma Press, 1964), 222.
5   "Arrival of the Indians," *Carlisle Weekly Herald*, October 9, 1879, 3.
6   Todd Leahy and Nathan Wilson, eds., "My First Days at the Carlisle
        Indian School by Howard Gansworth An Annotated Manuscript,"
        Pennsylvania History: A Journal of Mid-Atlantic Studies 71, no. 4: 479–493.
7   "Montana Indians Big Cattle Men," *Fallon County Times* (Baker, MT),
        May 9, 1918, 12.
8   Katie Snyder, "Eleanor Houk: An Indigenous Woman of the
        Blackfoot Nation," Oregon Women's History Consortium, accessed
        January 13, 2024, at oregonwomenshistory.org/eleanor-houk-an
        -Indigenous-woman-of-the-blackfoot-nation/.
9   "Tony Bleish on Trial for Life in Court Today," *Great Falls Tribune*,
        May 19,1950.
10   David Murray, "Remains of Blackfeet Man Returned to Family
        for Burial 128 Years after Abduction," *Great Falls Tribune*, July 2,
        2028.
11   Nora Mabie, "Bringing Lawney Home: More than a Century Later,
        Blackfeet Bury Boy Who Died at Carlisle," *Missoulian*, November 9,
        2023.

Chapter Three: Under the Bird Tail

1   "Arrival of the Indians," *Carlisle Weekly Herald*, October 9, 1879, 3.
2   McBride, *The Bird Tail*, 101.
3   *The New North-West* (Deer Lodge, Montana), March 20, 1885, 3.
4   Sources vary widely as to the origin of the name "Hill 57." The most
        complete version of the name's original was reported in the *Great Falls
        Tribune* in 2009 by Ralph Pomnichowski, who wrote that in 1926
        Heinz 57 salesman Art Hinck (or Henck) arranged rocks on the hill
        into the form of a gigantic "57" and then painted them white.
5   Travis R. Annette, "Where the Buffalo Roam," Montana State
        University, posted at www.montana.edu/history/documents/papers
        /TravisArnette.pdf.
6   Erin Blakemore, "Meet Stagecoach Mary, the Daring Black Pioneer
        Who Protected Wild West Stagecoaches," *Inside History*, posted
        September 14, 2017, at www.history.com/news/meet-stagecoach-mary
        -the-daring-black-pioneer-who-protected-wild-west-stagecoaches.
7   McBride, *The Bird Tail*, 86.
8   Seaborn Larson, "Great Falls-Billings Catholic Diocese Reaches
        Settlement with Sex Abuse Victims for $20 Million," *Great Falls
        Tribune*, posted April 17, 2018, at www.greatfallstribune.com/story

/news/2018/04/27/great-falls-billings-diocese-reaches-settlement
-terms-sex-abuse-victims-20-million/557986002/.

9   www.stlabre.org/wp-content/uploads/2022/01/St.-Labre-FY21
-Audited-Financial-Statements.pdf.

10   Jenna Kunze, "Catholic Group Investigates Unmarked Graves and
Student Deaths at its Montana Indian Boarding Schools," Native
News Online, posted July 8, 2023, at nativenewsonline.net
/sovereignty/catholic-group-investigates-unmarked-graves-and
-student-deaths-at-its-montana-indian-boarding-schools.

11   "Cascade vs. Ft. Benton," *The River Press* (Ft. Benton, Montana),
June 12, 1912, 5.

12   Joseph Kinsey Howard, *Strange Empire* (New York: William Morrow
and Company, 1952), 343.

13   Harry P. Stanford Reminiscence, "Louis Riel," Special Collections
775, Folder no. 1, Montana Historical Society Archives, 1–2.

Chapter Four: The World's Wealthiest Nun

1   Consuela Marie Duffy, *Katharine Drexel: A Biography* (Cornwells
Heights, Pennsylvania: Sisters of the Blessed Sacrament, 1941).

2   Cheryl Christine Dempsey Hughes, *Katharine Drexel: Mystery,
Mission, Spirituality and Sainthood*, Ph.D. thesis, Durham University,
Department of Theology and Religion, 2007.

3   Katharine Burton, *The Golden Door* (Whitefish, Montana: Kessinger
Publishing, 2009), 106–07.

4   William Ketcham, "Report of the Director of the Bureau of Catholic
Indian Missions for 1903–1904," Washington, D.C.; Bureau of
Catholic Indian Missions, 1904, 2–3.

5   Amanda Bresie, "Mother Katharine Drexel's Benevolent Empire:
The Bureau of Catholic Indian Missions and the Education of Native
Americans, 1885–1935," *U.S. Catholic Historian* 32, no. 3: 1.

6   "A Finely Furnished Convent," *Great Falls Tribune*, 1912.

7   John G. Neihardt, *Black Elk Speaks* (New York: William Morrow and
Co., 1932), 156.

8   Clovis Lugon, La République des Guaranis (1610–1768), FeniXX
digital reprint: Paris, France, 1970.

9   Nicole Winfield and Pedro Servin, "Pope Praises Jesuit Missions in
Paraguay after Apology," Associated Press, posted July 11, 2015, at
apnews.com/article/9a32ad64a0de43a1a04d652dda8bf2be.

10   Hiram Martin Chittenden and Alfred Talbot Richardson, *Life,
Letters, and Travels of Father Pierre-Jean DeSmet* (New York: Francis
P. Harper, 1905), 318.

11   L. B. Palladino, *Education for the Indians* (New York: Benziger Bros., 1892), 14.

12   Angela Lincoln, *Life of the Rev. Mother Amadeus of the Heart of Jesus* (New York: Paulist Press, 1923), 96–97.

13   Mark Clatterbuck, *Demons, Saints, and Patriots: Catholic Visions of Native America through the Indian Sentinel, 1902–1962* (Milwaukee, WI: Marquette University Press, 2009), 39.

14   Bresie, "Mother Katharine Drexel's Benevolent Empire," 3.

15   Robert Utley, ed., in the introduction to Richard Henry Pratt's autobiography, *Battlefield and Classroom* (Lincoln: University of Nebraska Press, 1981), p. xx.

16   Wilson O. Clough, "Mini-Aku, Daughter of Spotted Tail," *Annals of Wyoming* 39 no. 2, (1967): 187–216, posted online at archive.org /details/annalsofwyom39121967wyom/page/186/mode/2up?view =theater.

Chapter Five: The Hostages

1   Mary Annette Pember, *Buried Secrets: America's Indian Boarding Schools Part 2*, Reveal podcast, accessed at https://revealnews.org/podcast /indian-boarding-schools-part-two/

2   Tim Giago, "Boarding School Trauma Still Haunts Indian Country," *Indianz.com*, posted February 5, 2018, at indianz.com/News /2018/02/05/tim-giago-boarding-school-trauma-still-h.asp.

3   Laura Johnson, "Former Boarding School Establishes Truth And Healing Committee To Reconcile With Its Past," July 19, 2021, South Dakota Public Broadcasting, posted online at https://www.sdpb.org /blogs/news-and-information/former-boarding-school-establishes -truth-and-healing-committee-to-reconcile-with-its-past/.

4   Chris Laughery, Lori Walsh, Steven Zwemke, "In The Moment: The Return Of Native Children's Remains from Federal Boarding Schools," South Dakota Public Broadcasting, posted online July 16, 2021, at listen.sdpb.org/news/2021-07-16/in-the-moment-the-return -of-native-childrens-remains-from-federal-boarding-schools.

5   Hilary Giovale, "Conversation with Oglála Lakȟóta Elder Basil Brave Heart: Part One," *Bioneers*, posted online August 3, 2023, at bioneers. org/conversation-with-oglala-Lakȟóta-elder-basil-brave-heart-part-1 -zmbz2108/.

6   Talli Nauman, "Youth Demand Redress for Indian Boarding School Atrocities," *Esperanza Project*, posted online August 4, 2023, at esperanzaproject.com/2021/native-american-culture /youth-demand-redress-for-indian-boarding-school-atrocities/.

7   "Fort Laramie Treaty," National Museum of the American Indian,
        posted online at americanindian.si.edu/nk360/plains-treaties-fort
        -laramie/#introduction.

8   Mary Claudia Duratschek, *Crusading Along Sioux Trails* (Yankton,
        South Dakota: Grail Publications, 1947), 17–18.

9   James C. Olson, *Red Cloud and the Sioux Problem* (Lincoln: University
        of Nebraska Press, 1965, 250).

10   Richard G. Hardorff, *Indian Views of the Custer Fight: A Source Book*
        (Norman: University of Oklahoma Press, 2005), 16.

11   Keven Abing, "Directors of the Bureau of Catholic Indian Missions:
        Reverend Joseph A. Stephan, 1884–1901," 1994, posted online at
        marquette.edu/library/archives/Mss/BCIM/BCIM-SC1-directors2.pdf.

12   Ibid.

13   Stephanie Woodard, "South Dakota Sex Abuse Scandal: A Peek
        Inside the Church's Drawers," posted online 19 April 2011 at huffpost
        .com/entry/south-dakota-catholic-sex-abuse_b_850102.

14   Stephanie Woodard, "South Dakota Sex Abuse Scandal: a Peek inside
        the Church's Drawers," *Huffington Post*, April 19, 2011, https://www
        .huffpost.com/entry/south-dakota-catholic-sex-abuse_b_850102.

15   Peter Cozzens, "Ulysses S. Grant Launched an Illegal War Against
        the Plains Indians, Then Lied About It," *Smithsonian Magazine*,
        November 2016.

16   Rowan Moore Gerety, "The Dark Secrets Buried at Red Cloud
        Boarding School," *Wired* magazine, posted online July 13, 2023, wired
        .com/story/marsha-small-red-cloud-boarding-school/.

17   Gerety, "The Dark Secrets."

18   Ibid.

19   Mary Annette Pember, "Pine Ridge Tribal Council Votes to Ban
        Missionary from Tribal Lands," *Indian Country Today*, as reported in
        the *Billings Gazette*, posted online August 22, 2022.

20   Crystal Echo Hawk and Lashay Wesley, "The Crimes of Native
        American Boarding Schools," *IllumiNative*, posted online at
        illuminative.org/americangenocidepodcast/. IllumiNative is a racial
        and social justice organization led by women dedicated to increasing
        the visibility of Native peoples.

Chapter Six: Custer Had It Coming

1   Chavers, Dean, "Alcatraz Is Not an Island," *World Literature Today* 93,
        no. 4 (2019): 61–64.

2   Howard Zinn, *A People's History of the United States: 1492–Present*
        (New York: HarperCollins, 2003), 52.

3   "Ghetto Spread over 1.6 Million Acres," *Borrowed Times* (Missoula, Montana) 1, no. 15 (April 4, 1973): 14.

4   Telephone interview with CBS News as reported in the Palm Desert, California *Desert Sun*, March 1, 1973.

5   Makenzie Huber, "Mission of Wounded Knee Activists Continues 50 Years Later with Children, Grandchildren," *Idaho Capital Sun*, February 28, 2023.

6   Annette McGivney, "Skiing on a Sacred Mountain: Indigenous Americans Stand against a Resort's Expansion," *Guardian*, June 21, 2022, posted at theguardian.com/world/2022/jun/19 /Indigenous-native-american-ski-resort-sewage-water-arizona.

7   Nina Lakhani, "US Supreme Court Rejects Dakota Access Pipeline Appeal," *Guardian*, February 22, 2022.

8   Derek Hawkins, "Dakota Access Protesters Accuse Police of Putting Them in 'Dog Kennels,' Marking Them with Numbers," *Washington Post*, November 1, 2016. Sam Levin and Nicky Woolf, "Dakota Access Pipeline: Police Fire Rubber Bullets and Mace Activists During Water Protest, November 2, 2016, theguardian.com/us-news/2016/nov/02 /dakota-access-pipeline-protest-arrests-standing-rock.

9   Echo Hawk and Wesley, "The Crimes of Native American Boarding Schools."

10   Huber, "Mission of Wounded Knee Activists."

11   "Native American Leader Dennis Banks on the Overlooked Tragedy of Nation's Indian Boarding Schools," *Independent Global News*, aired October 8, 2012, posted online at www.democracynow.org/2012/10/8 /native_american_leader_dennis_banks_on. Pipestone was built illegally on Yankton Sioux reservation land by the BIA. It took its name from the malleable red rock carved by Indigenous people into pipes and effigies. During the school's existence from 1891 to 1953 management of the pipestone quarries was taken over by the school's White superintendent, another reason the Yankton people hated the place.

12   Huber, "Mission of Wounded Knee Activists."

13   Mary Annette Pember, "Buried Secrets: America's Boarding Schools," *Reveal*, revealnews.org/podcast/indian-boarding-schools-part-one/.

14   Marsha Small and Jarrod Burks, "Excavation Results: Testing Two Ground Penetrating Radar Anomalies Detected in the Basement of Drexel Hall, Red Cloud Indian School, Pine Ridge, South Dakota, 2023 Report to the Red Cloud School posted at www.redcloudschool. org/file/web-admin-documents/Final-Report_2023.pdf.

15   Gerety, "The Dark Secrets."

Chapter Seven: The Lord's Vineyard

1   Associated Press, "Trump Visit to Mount Rushmore to Be Greeted by Protests, Wildfire Fears," July 3, 2020.

2   William Cummings, "Trump Says Adding His Face to Mount Rushmore Would Be a 'Good Idea,'" *USA Today*, August 10, 2020.

3   John Taliaferro, *Great White Fathers* (New York: Public Affairs, 2002).

4   Nick Estes, "The Battle for the Black Hills," *High Country News*, January 1, 2021, posted online at hcn.org/issues/53-1/Indigenous -affairs-social-justice-the-battle-for-the-black-hills/.

5   Nina Lakhani "South Dakota Governor Threatens to Sue over Sioux's Coronavirus Roadblocks," *Guardian*, posted May 14, 2020, at theguardian.com/us-news/2020/may/14/sioux-coronavirus-roadblocks -south-dakota-governor.

6   Associated Press, "Trump visit to Mount Rushmore to be greeted by protests."

7   Makenzie Huber and Erin Woodiel, "Protesters in Keystone Arrested after Blocking Road to Mount Rushmore for Hours," *Sioux Falls Argus Leader*, July 4, 2020.

8   Tim Giago, *Sioux Falls Argus Leader*, November 13, 1988.

9   Kyle Swenson, "'Long Time Coming': Army Returns Remains of Arapaho Children Who Died at Assimilation School," *Washington Post*, posted August 9, 2017, online at washingtonpost.com/news /morning-mix/wp/2017/08/09/a-long-time-coming-army-returns -remains-of-arapaho-children-who-died-at-assimilation-school-in -1800s/.

10   Makenzie Huber, "'They are important to us': Remains of Sisseton Wahpeton Children Returning Home," *Pennsylvania Capital-Star*, posted September 21, 2023, online at penncapital-star.com/civil-rights -social-justice/they-are-important-to-us-remains-of-sisseton-wahpeton -children-returning-home/.

11   David Paulsen and Egan Millard, "Indigenous Children Who Died at Boarding School Finally Make It Home as Tribes Repatriate Remains," *Episcopal News Service*, posted January 20, 2022, at episcopalnewsservice.org/2022/01/20/Indigenous-children-who -died-at-boarding-school-finally-make-it-home-as-tribes-repatriate -remains/.

12   Andrew Kennard, "Oneida Families to Hold Service for Relatives Buried at Carlisle Indian School," *Native News Online*, posted June 30, 2022, at nativenewsonline.net/currents/oneida-families-to-hold -service-for-relatives-buried-at-carlisle-indian-school.

13   Vine Deloria, "The Indians," in Brooklyn Museum, *Buffalo Bill*, 56.

14 L. G. Moses, *Wild West Shows and the Images of American Indians, 1883–1933* (Albuquerque: University of New Mexico Press, 1996), 277.

15 Charles Fox, "Fighting to Get Home," *Belt Magazine*, September 25, 2023, posted online at beltmag.com/fighting-to-get-home/.

16 Michael E. Krauss, "Native Languages of Alaska," in O. Miyaoka, O. Sakiyama, and M. E. Krauss, eds., *The Vanishing Languages of the Pacific Rim* (Oxford, UK: Oxford University Press, 2007).

17 Jacquelin B. Pels, *Family After All: Alaska's Jesse Lee Home: Seward, 1925–1965*, (Walnut Creek, CA: Hardscratch Press, 2007).

18 Amy Worden, "More than a Century Later, Disinterment Starts a Native American Girl toward Home," *Washington Post*, June 26, 2021.

19 Jenna Kunze, "Home From Carlisle: Rosebud Sioux Youth Council Reclaims Their Ancestors," *Native News Online*, posted online July 14, 2021, at nativenewsonline.net/currents/home-from-carlisle-rosebud -sioux-youth-council-reclaims-their-ancestors.

20 *"Jesuits: Slavery, History, Memory and Reconciliation Project,"* posted online at jesuits.org/our-work/shmr/what-we-have-learned/missouri/.

21 For more about De Smet see Pierre-Jean De Smet, *Life, Letters and Travels of Father Pierre-Jean DeSmet, S.J. 1801–1873* (Aurora, Colorado: Bibliographical Center for Research, 2010). Pierre-Jean De Smet, *De Smet's Letters and Sketches, 1841–1842*, Leopold Classic Library (South Yarra, Victoria, Australia, 2016). L. B. Palladino, *Indian and White in the Northwest* (Baltimore, Maryland: John Murphy & Company, 1894).

Chapter Eight: The Long Walk

1 Michael J. Warner, "The Fertile Ground: The Beginning of Protestant Missionary Work with the Navajos, 1852–1890," in Albert H. Schroeder, ed., *Changing Ways of Southwestern Indians: Historical Perspectives* (Glorieta, New Mexico: Rio Grande Press, 1973), 197, 199.

2 Cora Salsbury, *Forty Years in the Desert, A History of the Cariado Mission, 1901–1941* (Ganado, Arizona, 1948), 2.

3 Michelle Kahn-John and Mary Koithan, "Living in Health, Harmony, and Beauty: The Diné (Navajo) Hózhó Wellness Philosophy," *Global Advances*, posted online May 1, 2015, at www.ncbi.nlm.nih.gov/pmc /articles/PMC4424938/.

4 Consuela Marie Duffy, *Katharine Drexel A Biography* (Philadelphia, Pennsylvania: Mother Katharine Drexel Guild), 219.

5 Haile, Berard, *Learning Navaho* (St. Michaels, AZ: St. Michael's Mission) 1941–1948.

6   Patricia Lynch, *Sharing the Bread in Service: Sisters of the Blessed Sacrament: 1891–1991* (Bensalem, PA: *Sisters of the Blessed Sacrament*, Volume 2, 2001), 111.

7   Murray Bodo, editor and translator, *Tales of an Endishodi* (Albuquerque, New Mexico: University of New Mexico Press) 1998, 184–188.

8   Cheryl C. D. Hughes, *Katharine Drexel* (Grand Rapids, MI: William B. Eerdmans) 2014, 117–118.

9   Ross Enochs, "The Franciscan Mission to the Navajos: Mission Method and Indigenous Religion, 1898–1940," *Catholic Historical Review* 92, no. 1 (January, 2006): 46–73.

10   Egbert Fisher, "Our Mission Work at Fort Defiance," *Franciscan Missions of the Southwest*, 3, 1915, 9.

11   "Report to the Commissioner of Indian Affairs," 1903, House Document no. 5, 58th Congress, 2nd Session, SN 4645, p. 129.

12   Michael J. Warner, "Protestant Missionary Activity Among the Navajo, 1890–1912," *New Mexico Historical Review* XLV no. 3 (1970): 223.

13   Michael C. Coleman, "Not Race, but Grace: Presbyterian Missionaries and American Indians, 1837–1893." *Journal of American History* 67 (June 1980): 41–60.

14   Sally J. Southwick, "Papists presbyters and primers : A comparative study of Catholic and Presbyterian mission schools among the Navajo 1898–1928," master's thesis, University of Montana, 1993.

15   John Dolfin, *Bringing the Gospel In Hogan and Pueblo* (Grand Rapids, MI: Van Noord Book and Publishing Company) 1921, 130.

16   William Campbell Posey, M.D., "Trachoma among the Indians of the Southwest," *Journal of the American Medical Association* (May 21, 1927): 1618.

17   *Contagious and Infectious Disease Among Indians*, U.S. Public Health Service, Washington, D.C., Government Printing Office, 1913, 29.

18   Christian McMillan, "Indigenous Peoples, tuberculosis research and changing ideas about race in the 1930s," *Canadian Medical Association Journal* 1 (November 2021): 193.

19   Fred. T. Foard, "The Health of the American Indians, The American Journal of Public Health 39, no. 11 (November, 1949): 1403–1406.

20   Valerie Rangel, "Biography of Annie Dodge Wauneka," New Mexico History posted at newmexicohistory.org/2015/07/21/biography-of-annie-dodge-wauneka/.

21   Spencer Kimball in "Conference Reports of The Church of Jesus Christ of Latter-day Saints," The Church of Jesus Christ of Latter-day Saints, Salt Lake City, Utah, 1960, 34.

22   Yoonji Han, "In the 1950s, thousands of Native American children were placed in Mormon homes for 'racial assimilation.' Now, experts fear an upcoming Supreme Court ruling could allow that to happen again.", *Business Insider.* posted Oct.24, 2022 at https://www .businessinsider.com/latter-day-saints-church-mormon-native-indian -placement-program-icwa-2022-10.

23   Elizabeth Hardin-Burrola, "Sex Abuse Claim Filed by Navajo Siblings," *Gallup Independent*, Gallup, New Mexico, posted online at www.bishop-accountability.org/news66/2016_03_25_Hardin-Burrola _Sex_abuse.htm.

24   Suzette Brewer, "'I am X:' Mormon Church Faces Growing Sex Abuse Scandal," *Indian Country*, October 19, 2016, posted online at ictnews.org /archive/i-am-x-mormon-church-faces-growing-sex-abuse-scandal-pt-1.

25   According to the LDS Church, the Relief Society is a female Mormon organization "whose purpose is to help prepare women for the blessings of eternal life as they increase faith in Heavenly Father and Jesus Christ and His Atonement; strengthen individuals, families, and homes through ordinances and covenants; and work in unity to help those in need. All Mormon women are members."

26   Connor Richards, "At 12 Years Old, She Says She Was Raped Repeatedly by a Man Working for the LDS Church Indian Student Placement Program," *Salt Lake City Tribune*, October 1, 2018.

27   Han, "In the 1950s, thousands of Native American children."

28   Suzette Brewer, "'I am X.'"

29   Molly Ivins, "Mormons' Aid to Indian Children Preserved by New Law," *New York Times*, December 1978, A16.

30   "Native Americans Recall Torture, Hatred at Boarding Schools," at KSAT.com, accessed Feb 9, 2024.

Chapter Nine: Blackfeet Warrior

1   "Conditions Among Indians Deplored," *The Butte Daily Post* (Montana), Sep 29, 1950, 2.

2   J. Michael Kennedy, "Truth and Consequences on the Reservation," *Los Angeles Times*, July 7, 2002.

3   Pauline Arrillaga, "Indian Woman Steps in to Call U.S. to Account," *Seattle Times*, November 7, 1999.

4   Bethany R. Berger, "Elouise Cobell," posted online at cobellscholar. org/wp-content/uploads/2015/11/cobell_chapter.pdf.

5   Tom Kerin, "Browning Could Have Bank in 60–90 Days," *Great Falls Tribune* (Montana), Dec 2, 1983, 17.

6   In 2023 there were eighteen Native-owned banks operating in the U.S.

7   Bill McAllister, "Indian Trust Accounts: A Plan to Take Control,"
         Washington Post, February 27, 1997.

8   Julia Whitty, "Elouise Cobell's Accounting Coup," *Mother Jones*,
         September–October 2005.

9   Royce Lamberth, Memorandum Opinion, Contempt Trial, February 2,
         1999, cited in Whitty, "Elouise Cobell's Accounting Coup."

10   Carol Schmidt, "MSU Announces $12 Million Gift toward $20 Million
         American Indian Hall," MSU News Service, October 8, 2018. Helena
         Dore, "A promise fulfilled: Montana State University celebrates completion
         of American Indian Hall," *Bozeman Chronicle*, October 16, 2021, 1.

11   Robert Lee and Tristan Ahtone, "Land-grab Universities," *High
         Country News*, March 20, 2020.

12   Jenna Kunze, "Cornell University Should Work with Tribes to Mend the His-
         tory of Its Massive Land Grab, Report Says," *Native News Online*, October 11,
         2023, posted at nativenewsonline.net/sovereignty/cornell-university-says
         -it-will-work-with-tribes-to-mend-the-history-of-its-massive-land-grab.

13   Bill Bell, "The St. Boniface Indian/Industrial School: Frozen in
         Time," *Banning Record Gazette*, September 9, 2011, 15.

14   Alta Rutherford, "St. Boniface Indian School Condemned; To Be
         Demolished," *San Bernardino County Sun*, April 3, 1974, 41.

15   "Annual Report to the Commissioner of Indian Affairs," Washington,
         D.C., 1851, 281.

16   Nick Woltman, "U.S.-Dakota War's Aftermath a 'Dark Moment' in
         Fort Snelling History," *Pioneer Press*, St. Paul, Minnesota, June 24, 2016.

17   Associated Press, "Report: U of Minnesota 'Committed Genocide' of
         Native people," Published 1:12 PM MST, April 11, 2023.

18   Tristan Ahtone, Robert Lee, Amanda Tachine, An Garagiola,
         Audrianna Goodwin, Maria Parazo Rose, and Clayton Aldern,
         "Misplaced Trust." *Grist*, posted online on February 7, 2024 at grist.
         org/project/equity/land-grant-universities-Indigenous-lands-fossil-fuels/.

19   Tenzin Shakya and Anthony Rivas, "To Native Americans, Reparations
         Can Vary from Having Sovereignty to Just Being Heard," ABC News,
         September 25, 2020, posted online at abcnews.go.com/US/native
         -americans-reparations-vary-sovereignty-heard/story?id=73178740.

20   Vine DeLoria Jr., *American Indian Quarterly* 19, no. 1 (Winter, 1995):
         143–214.

21   Mary Annette Pember, "The Catholic Church Siphoned away $30 Million
         Paid to Native People for Stolen Land," *In These Times*, July 7, 2020, 1.

22   Sharlee DiMenichi, "National Grant Is Funding Digitization of
         Documents from Quaker-Run Indian Boarding Schools," *Friends
         Journal*, October 16, 2023.

23 Michael Wyland, "Jesuit Mission Gives Up Colonial Approach, Returns Land to Native American Tribe," *Nonprofit Quarterly*, May 24, 2017.

24 Ryan Burge, "The Catholic Church is in Trouble in Places Where It Used to Dominate," *Substack*, October 12, 2023. The platform's information is based on data collected by the Cooperative Election Study.

25 "Interior Transfers National Bison Range Lands in Trust for the Confederated Salish and Kootenai Tribes," Interior Department press release, June 23, 2021.

26 bishop-accountability.org/complaints/2011_10_05_John_Does _1_16_v_Ursulines_and_Helena.pdf

27 Gwen Florio, "Anguish Has Never Healed for Natives Physically, Sexually Abused at St. Ignatius Mission," *Missoulian*, (updated) April 22, 2014.

Chapter Ten: The Vanishing Indian and Other Myths

1 "Reclaiming Native Truth," https://rnt.firstnations.org/#top, accessed February 13, 2024.

2 Stuart Miller, "A Slice of Indigenous Life, With an Edge," *New York Times*, August 8, 2021, Section AR, 13.

3 Carolyn Kormann, "Tribe to Table," *New Yorker*, September 19, 2022, 22.

4 Jim Robbins, "With Bison Herds and Ancestral Seeds, Indigenous Communities Embrace Food Sovereignty," National Public Radio, posted December 9, 2023, at www.npr.org/sections/health-shots /2023/12/09/1217920232/buffalo-seed-native-american-food-diet.

5 Native Ways Today, "Montana Food Distribution Study," November 2020, (https://img1.wsimg.com/blobby/go/ed097c30-58d2-48db -80c9-d85c8e28ef32/downloads/MT%20Food%20Distribution%20 Study.pdf?ver=1690299819788).

6 This is not to say that boarding schools have completely disappeared, only those that attempted to assimilate Indians in order to take tribal land. Although 90 percent of Native students attended local, taxpayer-funded public schools in 2024 the others were enrolled in institutions operated by the Federal government and the tribes. These 183 schools are funded by the Bureau of Indian Education. Four of them are boarding schools.

7 Anna Paige, "New Music Considers Complex History of Montana's Catholic Missions," *Montana Free Press*, posted October 18, 2022 at https://montanafreepress.org/2022/10/18/new-music-considers -complex-history-of-montanas-catholic-mission-churches/.

BIBLIOGRAPHY

Bodo, Murray, ed. *Tales of an Endishodi*. Albuquerque: University of New Mexico Press, 1998.

Duthu, Bruce N. *American Indians and the Law*. New York: Viking Penguin, 2008.

Howard, Joseph Kinsey. *Strange Empire*. New York: William Morrow and Company, 1952.

Hughes, Cheryl C. D. *Katharine Drexel*. Grand Rapids, MI: William B. Eerdmans Publishing Co., 2014.

Jenkins, Sally. *The Real All-Americans*. New York: Doubleday, 2007.

Kreis, Karl Markus, ed. *Lakotas, Black Robes, and Holy Women*. Trans. Corinna Dally-Starna. Bochum, Germany: Projectverlag, 2000.

Mails, Thomas E. *The Mystic Warriors of the Plains* (1972). Reprint, New York: Marlowe & Company, 1996.

McBride, Genevieve. *The Bird Tail*. New York: Vantage Press, 1974.

McClintock, Walter. *The Old North Trail*. Lincoln: University of Nebraska Press, 1968.

McDonnell, Janet A. *The Dispossession of the American Indian, 1887–1934*. Bloomington and Indianapolis: Indiana University Press, 1991.

Paul, Eli R., ed. *Autobiography of Red Cloud: War Leader of the Oglalas*. Helena: Montana Historical Society Press, 1997.

Vaughn, Robert. *Then and Now: Thirty-Six Years in the Rockies*. Helena: Farcountry Press, 2001.

INDEX